David Liebman
Self-Portrait of a Jazz Artist

David Liebman

SELF-PORTRAIT OF A JAZZ ARTIST

musical thoughts and realities

second, revised and enlarged edition

This book is dedicated to all of those people throughout the world – past, present and future – who have helped me realize who and what I am through their love, respect, patience, inspiration, companionship, knowledge, devotion and sensitivity.
With special gratitude to my parents, Leo and Frances.

David Liebman

This second edition is dedicated to Caris, Lydia, Natalie and Harold who have given me the best years of my life.

These are the two themes from which the entire Lonliness of a Long Distance Runner recording were based on (see Discography).

© 1996 by Advance Music
All rights reserved.
No part of this publication may be reproduced, stored in retrieval system, or transmitted, in any form or by any means, electronic, mechanical, photocopying, recording, or otherwise, without prior written permission of Advance Music.
International copyright secured.

Editing: Caris Liebman, Richard Beirach, Bobby Burgess, Bill Dobbins, Gale Courey Toensing, Chuck Marohnic, Frances Liebman, Hans-Jörg Rüdiger
Cover design: 10eg

Printed by TC Druck, Tübingen
Production: Hans Gruber, Hans-Jörg Rüdiger

Published by Advance Music.
Rottenburg N., Germany

Order No. 19100

ISBN 3-89221-013-6

Table of Contents

Preface..11

Preface to Second Edition..............................12

Chapter 1
The Artistic Process......................................15

Chapter 2
Creating the Music 31

Chapter 3
Musical Autobiography 61

Chapter 4
The Basis of My Art 87

Chapter 5
Education 107

Chapter 6
Ruminations on Jazz 131

Appendices
1 A Conversation with David Liebman 153

2 In Pursuit of Balance 177

3 The Artistic Triangle ("The 3H Club")....188

4 Top Ten Jazz Recordings 189

5 What Jazz Means To Me 193

6 Miles Davis and David Liebman -
    Jazz Connections: An Oral History..........195

7 Proposal to form the
    International Association of Schools of Jazz 197

8 Return of the Tenor 200

9 Postscript 202

Books and Records – A Personal List 203

Discography 208

Publications 214

At the Eastman School of Music, Rochester, NY, USA 1996, rehearsal for a performance of Bill Dobbins' Concerto for Soprano Saxophone and Orchestra *(© Louis Ouzer)*

"What else is the whole jazz trip? You take your seat in the cat's head, like you're stepping into one of those little cars in a funhouse. Then pulled by some strong dark chain that you can't shut off, you plunge into the darkness, down the inclines, up the slopes, around the sharp bends and into the dead ends; past bizarre, grotesque window displays and gooney, lurid frights with spectacles and whistles and sirens and scares and even along a dark moody tunnel of love. It's all a trip-and the best of it that you haven't the faintest idea where you're going!!"

From "Ladies and Gentlemen – Lenny Bruce" (Albert Goldman)

"Bright moments is loving to play music if I'm allowed to play under good conditions. Bright moments is being dealt with as a man first. Bright moments is coming home late at night or early in the morning from a gig and if you're real relaxed and it's raining, you can hear the raindrops hit like in cluster chords-like little bells in tune with each other – a melting kind of thing. It's also not being afraid when you hear the thunder because it's probably Chick Webb and some other drummers playin' up there across the sky."

Rahsaan Roland Kirk

David Liebman Group: Vic Juris, guitar; Jamey Haddad, drums and percussion; David Liebman, soprano saxophone; Phil Markowitz, piano; Tony Marino, bass (left to right) (© 1996 Patrick Hinley)

Preface

I was raised in a family of teachers; both my parents and my brother. Maybe this is why I have a natural energy and inclination to explain how things work. This desire and ability to verbalize concepts is useful when I am actively teaching. On the artistic level, it means I am a perpetual student, always attempting to see and realize more about my work.

This book is a compilation of thoughts related to the art of jazz improvisation, gathered over three decades. The material derives from interviews, articles and workshops that I have given over this period. At first I gathered these bits of information for use as a teaching tool, attempting to be clear in my instruction. Over the years, my perceptions evolved and began to coalesce in my mid-thirties. I realized that a good deal of what I was alluding to is rarely described or discussed in musical circles. This is the sort of inside information which is seemingly understood, but never specifically articulated. That is the purpose of this book: to give a picture of how one musician deals with the creative process in the context of improvising jazz. The myths of creativity are not destroyed here, only explained.

In 1976, *Lookout Farm – A Study of Small Group Improvisation* (Almo Publications) was written cooperatively by the members of that group. In it we discussed five original compositions from the standpoint of how they were conceived and evolved during the course of performance. The ideas reflected our individual and collective insights into the creative process. Other books I've written deal with more technical matters like harmony and the saxophone. This present book is at times musically specific but it also is concerned with the broader implications of creating art. In its way, it reflects one man's philosophy about life, society, the individual and recent cultural history. It is in essence my creative diary, recounting how I grew as an artist and human being. Because of this underlying premise, I feel that much of the book should appeal to people interested in the creative process in general, as well as to musicians. I know that in my readings, I have learned a lot from similar books by artists in other fields.

The book is written on three levels of perception: from the standpoint of artists and humanity in general; from the point of view as part of the jazz tradition and a member of that specific community; and lastly from my own personal perspective. The views, judgments and opinions are my own, though much is collective knowledge.

Note: All references to "he," "man," or "men," are meant to include "she," "woman," and "women," also.

Preface to Second Edition (1996)

Since publication in 1988, I have been gratified at the wonderful response to Self-Portrait. As I hoped would be true, musicians and educators alike commented that the book confirmed many of their thoughts and verbalized matters of concern. As I described in the book, its contents were subjects which musicians often recognized among themselves but seldom discussed in public. Because so much of an art form like jazz is beyond verbal description, I suppose it is comforting, especially to young artists to be, to have one's questions addressed. The entire process of self discovery through the artistic quest is fascinating and continually revealing.

As I approach my 50th year I naturally have further reflections and insights to share in this edition which have evolved during the period since I wrote the original manuscript in 1986. Some of the new material will appear in different places throughout the original. Included are also two interviews, an updated discography and bibliography, a more extensive layout with photos, some appendix materials, and a French translation to be published simultaneously. As I get older and my students obviously continue to be for the most part around 20 years of age, I realize more and more that what sociologists call the "passages" of life, referring to various stages of personal evolution, become more and more clear. The clicking off of decades on the chronological time clock is meaningful and in terms of one's attitudes and activities, there are significant and observable changes. Of course, these descriptions are generalized and they certainly didn't occur on the strike of midnight on my 30th or 40th birthday, but somewhere in the period surrounding those markers on either side.

It was in my twenties that I went to the jazz equivalent of graduate and post-graduate school. Playing with Elvin Jones and Miles Davis, beginning my own solo career, touring and recording, were all primarily learning experiences. I observed and experimented both with and without success. I learned to deal with my ego and the world at large. Musically, I spewed out all the influences I had learned up to that time. I was satisfied with action and movement, self-reflecting little. Succinctly put, I had a lot of fun and experienced many emotional ups and downs in both my personal and public life.

A few years after turning thirty, I realized that this state of being was not so satisfying. First of all, the sweet smell of success and flush of fresh victories waned as it often does for those given early rewards. More crucial was that I heard repetition with little freshness in my playing. The decision to play soprano saxophone exclusively took time to make, but within a few years, by the mid 1980's, I knew the move had been eventful and would set the tone for the ensuing decade. As I approached forty in 1986, with a great band (*Quest*), a settled personal life and a deeply felt dedication to education, I began to feel secure and rooted, looking forward to the future. As befits the present midpoint stage, the conviction that what one does in life is the correct path does provide comfort and allows you to proceed with renewed vigor and enthusiasm, hopefully towards leaving a positive mark on the planet. I would say that my best and longest lasting work occurred during these last ten years.

What is happening as fifty approaches is that the personal center expands outward towards the world at large. Having a child does precipitate this, but equally concrete is the reality that barring the unforseen, where you are is where you will be. If it were only because of the way you are perceived by the immediate communtiy itself, this would be true. In other words, we all know what to expect from an individual by this point, or at least we think we know!! This can be problematic if it is far off the modus operandi that one feels he has created. With people who have been under the glare of public scrutiny, this can easily occur because of miscommunication and the propensity of the media to over simplify and generalize a person's actions and utterances. But no matter how private one's life has been, if you have more or less pursued the same course for several decades, the way you are perceived is well in place by this stage of life. And because of that as well as the inevitable perception of one's impending mortality, you naturally turn outward towards the world at large and try to contribute something of worth which will exert a positive and permanent effect. In other words, how can I use my talents and experience to influence the future?

I can only speculate, but my gut feeling is that the ensuing decade(s) will increasingly deal with that challenge. In order to confront that task, I have to try and insure that my personal health as well as the safety and sanctity of my home and family are intact consistently. Balancing all of these facets along with the natural conservative bent one experiences as time passes and age increases is quite a challenge for this coming decade. Is the search for a real, concrete form of spirituality the major concern of the sixties as I have perceived in some of the lives of artists who attain longevity? And how does one stay inspired, productive and non-repetitive in a performing art? Also, as one's stature as a "survivor" increases and the legend grows, how can artistic closed-mindedness be avoided? Hopefully, in ten years I will attempt to answer these questions. For this new edition I'd like to share some of the thoughts and ideas experienced in the last decade.

The Duo Live *recording session, 1985, Tübingen, Germany (© Hans Gruber)*

The Artistic Process   1

In a letter to his brother Theo, Vincent Van Gogh wrote: "Great things are not done by impulse, but by a series of small things brought together. And great things are not something accidental, but are willed. What is drawing? How does one learn it? It is working through an invisible iron wall that seems to stand between what one feels and what one can do."[1]

    This chapter deals with my reflections on working through that wall. The problems are concerned with all facts of life ranging from the purely technical to the spiritual, and finally to everyday affairs. Being an artist is a full-time job; there are no office hours or vacations. Even when not physically working on creating, the artist is thinking, feeling and reflecting in order to gain more insights and material for the creative act. In a sense, the artist is constantly attempting to combine the left and right sides of the brain: intuitive and intellectual.

    The first section defines the artistic process and explores the social, psychological and cultural factors which makes a human being identify himself as an artist. The next section deals with art in general, including some comparisons between the different disciplines. Following this is a more in-depth analysis of the personal process one goes through as an artist. The final section traces the chronological stages through which a jazz musician passes based on my own observations.

What is an Artist?

An artist is a person who spends his life trying to be in touch with his inner self and attempts to communicate these perceptions to the world through a chosen art form. One's works of art are a mirror of personal thoughts and feelings which are reflected for all to see and consider. A body of work over a period of time is similar to an autobiography, for the artist's entire being is revealed. What an artist experiences and feels are hopefully shared by all people on one level or another; this is what is meant by universality. All human beings have the potential to experience similar feelings somewhere within themselves at one time or another during their existence. Art acts as a catalyst to remind and help clarify these feelings. There are some artists who qualify primarily as technicians and craftsmen. This means they possess works which may appeal to a portion of the audience, but behind the facade there is emptiness and lack of depth. The true artist has considered the meaning of his work as

[1] Vincent Van Gogh, *Dear Theo: The Autobiography of Vincent Van Gogh* (New York: Signet Books, 1969).

well as the technical aspects and attempts to portray this to others. This gives great art depth, relevance and timelessness which is not usually observed in the popular art of a given period. Art should be both entertaining and educational: *edutainment*.[2] In this way, art is not just transitional, but eternal.

In sum, individuality of expression revealed in a creative and instructive form is the general axiom of an artist. His constant search for beauty, truth and knowledge should be an example for all to be inspired by. The creation of art itself is representative of the ultimate act of individual freedom and is an expression of this basic human need which no political or cultural taboo can stifle. This is why in theory, the artist and revolutionary share a common bond. They both serve to inspire people to better themselves and the world around them.

In order to be universal, the artist's task is to integrate his own individuality with those attributes and feelings that are common to mankind as he observes it. This goal of integration underlies all artistic achievemant. Each individual has feelings that are different from others and need to be expressed. But in order to comprehend the uniqueness of one's vision, these perceptions have to be in the context of a world view also, for then the comparison is more clear. Artistically, a work should include some features that are recognizable upon careful analysis. The balance between the known and unknown is one of the factors having the greatest effect on the communicative value of a piece of art. People should be able to discern the obvious in order to recognize any new ideas being presented.

An artist is constantly confronted with the dilemma of his need and ability to communicate to others what he feels. If his art is complex by nature or truly abstract, the difficulty in obtaining a response is obvious. Sometimes the only recourse is to create only for oneself and an immediate circle of enthusiasts. This can be quite satisfying for a while, but in the end there is frustration in not having one's message appreciated by more people. Some of the desire to be recognized may be purely egotistical but at the same time an artist may truly feel that the world will be a better place if his work could be appreciated. However, the problem exists on both sides of the question. If the artist achieves recognition and the market place exerts an influence on him, he may eventually compromise in one way or another, possibly without even being aware that he is doing so. On the other hand, the image of the non-compromising artist in an ivory tower can be self-defeating because in the end, art is for the world to appreciate and enjoy. This applies also to an artist who is ahead of his time and whose work will be valued by future generations.

Finally, it is the artist's sense of humanity that is felt. Com-

---

2 *edutainment* – the twin sided goal of educating and entertaining an audience.

passion, love, and respect for all forms of life are common attributes which human beings aspire to. The artist's code of morality and decency will underlie his work as will the conduct of his everyday life. But because of the artist's example and inspirational value to others, he must be even more aware of these things. An artist has to delve into matters of ethics, morality, justice, etc., so that his work reflects a vision of humanity which includes these eternal questions. An artist is the very subtle voice of our subconscious, disguised in the creations themselves.

Over a lifetime, the artistic process usually follows a three fold path: imitation-style-innovation. Within each individual's own framework, timing and idiosyncracies, all artists somehow traverse at least part of this process.

The Stages of Learning the Art

Imitation is the learning one gathers from predecessors in the field. Writing out, playing with and analysis of the masters (which I refer to as the transcription process) is my recommendation for the most effective form of imitation in jazz. It is clearly described in my video *The Improviser's Guide To Transcription,* as well as being a permanent fixture of my lectures to students around the world. The imitation stage assumes understanding the history of jazz, meaning the major milestones and important individuals as well as the basic repertoire and how the music is itself constructed. This learning of what came before never ends, but the highest intensity of this stage comes early in terms of overall development.

It is important to be clear about this sometimes misunderstood imitation phase. I acknowledge that one of the overriding goals of artistic development is the discovery and nurturing of one's own individual voice. It is a pinnacle of the artistic search to be able to recognize a musician's identity from the first note played. On the surface, imitation might seem to not reconcile with this search for individual identity. In fact, some artists discover that moving beyond imitation is an insurmountable obstacle. But there are some methods available to help this movement along which I will discuss under "Finding Oneself" later in this chapter. Suffice to say, on some level all artists go through imitation, if only when they copy someone else on their instrument, even their first teacher.

Style means that an artist becomes proficient in the idioms of the period and musical environment he is a part of. In practical terms, this student has probably become a working musician and is taking part in the musical scene around him. He may be borrowing from his predecessors at the same time that he is dealing with experimentation and trial/error on his own. Progress is measurable in smaller chunks than during the previous imitation period. During the beginning of this stage, a relentless desire to improve by practicing, playing, and learning is often prevalent. It is also a period of self discovery as the budding artist reacts to others around him and has to deal with the ego, criticism and his place in the musical community. This can be an ordeal by fire especially if the artist gets the opportunity to play alongside older, more established musicians.

(Private collection)

It is often during this stage that the young artist discovers the sheer pleasure of playing. Slowly, he becomes more and more immersed in this spontaneous joy. Soon he may discover that the urge to practice abates, which can be accompanied by a feeling of guilt after years of so much enforced discipline. What is happening is natural – the young artist is encountering life situations in a more serious way as he makes his way through the business of being a musician and increasingly, a wage earner. The *practice* is now life itself. Social, personal and business encounters become the new learning field. The effect on the music is long term, for the young artist is beginning to build a real framework for a full blown musical and personal life to evolve. The habits which are ingrained at this stage will probably be there in some form or another for life.

Finally, very gradually and in an ongoing, never ending process, one MAY begin to notice the beginnings of an individual approach. Usually this can be observed by peer recognition and comment. The individual himself might be the last to notice what others hear. I call this stage innovation, when in actual fact a true innovator in the real sense of the word is extremely rare. Describing someone as an innovator is very subjective and usually requires years to pass before a fair judgement can be made. However, I consider signs and proof of individuality as grounds for entering this stage. It can be manifested in many forms including from the instrumental standpoint or the music itself evidenced as a new way of conceptuallizing. An artist can exhibit individuality solely technically, in terms of tone, articulation, fingerings, nuance, etc. It may also stem from a compositional approach. It is most often that such discoveries combine at least several aspects in tandem.

Innovation in the way I describe it does not spring out of the air from nowhere. It is a slow, sometimes not straight line of development and it always has its roots somewhere in the past. Everything comes from something – it is the natural law of nature and life. Only those who are ignorant of the past will consider something new and bestow upon it an aura of incredibility. If you search deep enough, the antecedents of most acts of creation can be discovered somewhere. It is only a matter of research and examination. In any case, looking backwards or sideways provides sources for the search in the innovation stage.

Finding Oneself

I am often confronted with accomplished students who have passed through a great deal of the stages of imitation and style. They are ready to move forward but come up against this obstacle of how to accomplish it. This is the most frustrating of stages and although each individual's response is unique there are some guidelines to be aware of.

First and foremost, there must be a burning desire and ambition to find one's own musical identity. It is not an easy or comfortable situation and it may take years to discern tangible results. Frustration may be an integral part of the process, therefore the inner light must be bright in order to persevere. Practically speaking, an artist may have to accept a period where he doesn't sound as good as previously. It is a stage when as technique and concepts change, the actual playing may temporarily suffer. This is natural and necessary while the process is occurring. Ideally, it would be great to be able to stop playing when one enters this transition and begin again fully evolved. Except in rare instances (like the famous sabbatical which Sonny Rollins took in 1959 to practice new techniques as evidenced on the recording called *The Bridge*), this is not realistic for most people, if only because of the financial burden.

Along with this acceptance and desire for change there should also be present a strong commitment to leaving behind one's influences. In some cases, what one loves most about his playing can be just that element which needs to be dropped. This demands a certain ego-less state in order to be able to defer one's strongest attributes for a time, in order that creative space will be available for the new to enter. It needs to be accompanied by the real belief that indeed you are capable of change and ultimately of finding a unique and individual approach. The artist must believe that it is indeed possible to excel and find his place. This necessitates a combination of conviction, honesty, hope, and self confidence. Such a mixture doesn't occur everyday, which is why developing individuality is so rare.

Let's consider the actual steps along the way to self discovery. The artist must listen to his performances in a completely objective and dispassionate manner in order to find something to isolate in his playing which is not directly traceable to a known source. This could be exhibited in the music itself: for example the notes used, the rhythms played, the harmonic implications, etc. Or more commonly, it could be evidenced through the instrument itself as a technical manifestation, most probably in the tone or expressive devices used. It could be as simple as the manner in which the artist punctuates or slides into a particular note; or the use of a certain dynamic range somewhere on the instrument; or an unusual color on even one or two notes of the instrument's range. The point is to notice this aspect no matter how trivial, isolate it and develop it by expanding and spreading it to other notes or areas. In any way possible, the artist must nurture this little seed into a full blown flower. The main challenge is to notice the existence of something musically, which has the potential of becoming an individual trademark.

As mentioned before, in order to encourage the introduction of unique characteristics into one's music, the direct influences that an artist pursued in the imitation and style stages have to be let go of. The musician must make a concerted effort to avoid these patterned responses from his early studies, no matter how good they sound. This takes a great deal of strength because what one loves the most and sounds best are often the same element. To help this process along, the artist should turn to other, non-direct influences, meaning music and art not directly related to the idiom or area he is involved in. This could mean music from foreign cultures using different instruments. Or classical music from a specific era. Even jazz itself from an earlier period can be useful. The challenge then becomes to transfer or graft some musical element from the new music to one's own personal situation. The same process applies to examining and possibly becoming immersed in another art form, such as poetry, painting, literature, etc. Readings in the spiritual realm may also inspire fresh and new directions.

The point is that this is where the differences in quality between the great and merely good in any field usually can be observed.

Outside the rare, natural genius, most great art is the result of hours of study, disciplined practice, thoughtful reflection, intense curiosity and personal courage with little fear of failure or alienation. Mixed with even a little bit of imagination, the truly motivated artist can find something that will mark him apart from the vast surrounding field. This stage of self discovery is fraught with obstacles and at times, severe emotional distress which in itself can lead to problems, hopefully not of extended duration. But this is the challenge one must take to find something of value. There is no turning back once this process begins. It is a lonely voyage which at times can appear to be heading nowhere, but with sheer perserverance it is within reach.

Refinement and consolidation are the next stages of innovation and for many fine artists, the final. It is a rare artist who continues to push the envelope in order to find out even more about himself. Most are content to have discovered something and use that as a basis for the remainder of his creative years. As long as development is apparent and continual, such an artist will not suffer from boredom, either personally or in the work. Of course, as a human being, the artist may go through periods of instense creativity or the opposite, but this is to be expected. The bottom line is that the quest for self discovery never completely leaves. The other aspect to be vigilant about is to avoid becoming close-minded and oppose new views which inevitably surface from time to time. Being defensive in order to consolidate one's position is dangerous because it can lead to isolation and even paranoia. To love something just because it is new is not healthy either. It is a real challenge to stay open, sensitive and balanced in all ways.

The Mature Artist

If all of the above takes place for the most part in the first several decades of artistic growth, how does the older, established artist continue to develop without falling into the traps described above? It is in large part up to a changing perspective from the early years when progress is so obviously measurable and manifested as a kind of forward motion.

The mature artist must be able to move both sideways and backwards for the purposes of refinement and even recycling. Similar to taking an original tone row and using its several variational forms (inversion, retrograde, retrograde inversion) as the basis for new compositional material, variation of earlier discoveries can lead to fresh work. Just as jottings in Beethoven's notebooks were sometimes used for pieces even if they were written years before, the artist can go back to older material or styles that he was involved in and because of his growth, see them in a completely different light. After all, as one's life and views change inevitably through the years, wouldn't the same be true for the music? It's simply a matter of accepting the need to regroup and re-think the old.

There is a natural tendency as one matures to want to simplify and edit. The dictum that "less is more" becomes a self-fullfilling prophecy. Maybe it's a side effect of life's passages and the shift from egocentrism to the world at large which results in less need to prove oneself. In any case, the evolving artist learns more and more to edit out what it is unnecessary; to maximize the relationship between cause and intended effect; to economize one's shifting physical and mental powers; to be more universal and truly attempt to reach a wider audience within the limits of one's own acceptable aesthetics. It is not that the flame withers; it is that the white heat in the middle of the flicker grows more intense. You can hear in older instrumentalists a maturity of sound and touch. This is apparent with the writer who becomes more concise in the use of vocabulary; for the painter whose colors become more vivid; to the composer who arrives at a point more swiftly. The mode which the artist choses does not necessarily have to be simpler or less sophisticated. It is just that even within the complex, there is refinement going on.

The mature artist increasingly realizes that there is meaning beyond technique which becomes more attainable as mastery develops. Mastery refers to both the specific discipline as well as self mastery meaning clarity of thought and emotion in balance. There is inherent in the mature artist a desire to express beauty and truth as clearly as possible – maybe because the chronological clock is ticking. For the musician, there seems to grow a desire for expressing real lyricism, manifested in the eternal search for the perfect melody.

The Artist's Schematic: Body-Soul-Mind

Mastering anything in life is a matter of combining the three aspects of being human: mind, body and soul. The mind deals with ideas and concepts, the body with technique and the soul with emotions. Another way of perceiving this triad is that man must develop a world view, a way of expression and self-knowledge. Achieving a balance between discipline and flexibility establishes the temperament through which these goals are acquired and acted upon.

An artist needs to be able to communicate with himself on all three levels so that his art will reflect the whole without neglecting any necessary elements. If even one element is overlooked, the art will suffer and more likely fail to move others. At different stages of growth, the artist may find it necessary to exaggerate one aspect over another, for example, technique over substance, or emotion over technique. In the end, it is the balance between mind, body and soul operating at a consistent level which will produce the most worthwhile art.

For an artist, the concern of the body is technique. Being able to physically master the tools of the trade is particularly true for performers. A musician, especially the improviser, must be able to have his imagination and instrument united as one.

Technique also means that in any specific musical area, the artist is aware of the principle of tension and release. Some of the more obvious ways tension and release are manifested musically are the execution of extremes such as fast/slow tempos, soft/loud dynamics and other opposing pairs. The use and manipulation of such wide ranges of expression is a necessity for an artist to be totally convincing both technically and expressively.

The emotions (coupled with the intellect) provide the raw energy of creation. The emotional needs of an artist will find satisfaction in his creations. The usual growing pains of life and death, childhood experiences, relationships with the opposite sex, spiritual concerns, and other such matters are source materials for creativity. These are events and feelings which strike a responsive chord in all people. Feelings of love, hate, sadness, joy, etc., are necessary to make art realistic and grounded to life itself. It is sometimes easy for an artist to become self-indulgent by exaggerating these feelings. This is where the intellectual aspect serves a direct creative purpose, by balancing the emotions with ideas and content while also functioning to make certain that mere technique serves an artistic end.

For the initial creative impetus, one's intellect is by nature curious about how things operate. Asking why things are a given way leads to questioning the process. One of the functions of the intellect is to delve into the past history of the specific art form under study as well as other aspects of life. The artist who understands and can reasonably reproduce the works of the past stands well equipped with a vocabulary of responses that has been tested and is a known quantity. He has a basis by which to judge any twist of the creative impulse which may arise and, at the least, has a place to begin his own explorations.

The intellect analyzes and judges events so that the individual can decide on a course of action. To advance artistically, the artist must objectively evaluate what he sees and hears around him. It is impossible to go forward with clarity if there are doubts about one's immediate surroundings. An emotional response is not valid by itself; the intellect's responsibility is to assess incoming material and information in terms of what is useful and how it can be used. Teachers and other influences help to determine a way of conceiving reality and interpreting new information, but in the end, each artist is responsible for his own decisions and judgments.

Problem solving is another way of describing the role of the intellect in artistic development. Most artists exhibit the ability to absorb new information quickly and get to the heart of the matter. This is a result of discipline and concentration. The overall development of clarity in one's thinking directly influences the creations themselves. If it is difficult at times for an artist to understand something he is presented with in his own field of expertise, then he may be better able to emphathize with the great difficulty outsiders have with his work. Clarity of thinking helps to give needed objectivity in trying to foresee the effect a work might have upon others.

Finally, the intellect along with the emotions gives an artist awareness of man's eternal quest for beauty, truth and perfection. The end result of being a cultured being means that one gains respect and understanding of mankind's hopes, fears and behavior. This in turn adds to the emotional and intellectual reservoir that is called upon in creating art. All human beings are linked together through the timeless universal chain of history and events. Art is an important way of perceiving the continuum of man's past, present and future.

The Three H's

Over the years I have discovered other ways to summarize what I mean by the artistic schematic. Using what I refer to as the "3 H's", to mean head, hand, heart, it becomes clear that the artist is constantly struggling to balance these three aspects of creativity. The head is the intellect, referring to the necessary knowledge concerned with what one is playing as well as understanding the rules and conventions of the music. The hand translates to the technical expertise or specifically the hours spent mastering one's instrument. And the glue which holds the hand and the head together is the heart – the emotional, psychological and sensual feelings which an individual is able to conjure up and translate to the world at large. Without the heart, the others are meaningless. As one matures, all three continue to develop in different ways.

The head or learning aspect is definitely not as sensitive as in youth. Maybe the cup just becomes full and there isn't much more room to add to its volume? Raw facts are harder to retain for this reason, but also because of less need to amass information for its own sake. In other words, facts, figures, etc. become irrelevant to the real, deeper significance of what one does. Thankfully, this attitude is slowly progressive, because by this point there is usually enough information for several lifetimes of use.

Meanwhile the hand, or the technique changes but not necessarily in a straight line of evolution. One finds that instrumental technique becomes more subtle, less burdensome and more natural. What was formerly difficult to execute becomes more graceful. The instrument truly begins to feel like an extension of the body. For me, the soprano is like part of my arm and requires less effort to play than a decade ago. The ability to nuance and express has deepened to a point that almost every note has a personality of its own through the musical devices of attack, vibrato, sustain, decay, dynamics and vocal/embouchure effects. Speed and agility are less important than they used to be, because they are not a priority anymore. Now the concern is is about sound, color, tone, timbre, sonority – all equating to feeling and expressiveness.

Finally the heart truly rules supreme. With the hand as a servant or tool more immediately accessible to one's impulses, the ability to transcend knowledge and technique in order to express becomes the great gift of experience. More and more it becomes clear that nothing can stop the conviction and sureness from which one's playing springs forth. A negative situation such as a non-appreciative audience, bad sound or malfunctioning equipment can surely annoy, but concentration is possible to such a degree that little can halt the heart from functioning. This is the greatest gift of artistic longevity as an artist – what you want and need to express MUST find its way out. This affects my attitude towards the audience. Although I have the utmost respect for them in that they have come to listen to me and paid money for the event, I have become more objective about their reaction. I realize that given the right circumstances, they will respond to me positively, but in truth, they have no idea or should they of what I am actually doing. I truly want to play for the other musicians on the stage with me. I am convinced that for me personally, this is the best path to pursue even though possibly the results can lead to an even more limited audience than I already have. I am diminishing my appeal, but with clear purposeness and increasingly, no regrets. There really isn't any choice by this stage of life.

The Stages of the Process for the Improviser: Psychological Factors

In any art form there are usually some legendary artists who were seemingly born great. "He never had to practice… he was a real natural" is sometimes said about a particular artist. While this may be true to an extent in certain cases, such tales are often more romanticized than real. The folklore of an art form serves a purpose for inspiration and enjoyment, but the truth is that artistic development is a long process. Granted that to some degree, talent is inborn. Nonetheless, there are stages of growth that any artist invariably goes through, albeit at his own individual rate.

Even if technique is learned quickly and easily, to habitualize these skills to a level where they are spontaneous takes time. In jazz improvisation, this is particularly true. For the improviser, a body of personal *expressive devices*[3] used when phrasing as well as a generalized way of approaching any musical material are examples of skills which must be habitualized over time. These are matters of trial and error coupled with long-term experience.

The young artist is at first inspired to imitate his idols. The desire to emulate spurs the initiate on through a period of reproducing the past as well as a disciplined study of the rules of music and how

---

[3] *expressive devices* – the use of nuances in phrasing that give personality to music and include the aspects of articulation, dynamics, bending tones, intonation, smears, etc.

they operate. As one matures, everyday existence and life's normal passages become the basis for inspiration and the need to create. As the artist evolves, his works are a chronicle of his perception of events occurring to and around him. His relationship to the world slowly changes as he evolves from a view that is self-centered to one that is broader, including society and the world at large. Presumably, his later years reflect thoughts having to do with the cosmos, spiritual matters and other eternal verities. Each stage gradually passes to the next. Remembrances of past events and thoughts intertwine with present perceptions. The endless possibilities and mixtures of old and new realities help to keep creativity alive and active.

During this growth process, the individual's relationship to himself also undergoes changes. In the imitative stages, an individual's own impulses are de-emphasized in order to absorb the way others have thought. Once a good grounding of the past is accomplished, any future study of older techniques and processes will only increase the development of an artist's individuality. The past need not be an obstacle to the future, because as one's own artistic personality develops, history takes on a fresh look.

The young student practices and learns on a mechanical, rote level. To a large degree, the beginning is memorization. His ego and consciousness don't have time to reflect upon the implications of what is being studied or how it could be utilized.

He should notice vast improvement almost from day to day at this level because the new material is so fresh. This constant reinforcement spurs him on to where his own personal way of duplicating past and present styles becomes more apparent. Accompanying these beginning stages, the separation between life and art can easily become confused and frustrating. This is the period when an artist may in a sense pay his "dues" emotionally and psychologically. Handling this stage of self-development positively can play a major role in determining his future both artistically and on the level of everyday living in the world.

Objective evaluation of oneself becomes increasingly difficult. As the artist improves, he becomes more critical because he begins to realize the details and specifics of the art. Because of his heightened sensitivity, the response of peers, critics, audiences and the world at large effects him to a greater degree than when he was simply a student. If he accepts solely the views of his peers, there is danger of falling into a clique whose norms only pertain to the group itself, thus shutting him off from outside influences. In any case, personal egos and competitiveness may naturally taint his peer's opinions. On the other hand, if there is critical and/or public acclaim, it may not necessarily be based on the depth of the art itself but can be a product of other superficial factors; such as merely being in the right place at the right time. In the case of huge public popularity, self-deception is easily possible because if the art seems to be communicating, the artist may feel that in accomplishing this, there is no need to grow or change.

The result of all these factors is that it takes great courage and strength to be honest about one's accomplishments. To be self-critical is very hard, but if the process initiates positive energy, then future development will be highly satisfying. On the other hand, if an artist is overly critical, then the lack of positive reinforcement can be frustrating and in turn cause inspiration and creative energy to suffer.

So there needs to be a balance at this early stage between self-criticism and positive feedback. This is extremely difficult and may be one of the key reasons why the developing artist is prone to some unhappiness in personal relationships. It is in such a period of artistic and personal turmoil that both the best and worst in an individual is called upon. For an artist, great advancement can occur at this time, but unfortunately, there is the possibility of finding refuge in self-destructive tendencies and lifestyles. Drugs and alcohol can seem to offer relief, which is why they are so dangerous at this sensitive stage. In the end, the artist will realize that surviving this personal storm is a necessary part of the artistic process.

Projecting further, an artist in his thirties has reached a particularly positive stage where personal artistic breakthroughs are finally evidenced. One still retains the energy and enthusiasm of youth, yet is experienced enough to recognize who and what he is. Any success and knowledge that has been accrued up till now can make an artist proud of his short history and yet ambitious enough to advance even further. Also, the thirties are a time for seeking financial and physical security. This desire for rewards and recognition can have a healthy impact towards stabilizing one's career at this time. But more important than all of the above is that by the mid-30's, by and large, the average serious artist in our culture has had approximately 10 to 15 years of experience. He is finally technically equipped to be freely creative and truly express his own vision.

What about the intuition? Intuition cannot be explained, but to some degree, most people possess it about something (although if it is not encouraged and used, it becomes negligible). This inexplicable element has to be trusted at times, especially for the artist, whose goal is to constantly strengthen the intuitive faculties at work during the creative process. The improvising musician is even more dependent on his intuition than other artists because of the spontaneous nature of his work. Developing intuition is one of the major results of the artistic process, for in the end who can explain the creative act? How much of it was intellect, emotion or intuition can never be definitely ascertained.

Art and Society

Art reflects the varieties of people and cultures throughout the world. Once again, the combination of the universal and the unique and personal attributes of an artistic statement are what give it life. Hopefully, the multiplicities of life and society which produce cultural differences do not override the universal qualities. Diverse styles are vehicles through which specific ideas are presented. A work of art should be able to include an individual's or a culture's vision of life in a vehicle that can be universally appreciated, assuming that the audience is sophisticated and educated enough to perceive the point.

The world of music is a great example of diversity from several standpoints. When one considers geographic differences, the rhythm of a culture's music is reflective of the feeling of life in that place. Rhythm is a basic component of the human condition. It is in everything people do, not only in the art forms. In a sense, rhythm is a direct manifestation of the ebb and flow of life and therefore always very obvious. Think about the rhythmic and geographical differences between Brazilian sambas, German polkas and African ritual music, for example.

Cultural differences are also apparent in the meditative music of a society. For example, the European-based Gregorian chants are quite different from Hindu ragas or Jewish cantorial music though their functions are similar. Even in the same country, differences are obvious. In the United States, there has traditionally been a musical difference between East and West Coast jazz. In India, the music of North and South exhibits wide differences in form and content. An artist usually finds his voice within the framework of his immediate culture before mixing together diverse elements.

Western View of the Artist

In the Western world, the artist has a status quite different from that of primitive societies where his function is considered a necessity. On one hand he is a non-entity and has little respect accorded him. This means that the artist's life is a constant battle of survival which of course has its effects on the work. On the opposite side, the artist who is popular becomes a celebrity. This may enable him to create more easily because success translates into financial independence which can mean artistic freedom. But the big danger is the deadening influence of commerciality upon creativity. The success of a creation is not necessarily a barometer of its artistic or philosophical merits. An artist can be fooled like anybody else into thinking that his work is more than it really is, because it is being acclaimed. Our culture has created quite a dilemma for the artist who strives for acceptance.

Comparison of the Arts

The performing arts differ from the more solitary art forms such as writing and painting. They involve group interaction first and foremost and need a stage or performance area in order to be consummated. By the nature of this action, the public is immediately involved in the creation itself. The performing arts are thus divided very clearly between form and content. The need to balance these two factors is what makes these art forms so challenging. What the artist says and how he says it must be reconciled.

Instrumental music (as distinct from music with lyrics) is the most abstract of the performing arts. Often there is little action to see, yet a performance is taking place. There are no words or descriptions most of the time, but the feelings and impressions created can be quite compelling. Musical relationships are similar to mathematical ones; they exist temporarily in space and once they have served their purpose are gone into the ether. Music cannot be seen or touched, only heard and felt. In this way, music has the ability to raise art into a realm of pure feeling and thought.

At the COTA Festival, Deleware Water Gap, Pennsylvania, USA 1992, performing Coltrane's Meditations Suite *(© Walter Bredel)*

Creating the Music 2

This chapter is for me the core of the book. For musicians directly interested in specifics, there is more technical material here than elsewhere. But my intention is not for this to be a "how to" chapter; that is the subject of other writings.

I want the reader to be able to sense the process as it relates to the actual work. This is a tour of the universe where the music is created. The making of the music and some of the results generated form the basic guidelines for the beginning section, "The Act of Improvising." The next section gives a glimpse into how the "Elements of Music" are thought about in improvisation. The elements here refer to melody, harmony, rhythm, color and form. It is a description of the ingredients or alphabet of our musical vocabulary.

Finally, the sections on composition, recording and being a bandleader round out corollary areas which are of concern to those creating this music. This chapter describes the parameters we all work in. My own personal interpretations of these aspects are in the chapter "The Basis of My Art".

The Act of Improvising

In theory, improvisation is supposed to be spontaneous. There is an image of the improviser spewing out musical ideas in continuous fashion which have never been heard before and are not repeated. Although the overriding objective is to be fresh and new, this is hardly the case. Rather, the improviser is working on three levels interacting continuously in different relationships to each other.

The primary level is playing what is already known in much the same way that a person uses language when he speaks. There is a quantity of available words over which one has command. Within those parameters, a person expresses himself at any given moment. The sequence of the words or the way they're expressed may infer any number of meanings, but the ingredients themselves are a known quantity. Likewise, the musician has a command of a certain amount of musical ideas depending on the context in which he is improvising. The depth of content and intensity of these ideas differ for each artist, depending upon one's personal creativity, extent of practice and experience in that area. This is referred to as having ideas "under your fingers" or, more accurately, immediately ready to be reproduced in a real playing situation. A *cliché*[1] falls under this category when a musician repeatedly uses the same musical idea

[1] *cliché* – a musical phrase that has become commonplace, as representative of a particular sound or style

without variation and often at the same place. A creative improviser can make a cliché sound fresh by stamping his own personality on it.

The second level of playing involves instant creativity and highly developed musicianship. It is concerned with the working out of a newly formed, not yet perfected idea during the real playing situation itself. A musician may have an idea in his mind or ear but not yet under his fingers. Although he can practice the main thrust of the idea away from actual performance, the nature of improvisation demands that at some point, theory becomes reality. The experienced musician does not fear becoming confused or lost while playing if he tries to work an idea out, because his basic musicianship will insure against this. But the improviser must be careful not to use stage time for practicing because the success of his and the entire group's creations will suffer in the end; both in relation to the music itself and the audience. When kept in balance, this "work in progress" attitude is one of the best aspects of great live jazz. It is the excitement of living on the edge, comparable in theory to a race car driver or athlete. Depending on one's viewpoint, saxophonist John Coltrane's playing was either criticized or praised as an example of this attitude in jazz.

Finally, there is the highest creative level of playing which is extremely rare, even for the greatest musicians. This is where pure inspiration results in a sudden creative flash and a musical idea is born. There might be only the smallest thought realized, but the artist knows he has heard the seeds of something different. Now he must figure it out and develop it to the point of immediate recall and accessibility. These moments are rare because two events must coincide: a comfortable musical environment should exist with the other musicians and with the audience. It is a state of mind in which the improviser has attained a balance between looseness of thought and feeling along with the necessary control and discipline.

All three levels are theoretically possible at any given moment for the improviser. The true professional never reveals artistically on what level he is operating. The demonstration of a consistently high performance level is what separates some improvisers from others. A judgment based on a few performances or recordings is not truly valid, because in some cases either the artist or listener might not be psychologically in tune with the music at the moment. It is the overall level over a substantial period of time which reveals the true worth of an artist's creativity.

As a performing artist, the improviser is obviously effected by his psychological and physical state at the time of playing. The events of a particular day, either positive or negative, must influence the musician's temperment and therefore his performance. And of course if there is a physical ailment, it can directly influence technique and execution as well.

How does the improviser's mind calculate all of the above? The technical aspects of the music combine with the creative energies of each individual at a break-neck pace during improvisation. And then, there are the inevitable non-musical factors which may affect the musicians, such as distractions of where and for whom one is playing. Of course, historically, most jazz has taken place in night clubs where musical creativity was not the primary reason why the people were in the audience. It is amazing that jazz has progressed at all in the face of such difficult creative situations. The people who perform jazz in these settings must demonstrate strong concentrative powers and intense dedication in order to cope with such environments.

It seems that all of these above factors are operating in the improviser's mind simultaneously. For myself, I can sometimes recall what musical thought led me to a particular idea, such as a chord, or rhythm. At times I can also recall nonmusical thoughts. But most often, my mind is thinking about what I'm playing in relation to the other musicians and trying to keep in communication with them. That is the general thrust of what seems to be happening. Otherwise, I try to keep open and receptive so that anything which occurs either consciously or unconsciously can be included or at least not come as a surprise. In fact, I think a central philosophical aspect of the art of improvisation is strongly related to the Tao or Zen concept of being in present time as much as possible; neither the past nor the future should interfere with living fully in the moment.

Considerations of the Act: Listening

Listening stands as the paramount task for the improviser while playing. There are many levels of listening from obvious to subtle that should be clear to the artist. In traditional jazz where a *steady pulse*[2] is being played for example, the clearest indicators of this pulse are the drummer's *riding*[3] on the cymbal and the bassist's *walking*[4] quarter notes which mark off every beat. The cymbal beat is altered continuously by variation in addition to coloristic shadings played throughout the drum kit. Primarily, it is the cymbal which energizes and drives the momentum forward. As a corollary, the ability to hear the exact pitches as well as the pulse which the bassist is playing indicates a highly subtle and important aspect of listening for everyone in the group whether soloing or accompanying. The relationship between drums and bass for the rhythmic impetus as well as that of the piano (or guitar) and bass for harmonic reference points is a symbiotic one. It means that in jazz, the bassist is the anchorman, even though he usually is heard only in the background by the untrained listener.

2 *steady pulse* – when the rhythm is stated evenly.
3 *riding (ride beat)* – the basic propelling jazz feel (dotted eighth-sixteenth) played by the drummer on one cymbal.
4 *walking (walking time)* – when the bass plays every quarter note of the bar.

The instrument playing chords *(comping)*[5] is in a sense calling the plays like a quarterback in football ot the helmsman in rowing. This musician can by the nature of his function change the mood and direction instantly of the rhythm section and the soloist. He is the intermediary between the bass-drum team and the soloist. The importance of this role to the overall music cannot be underestimated. Truly, the "comper" can easily make or break a group's performance. The ideal musician for this role is one who has a thorough knowledge of rhythm and harmony, as well as an attitude of complete giving of oneself for the benefit of the group sound.

The format of mainstream jazz improvisation generally takes the shape of soloist with accompaniment. (Not included here are most collective improvisational styles). It is very democratic in theory, but in truth the soloist has the central role when his time comes. The accompanists are there to serve his musical ideas, translate his impulses and provide inspiration for further development. The interpersonal dynamics of the typical jazz group imply trust and confidence between the members. Because of the constant, ongoing nature of improvisation during any given solo, there is no time for the musicians to discuss what is, or has happened. This rapport-building process often takes time to develop and in many cases is either positively or negatively affected by the social give-and-take when members are not actually performing. The similarities between a band and a team engaged in competitive sports is very close. Living and working together become equal at some point.

In fact, my feeling is that what a jazz audience is reacting to is not really the soloists and their creations. On a deeper human level, they're responding to the degree and quality of communication which is evidenced between the members of the group. Besides the aforementioned points of freedom, spontaneity and the idea of being in present time which jazz brings to people, there is also the direct inspiration an audience feels when they have witnessed good rapport and communication between human beings.

The Concept of Soloing

The solo represents each man's version of the story. A group in essence agrees to the subject matter at the outset of a song by the act of presenting it in the first place. Of course, the material may not be everyone's taste in reality, but the physical act of performing means each member is in some way using the piece as a starting place. Once in progress, the soloist has a chance to express his feelings just as in a conversation.

One can easily compare aspects of soloing to certain literary concepts. If you analogize the idea of a concert to a novel, or an album to a short story, then each composition is similar to a chapter. Within the chapter, the solos are like paragraphs. In each solo, the

---

5 *comping* – the rhythmic and harmonic accompaniment behind a soloist.

pauses or changes in direction are equal to marks of punctuation and new sentences. Obviously, dialogue between instruments as well as soliloquies occur throughout. Also, a good solo will often have a period of introduction, exposition and a finale just as writing does.

The central point is that there is a sense of form to improvisation when it is well done. Musical ideas which only reflect clever relationships between the elements of music for their own sake result in empty technique. The goal of the art of improvisation is no different than in other art forms; to express something meaningful and communicate it to others.

"And then I look at them and say: 'Have you transcribed?'" (p.179) (Private collection)

The ideal physical and mental state while improvising is one of relaxed intensity. Being relaxed enables the mind to be open and flexible as well as allowing the body to execute technique gracefully. On the other hand, intensity refers to the clarity of ideas and the emotional conviction needed to express them.

Most artists have their own personal way of creating this mood prior to performance. But in general, the excitement and natural nervousness of public performance gives an artist a bit of an emotional edge before playing that can be channeled into the desired intensity of feeling. At the same time, a sense of relaxed confidence is felt because one is doing what he loves and is best at. The times spent on stage are unlike any other in either normal or artistic life. This is especially true for the typical jazz musician whose entire art leads up to those moments of spontaneous improvisation.

Relaxed Intensity

Making Mistakes

The more an improviser reaches towards the unknown, the more likely he will stumble and become temporarily lost in the music. In fact to my mind, when a performer is consistently perfect, I suspect that in terms of his own playing he is not attempting to explore. Musically, being lost means pitfalls such as ending or beginning a phrase in an awkward rhythmic or harmonic juncture, losing the pulse or form of the tune, etc. Reacting to momentary confusion is a true test of experience.

There are cues constantly being given along the way by the other musicians, especially if they're aware of the situation. These cues can come in many musical forms, but in general are concerned with one of the other musicians being simple and clearly laying out the ongoing structure to the confused player. This necessitates a willingness in one's accompanists to help the overall performance by demonstrating an unselfish attitude. But even more important, the confused musician must sacrifice his ego by not insisting that he is correct and all the others are mistaken. Nor should he be so discouraged that he feels he cannot remedy the situation. Only a fellow musician should be able to see a mistake in any case, as long as the group cooperates and does not aggravate the situation by making it more obvious than it is. In the end, being correct is not the point; being creative and flexible is.

Different Playing Situations

Up to now, I have discussed the act of improvisation from primarily specific musical standpoints. One should feel by now that the improviser's art is also a result of other factors besides musical aspects, the psychological state of mind being critical. An important influence in this area is the effect of different playing situations upon the improviser's art. I have found that these feelings become habituated after repeated exposure to a particular environment.

In live performance the emphasis is upon interaction (mostly unspoken) between the audience and the performer. Even if a performer tries to ignore the audience, the vibrations are present and must influence the music. In fact, most members of the audience come to the performance with a preconceived idea of expectations. This is especially true if a performer has a particular reputation for his stage demeanor.

Given a clean slate though, a performer can either ignore the opinions of the audience or give them what he thinks they expect. Obviously, this will affect his performance to a great degree especially in his attitude towards choice of material and manner of presentation. Ideally, there should be a good balance between educating and entertaining the audience.

The size of an audience can affect a performance. Large audiences which are physically distanced from the stage usually cause a performer to be more obvious than in a smaller intimate setting. When people are physically closer and fewer in number, there is a sense of immediacy which can lead to an even greater use of subtleties than found in a larger setting. Hopefully, a good improviser can make these kinds of shifts without sacrificing any artistic impulses. For myself when I was inexperienced, I seemed to take more musical chances in smaller settings while in front of larger audiences I play it safer.

The recording situation is quite opposite and because of its importance in documenting the history of jazz, I will discuss it more fully later in this chapter. Suffice to say, the inherent paradox in recording jazz is that spontaneity and impulse are captured forever, causing the concept of improvisation to imply more than its immediacy because it can be scrutinized much like a classically written or commercially planned piece of music. This exaggerates the whole premise of capturing the moment and the process of ongoing change which is essential to the improviser's art. In recording, a balance must be struck between spontaneity and planning.

One other playing environment is particularly special in jazz. I term it the "workshop situation". It ranges from the free-wheeling social comraderie and competition of the jam session to the highly critical expectations of the teacher-as-performer master class situation. Time spent rehearsing is also included. These situations give playing a different perspective from live or recording. What gives these settings a common denominator is the inherent element of looseness and relaxation. There is a sense of freedom which can contribute to a willingness for experimenting further than usual.

The consummate improviser should feel at home in each environment with its unique characteristics. A measure of greatness is the artist's ability to respond in an appropriate fashion to each situation and convey this in the music itself.

Rhythm is the element which gives cohesion to the music during improvisation. It is like the frame surrounding a painting for it provides the shape and overall flow. No matter what harmonic or melodic devices are occurring, rhythmical contrasts (for example between fast and slow) will be the outstanding feature heard, especially in jazz music.

The Elements of Music – Rhythm

The often neglected use of space creates a sense of breadth which helps to highlight ideas. The solo style of Miles Davis was a prime example of how space creates dramatic effect, as was also his extensive use of short, staccato rhythmic figures to offset long, sweeping melodic lines. Miles was a master of contrast which is a key for keeping the accompanists in the rhythm section creative and alert. They become aware that the soloist is using their accompaniment in an active sense rather than just playing over them as if they were only a back-drop.

The concept of *swing*[6] is peculiar to jazz and can best be described as an intangible feeling of lilt or bounce to the beat. In a group, swinging is the result of a tacit agreement about how to phrase and place the rhythmic aspects of the music in order to achieve this feeling in a comfortable manner. Individual differences of interpretation are integrated in a way which emphasizes a unified approach. If this is accomplished in a relaxed manner, it leads to a flexibility of beat whereby a sense of pushing or relaxing the feel of the rhythm is subtly felt. However, if pushing becomes rushing, or relaxing turns into dragging, then the drive and propulsion of a good, accurate pulse is lost and the rhythmic impetus of what is being played falls short.

Technically, the phrasing of the *dotted eighth*[7] note followed by a sixteenth is the crucial musical device which facilitates swing. There is a slight hesitation felt after the dotted eighth, before the sixteenth. The interpretation of this space is open to countless variations. This is coupled with a general tendency towards unaccented downbeats (in 4/4 the first and third beats), or conversely a predominant upbeat feeling (the second and fourth beats). Phrasing is the combination of: a) articulation, which is the kind of attack and release of each beat ranging from *staccato*[8] to *legato*[9]; b) the *dynamics*[10] of the rhythms as they're played ranging from inaudible "ghost" notes to double forte levels; c) the placement of the beat behind, on top or directly in the middle of the established pulse. Of course, all these factors are entirely personal and in constant flux for the master improviser, who approaches these rhythmic factors from the standpoint of their expressive values, similar to his subtle use of nuances when phrasing a melody. Lesser musicians see rhythm as a hurdle or obstacle that must be dealt with, rather than a major tool for expressive purposes.

The greatest use of rhythmical expression is how it can provoke or pacify a response coming from the accompanists to the soloist. In this sense, rhythm is the least verbalized element between musicians, which in turn leads to countless possibilities of personal interpretation on the spontaneous level. Experience is a crucial factor here as is knowledge of the repertoire so that a soloist is aware of what the commonly accepted responses usually are. He then can be free to attempt variations and see what the result will be.

Rhythmical interplay, vis-a-vis the pulse, tends to follow one of three possibilities. An improviser can choose to play directly *into the time*[11] with variations of placement (ahead to behind the beat); he can play *against the time*[12], superimposing other rhythms which may or may not eventually coincide with a particular downbeat (for

---

6 *swing* – the basic rhythmic momentum of jazz which has changed in concept as the music has evolved.
7 *dotted eighth* – the basic jazz rhythmic feel; interpreted as a dotted eighth note followed by a sixteenth (dotted feel); sometimes expressed in triplets.
8 *staccato* – short, usually percussive articulation.
9 *legato* – smooth articulation as opposed to tongued or staccato.
10 *dynamics* – volume levels.
11 *into the time* – playing in a rhythmical manner directly related to the existing pulse.
12 *against the time* – playing rhythmically in a manner implying another meter or time signature other than the stated one; as in polyrhythms and metric modulation.

example, playing a triplet against eighth notes); or he can ignore the pulse altogether and play *over the time*[13] in a free *rubato*[14] manner, either relating every so often or not to the established pulse. The artistic use of these principles will be present in the music of a mature improviser.

13 *over the time* – rhythmical playing in a manner that suggests complete independence from the basic pulse.
14 *rubato* – a manner of playing in which there is no established pulse, giving the rhythm a free interpretation.

Jazz Club Reutlingen, Germany, mid '80s (© Veronika Gruber)

Rhythmical Extremes: Fast Tempos

In the arts, the extreme poles of a given area are a challenge in themselves. Rhythmically, improvising at a fast tempo has always posed unique problems for the jazz musician. The obvious difficulty is being able to think at break-neck speed. And if the music is harmonically complex, this problem multiplies in difficulty. On one hand, playing fast is nothing more than the usual ideas sped up. But the nature of the quick rhythmic feel necessitates technical accomodations. The be-boppers loved to play fast!

At fast speeds it is imperative that the improviser limits himself to a specific idea over a given musical space. If the sequence of ideas is choppy or moving very quickly from thought to thought, the artist has placed tremendous difficulties upon himself above and beyond technical considerations. Trying to remain with one thought for a while is crucial.

Another clue to feeling a fast pulse is to consider groupings of bars as one unit instead of separately. For example, while one may feel the second and fourth beat in each bar at a normal tempo, it helps to place four bars together as a unit with only one downbeat when the bars are moving quickly. Large groupings of units give the player a wider space to think in. This mental slowing down of the pace can help the musical flow.

At faster tempos the eighth notes take on a more *even*[15], rather than dotted feel. In this way, articulation helps smooth out the fast rhythmic pace. There is usually less of a percussive attack physically (whether it be the tongue or fingers depending on the instrument) and the musician must learn to play lightly and relaxed. Fast tempos are a situation where the notion of relaxed intensity is particularly important, as well as having ideas "under the fingers". The overall challenge at fast tempos is to be expressive and interesting rather than stiff and mechanical.

[15] *even eighth note feel* – the dot of the eighth/sixteenth rhythm is understated.

Melody

Melody is the most personal element of music partly because a musician's tone or sound on his instrument is inextricably linked to melodic playing. This combined with the extremely personal nature of melodic ornamentation makes playing melodies a unique and challenging aspect of improvising. *Ornamentation*[16] means expressive nuances such as *slides*[17], *pitch bends*[18] dynamics, articulation, *grace notes*[19], *grupettos*[20] and more.

As soon as two different pitches are played, a melody has been heard. Using a variety of intervals when improvising is the key to sustaining melodic interest. Besides the obvious changes of shapes that result from varied intervals, there is the expressive factor. For the mature improviser, each interval elicits a different expressive nuance that is emotionally relevant to the actual improvisation. These interval choices will do much to dictate the feeling portrayed in the solo. The use of lyrical versus dissonant intervals are a clear indicator of expression to the listener. Another important fact about melody in the act of improvisation is that usually it will stand at the beginning and end of a piece; obvious focal points for establishing and leaving the listener with a clear impression of the performance which took place.

[16] *ornamentation* – a variety of musical devices used to enhance a basic pitch or pitch sequence.
[17] *slides* – a combination of glissandos and pitch bends as an expressive device.
[18] *pitch bends* – the altering of intonation for purposeful expressive nuance.
[19] *grace notes* – an aspect of melodic phrasing and expression using a neighboring tones quickly preceding the main pitch.
[20] *grupettos* – a melodic device whereby the main pitch is surrounded by neighboring tones above and below it; played in a similar manner as a grace note. (also called mordants).

Extremes in Melodic Playing: Ballads

At fast tempos, rhythm is more crucial to melodic interpretation than in a ballad, where a musician is called upon to excel melodically. The reason is apparent: there is a lot of space when the tempo is slow. All the nuances of every note including the beginnings and endings of the sound itself are exaggerated. In general, the slower the tempo of the music, the more obvious expressive subtleties become.

The art of ballad playing has more to do with experience than any innate talent, although there may arguably have been some improvisers who seemed better or more natural than others at ballads. However, the great jazz musicians could play fast and slow equally well. With age comes maturity and wisdom in life, so that the feeling of a ballad where sensitivity is are highly exposed usually improves over time. In the end, my judgment of an improviser's full worth is reserved until I've heard a few ballad interpretations. More specifically, the ballads should be a known quantity as in a *standard tune*[21].

21 *standard tune* – a song from the established repertoire in any genre; in jazz, the popular songs of American 20th century composers like Porter, Gershwin, Kern, Rogers and Hammerstein.

Throw-Away Phrases

I want to bring attention to one small point that falls under melody playing, which is quite interesting to me. A throw-away phrase is what I call the kind of trail off beginnings and endings of an improvised line which permeate improvisations. They are usually played softly and with what seems to be an unintentional attitude, as if they were an afterthought. The interest is that much like conversation, improvisation is a kind of stream of conciousness and these phrases are indicative of transitions between ideas and also harbingers of what is to come. These are the inner workings of the improviser's mind figuring out what exactly should be presented in the playing; sort of the improviser's private musical strategy.

Harmony

In music, this element is not essential as evidenced by the amount of world music in which harmony is simple or even non-existent. However, in the development of Western music, harmony plays an indispensable role in expressing feelings and ideas. In the broadest sense, harmony is essentially a way of coloring melody to enhance its effect. Another way of looking at it is that harmony is the result of many melodies intertwined.

Describing harmony can be quite complicated and highly technical. The history of harmony is one of evolving dissonance from the Gregorian chant through atonalism. In jazz, harmonic thought has encompassed all of the history of Western music and has accomplished this in less than a century. Knowing how to use harmony expressively and to advantage is truly a major challenge in playing jazz. Every artist has his own subjective feelings about a particular harmonic sequence. Possibly he sees hues and colors. In my case, harmonies evoke geometric shapes and designs like straight lines, circles, squiggles, curves, etc.

Harmonies are made up of the spacing of intervals as found in chord voicings. A specific chord exists also in relation to what precedes and follows it; the preparation and resolution. These two factors of voicings and root movement follow patterns, some of which are familiar through repetition and musical laws. The juggling of these voicings and their sequence is how harmony serves its purpose, which is to provide further means of expression and enhance the elements of rhythm and melody.

22 *chord changes* – the spelling of moving harmonic aggregates.
23 *cadential patterns* – harmonic and their accompanying melodic lines marking tension/resolution points.
24 *multi-noted clusters* – chords built of several close intervals on top of each other.
25 *root motion* – the intervallic sequences in a bass line indicating the tonal centers of a given harmonic movement.
26 *chord quality* – the specific harmonic color of a chord; major, minor, augmented, diminished, dominant.
27 *chord voicings* – the specific positioning of notes in a chord.

In jazz improvisation, moving harmonies are referred to as *chord changes*.[22] The ability to improvise new melodies spontaneously over these changes, taking into account the rhythmic feel of a piece, is a fundamental challenge of the art. Throughout its history, the harmonies have evolved in complexity, but whether the chords are simple triads that move in basic *cadential patterns*[23] or multi-noted *clusters*[24] with no set *root motion*[25], the challenge is still the same. Although a composition may prescribe a certain sequence and *chord quality*[26], the improviser who can hear and know what these changes are will make spontaneous alterations and substitutions. In this way harmony becomes as fluid an element as melody and rhythm. The basic guiding principle is the simple artistic ethic of tension and release in both root movement and chord *voicings*.[27]

with Jim McNeely preparing for a concert in Rottenburg, Germany. (© Hans Gruber)

28 *modal playing* – a way of improvising highly developed in jazz by John Coltrane in the 1960's; one scale as a point of reference rather than moving harmonies and scales; often stationary for a time.

Modal playing[28] is a more open use of harmony for since the root and mode are a known quantity, the colors or voicings can be freely mixed up. This also applies to progressions with a slow *harmonic rhythm*[29]. More use of *chromaticism*[30] or *polytonality*[31] is possible because once again if the root movement is stationary and predictable, the colors above it can easily be superimposed in other keys.

The artistic goal of chord changes is sometimes forgotten. A developing improviser must pass through a stage of enslavement to playing the correct changes. This discipline is a mathematical one which means that the notes being played all fit in some related and acceptable manner to the chords stated. However, if a musician takes this too literally, his melodies will sound stiff and unspontaneous. In the end, chords are only moving colors that help to specify the available notes for melodic invention, but do not preclude unrelated tones. Harmony is not an intellectual tool with no other purpose than to cause the music to be pedantic; it serves the element of melody.

29 *harmonic rhythm* – the duration of a specific harmony (harmonies) in relation to the ongoing meter.
30 *chromaticism* – a style of melodic and harmonic improvising in which tonal centers other than the established one are superimposed alongside.
31 *polytonality* – the use of three or more key centers together; bitonality is two keys.

Color

Color and expression are nearly interchangeable terms for the purposes of improvisation. Color is always present as soon as the first note is played and opbviously a manifestation of the instrument(s) timbre. But taken to a deeper level, color is the combination of expressive devices or personalized nuances that separate styles of music as well as artists themselves. The tone a musician demonstrates is the most obvious example of expression, for much like fingerprints, no two tones can be exactly alike. The more advanced artist will realize how his sound differs from others and exploit these aspects. He does this by a combination of experimenting with equipment (reeds, drum heads, guitar strings, etc.) and by technical manipulation. Although it may be true that one's sound is inborn and natural, much can be done to develop a unique tone.

Nuances include the whole concept of phrasing, which in turn involve articulation, dynamics and devices such as pitch bends, *smears*[32], *voice effects*[33], percussive elements and others, some of which may pertain to a specific instrument only. In a certain style of music, there may be an accepted area of expressive devices which have become associated with the overall sound. For example, the kind of phrasing common in dixieland as compared to be-bop is quite different. A musician must of course be aware of these unwritten rules through his knowledge of the legacy. Once recognized, the artist should be able to stamp the music with his own personal use of nuances and expression. This area, along with tone, is one of the most obvious places in music where an artist's personality can most easily be discerned. As a musician matures, his tone often becomes darker and more mellow as his rapport with the instrument continues to grow.

Another way of conceiving color is that of mood or atmosphere. The overall color of one improvisation, an entire album or concert of music is the sum of all the elements of music together. In the sense of what is really being communicated to a listener, color defined as mood may be one of the most important considerations in measuring the artistic success of the material.

32 *smears* – another vocal/glissando/bending/distorted coloristic effect, especially suitable for brass instruments.
33 *voice effects* – derived from singing, especially the blues; it is the use of vocal sounds on a wind instrument.

Form

The element of form is a basic fact of art. Everything has form, whether intended or not. In improvising, form is apparent all the time because of the nature of a spontaneous solo. Apart from the form of the composition itself, the exact form of an improvisation is not known prior to playing it, so the artist is improvising this element as well. This is a very unique challenge in jazz because it is so unpredictable and open to interpretation. Every improvisation has a beginning and end, obviously, but the manner in which the soloist connects these two is open for each and every solo.

In the compositional sense, form is an understood element to the mature musician. He must have the ability to be aware of the details of melody, harmony, rhythm and color at the same time that he conceives the form. In the case of an improviser, he will be handicapped if he must be thinking about where the *form*[34] of the tune is at any given moment. This innate sense of form is based mostly on experience and practice, but is essential to the jazz improviser.

[34] *form* – in this sense, the exact harmonic and bar structure.

Technique

Being able to manipulate the elements of music is a matter of technique. A musician must walk before he runs and the acquisition of naturalness and smoothness follows a gradual evolution. In the section on education, I will cover more specifics along this path. Here are some general thoughts concerning the perfecting of technique.

An artist must become one with his vehicle. There should not be a separation between what an artist hears in his imagination and his applying these creations to the instrument itself. For improvisers, there must be a direct rapport between mind and body, so that the immediacy of a musical thought finds its way through the instrument at will. If not, then the whole idea of spontaneity is defeated.

The instrument should be an extension of the improviser's body as well as his ideas. Just as body language and voice are indicative of personality, so is the physical relationship between a musician and his instrument. There should be in evidence a sense of grace and ease in the performer's stance and handling of the instrument itself.

Under the heading of technique is the need to develop great powers of concentration. There must be a high level of this to bring together all the elements of music as well as cognizance of the situation in which a performance takes place. Because the act of improvisation is spontaneous and incredibly intense, the artist must be able to coalesce his energies more quickly than in a situation where time is not of the essence. The ability to do this is a training in itself in which meditative and exercise techniques from Oriental and other philosophies can be quite useful.

When technical problems confront the improviser during the playing, there is great inner frustration felt because mental and physical energies have to be spent on correcting technique rather than creativity. A bad reed or faulty instrument for example can be quite unnerving to the inexperienced improviser. One must be able to overcome these types of physical impediments by a strong sense of will power and possibly compensating in other ways.

Composition

For the improviser, composition and recording hold a unique position. The challenge is that the improviser is in a sense freezing what might be another improvisation. The whole notion of spontaneity is undermined because now the improviser must plan and formulate his music methodically without many of the precarious conditions which exist in the act of improvisation.

Composition for the improviser may serve as a tool to facilitate the improvisations themselves. For most composers/improvisers, the reality is that they themselves will be interpreting and improvising their original pieces with other musicians. Because a composition serves as a vehicle or framework for the solos, there is an obvious advantage in creating one's own musical setting.

The other advantage in composing is that it slows down the musical decision-making process which during the act of improvisation is by definition spontaneous and therefore quite rapid. This retardation of what are usually split second musical choices concerning the elements of harmony, rhythm and melody, helps to refine the improviser's mind.

The overall result should be evidenced in more clarity while actually improvising. And if there is any overall goal to reach for in the act of improvisation, it is more and more clarity of musical thought. In sum, the musical skills necessary to compose will find their way into the spontaneous act of improvisation.

Inspiration

The often-heard statement that great art is 10% inspiration and 90% work is nowhere more apparent than in the act of composition. True, one hundred percent inspiration would mean that the artist hears and conceptualizes the complete composition in total. More often the case is that an initial musical idea grows from some sort of outside stimulation. It can be directly musical such as a scale, chord progression or mathematical intervallic relationship, or extra-musical stemming from a real life source such as a person or place and the rendering of that subject in a musical way. Whatever the source, the next step is to approach this germ idea as a problem to be solved. Possible questions concerning problem solving have to do with what framework or form to choose; what emotional feeling does the composer wish to portray through his melodic and harmonic choices; what rhythmical feeling will suit the mood; is there a special playing situation concerning certain individuals, an occasion, or particular instrumentation that is desired; and finally, do all the ingredients together create the color or mood which the initial idea intended to portray?

Thus the real work of composition begins and a musician's knowledge of its mechanics as well as its evolution will greatly affect the results. However, whatever technique or theory used, the final result is judged quite simply. Did the piece convey the composer's perceptions musically? Was the "problem" solved compositionally? After those considerations, it is up to the listener to form his own judgment as to the artistic merit and success of the composer's efforts.

Compositional Consideration: Simplicity vs. Complexity

If we assume for our purposes that composition in jazz functions primarily as an improvisational framework, there needs to be a correct balance between written material and improvisation. If the writing is overdone, the improviser may be forced into a strait-jacket situation where his best capabilities are not given room to breathe. Of course there are situations where this is desired and effective. But in the case of musicians who excel in the act of improvisation, it would be self-defeating artistically to place such strictures upon them. Miles Davis always created a musical situation where the capabilities and assets of his sidemen were given free rein (of course, within the limits he wished to hear from them!).

For the purpose of improvisational clarity, one salient musical element should serve as source material to trigger the improviser's mind. Out of the composition itself, there may be one aspect chosen from either the harmony, rhythm, melody, form or color of the piece which can become a guiding principle. This gives cohesion to both the soloist and composition itself. Sectional writing, whereby each soloist has one different aspect of the composition to improvise on, is very effective and has been widely used in contemporary jazz. In jazz composition, an important goal is to balance the formality of writing with the flexibility of improvisation. As a general guideline, a simple compositional scheme can absorb complex improvisation. Given just enough of an outline, the improviser can feel free enough to make his statement upon the original but yet adhere to the intended compositional goal of the composer.

Technique: Composer's Notebook

In classical composition, there exists the tradition of a composer's notebook. It's the place where any idea, no matter how insignificant it may appear, is written down for future use. There is a discipline about this which is very important to the art of composition. The fact that an entry is made, hopefully on a daily level, means that the compositional process is ongoing. The composer is always adding to his repertoire of ideas, melodies, harmonies and rhythms. On a practical level, future compositions may be in need of just such an idea registered in the notebook. A composer cannot wait for only full blown compositions to come forth. When there is time to compose with some kind of regularity, many compositions can come forth from small sketches. The real work of composing is very time consuming and rigorous, but the rewards seem more immediate than, for example, practicing improvisation. At least when a piece is completed, there is a real satisfaction because physically, a creative work has been born.

Club in Paris, early '90s (Private collection)

In jazz more than other music, the birth of a written composition is only the beginning of a process which in the case of some musicians is constant. That is the ongoing revision or change of the original to suit the needs of improvisation as the situation changes. Conditions such as instrumentation and exact personnel are often in flux as well as whether the composition is to be recorded or not. Sometimes, ideas that work well for the recording situation where there is less playing time available are not suitable to live performsnce and visa versa. Room must also be allowed for changes in the composition as the act of improvisation takes place and new or different ideas become clear over a period of time. Of course in most real situations, after a composition is rehearsed and played a few times, it usually takes on a permanent character.

Compositional Technique: Ongoing Process

Compositional Technique: Using the Elements

If one is looking for a memorable melody in the composition, it is important to test the melody without any harmonic accompaniment. Harmony should further enhance a melody that already can stand by itself. A strong melody is a very sure organizing device in that it ties together the other musical elements no matter how diverse they may be. After all, the melody is the most obvious feature of music to the average listener. This is even more apparent if lyrics are involved.

Since harmonic choices for any one chord are so varied, this is where the subtlest of emotions can be musically described. The composer can change the entire color or mood of a melody and therefore the whole piece just by the change of a minor to major chord. The deeper knowledge and experience a composer has of harmonic styles past and present, the more he can choose from and hopefully find just the right color that will enhance his basic thoughts and feelings.

In jazz composition particularly, the rhythmical setting is of extreme importance because it clearly sets a mood to the improvisations by association of a given *rhythmic feel*[35] to a style of improvising. A *straight ahead*[36] *jazz feel*[37] means an entirely different set of nuances, melodic and harmonic choices differing from, for example, a rock or bossa-nova setting. It's like the difference between a Chopin ballade and Mozart minuet. Each feeling connotes a certain syntax and way of expression which although not ironclad, are associated with the given context for proven, time-worn aesthetic reasons. The rhythm definitely has a major role in determing the vocabulary and syntax which the improviser will use.

In jazz composition, form becomes crucial because it will not only apply to the written material, but it helps to guide the improvisations as well. Therefore, much care must be accorded this often neglected musical element. Use of sectional writing, introductions, transitions and codas can make or break the effect of a piece. Form is an area where constant juggling and change is often found. Although a composition may look correct and sound right, the feeling of a form that is comfortable to the improviser is something that cannot be known until a piece is played a few times. Of course, the composer/improviser as a single artist has a great advantage in this particular area.

Just as in improvisation, the color of a composition is the overall mood resulting from the other elements combined. In the end, the color of a piece and its improvisations have to fulfill two goals: it should accomplish the composer's musical and aesthetic desires; and the listener should be able to feel something akin to what was intended.

---

[35] *rhythmic feel* – the underlying rhythmical basis of a piece of music.
[36] *straight ahead feel* – refers to a walking bass line and typical swing ride beat on the cymbal.
[37] *jazz feel* – as distiguished from other rhythmic feels inferring "swing" as the intrinsic element.

Material: Larger Settings

One major compositional consideration is whether the music is for large or small groups. There is a natural tendency for most composers to eventually want to hear their pieces played by instruments of various colors in larger, more formal contexts than solely the small intimate jazz group. It is a very rewarding experience for a composer to hear his music on a grand scale. It is also an ambitious undertaking because in order to do something with all those musicians and instruments, more written material may have to be added. The composer is forced to go back to his original sketches and search further for seeds to bring forth more composed material, yet it must still be related to the original. The process of taking an idea and expanding it way beyond the original setting is the main challenge at this point. How to create a lot of material from very little and still be unified is what real deep composing is about. And then there is the *orchestration*[38].

There is one inherent danger in this enlarging process for the jazz composer/improviser. In order to arrange music for more musicians and instruments, a certain degree of tightness and disciplined planning will be necessary in the writing. The possibility of pretentiousness that one may abhor in academic and classical environments must be guarded against. Complexity is all right in any music, but the essential need for freedom and looseness should not be lost in jazz. Those qualities stand as two of the greatest contributions that jazz has made to the art of music.

[38] *orchestration* – part of the overall sound of music; specifically achieved by assigning instrumental colors.

Interpretation

Concerning interpretation, there may be occasions when the composer is aware of whom the musicians will be playing the music. Duke Ellington was a great example of a composer who knew in advance how the phrasing and interpretation would most likely sound, because the musicians were always the same. This greatly affects the composing process.

One definition of a great composition is its ability to absorb many interpretations by numerous artists. This attests to an ever-lasting challenge to personalize the music. It is even more outstanding when a song written and conceived in an older historical period transcends its boundaries and is adapted to diverse and modern stylistic concepts. The largest collection of this kind are the so-called standards of American popular music throughout the twentieth century as well as a few classic jazz tunes from different eras.

One common way to alter interpretations is to change the customary tempo at which the tune is known. The *be-bop*[39] generation of Charlie Parker, Dizzy Gillespie, Miles Davis and others often employed this device. Another more complex route is *reharmonizing*[40] the melody, in a sense, creating a new set of colors which in turn alters the mood of the piece. Pianist Bill Evans was remarkable in

[39] *be-bop* – the style of jazz established in the 1940's setting the modern standard for improvising on chord changes with a certain "swinging" feel to the rhythm.

[40] *reharmonization* – altering the given harmony, usually in close connection to the melody.

this respect. Another method is to add a new, composed section or *ostinato vamp figure*[41] to improvise over, alongside or instead of the chord changes to the tune itself. Reinterpreting a standard song can be considered a form of composition. It is especially effective because when something is well recognized in one format or style, the changes made to it appear more obvious. Thus the creativity and uniqueness of the new arrangement is easily appreciated.

41 *ostinato vamp figure* – an ongoing bass line and/or rhythmic idea played by the rhythm section.

Recording

Recording the act of improvisation is in a sense contrary to the whole concept of spontaneity, which emphasizes ongoing change and endless variation. The loose flexible attitude necessary while improvising can be at odds with the scrutiny that a recording receives. Also the usual conditions of live performance do not exist either in the recording studio (except for the live recording date), nor when and where the record will be listened to. To be sure, many jazz records do capture the true improvisational spirit, but the demands of recording necessitate other skills also.

There is the overriding fact that nothing slips by the microphone. I remember the first time hearing myself isolated on one track. The experience was quite instructive for discovering inaccuracies of technique such as faulty *intonation*[42], unclear tone or articulation. Isolated, these are immediately noticed by even the casual ear. Not only does the microphone capture everything, but it seems to magnify both the positive and negative elements of an improviser's sound and technique. In the sense of improving one's art, the studio situation is a great source for showing a musician his strengths and weaknesses.

In general, the act of improvisation is changed in one major aspect. Recording calls for a conciseness and clarity of ideas that is necessary because the performance will be listened to repeatedly and usually be shorter compared to the normal length of a jazz performance. In live improvising, the excitement of the situation and the visual aspect of seeing musicians interact together can blur the details of the music. Recording music means it will live forever in a neatly tied package. These challenges make recording indispensable to the development of an artist.

42 *intonation* – the relative sharpness (high) and flatness (low) of a given pitch in relation to an accepted tuning note; an important aspect of expression in jazz.

Recording Agenda

The ideal situation is one where an artist would be able to decide on when and what to record as his interests and work develop in a given direction. This would result in the necessary time to develop ideas and to experiment so that the album concept is clear (an album also means CD, cassette or whatever future technology will reveal). Of course, improvisational performances can't be prepared in the same manner as the written material, but by trying out a feeling or specific musical element the artist may get a clearer picture of what direction his improvisation might take when finally recorded. The chance to rehearse written music with musicians for some time before recording is a great advantage. If the group is a working band, recordings can be balanced between the studio and live situations, giving a full picture of the improviser's art revealing both the planned and spontaneous side of the music. Except for a few musicians, the opportunity to execute projects in such an orderly fashion is rarely the case.

An album is much like a novel with several chapters or a collection of short stories. In other words, it is a complete physical product with a definite beginning and end. The novel analogy can be further compared to a concept album in which each recorded track is like a chapter representing a part of the overall story. The short story concept is similar to what is called a *blowing date*[43], which simply means each track is not necessarily related in any direct conceptual way. In the career of a jazz artist, both extremes are revealing for the former presupposes a vision or concept where the parts are related to the whole; while the latter is a looser, more spontaneous setting.

Recording: Album Concepts

A careful artist will insure that an album is balanced in terms of tempos, harmonic textures, rhythmic feels and other facets of the overall sound. (Exceptions are albums which purposely address themselves to one or two elements for specific artistic reasons). Balance is crucial because it must be considered that the music may be listened to in many environments, some quite different than the one imagined by the artist.

[43] *blowing date* – a recording date where the musicians play in a jam session or informal atmosphere, using familiar repertoire such as standards and blues formats.

The hours spent recording are different from all other musical situations for reasons described earlier. Because of these influences, the act of improvisation undergoes some variations in the studio.

The Recording Process and the Act of Improvisation

The question of how many *takes*[44] or attempts to allot for one track is crucial. This is because "time is money" in the studio and artistically, the well may run dry at some point. Every musician who has recorded finds his own formula, but in my experience three takes seems to be the maximum for jazz improvisation. For written material or music where the outcome must be suitable for certain situations (pop, sound tracks, commercials) the takes go on until they are perfected and are often recorded in in a segmented fashion.

During the first take, the musicians usually try to find their way through the composition and discover what will work for the recording. After listening back, the experienced improviser will at first correct mistakes and then figure out the best way to approach the song. Often, the second take will work as the final version, but since the improviser has only just tried his approach for the first time on take two, there may be a third attempt to improve upon it or maybe try something new such as a different tempo or mood.

[44] *takes* – multiple versions of a song in a recording session.

As in all matters pertaining to recording, experience is the key. Listening to playbacks can upset the inexperienced musician and throw him off balance for the following takes. If the artist gets too critical, he may become nervous and technique as well as spontaneity will suffer. Also, the actual sound being engineered can be upsetting because the tone of the instrument is so different from what it usually appears to be. Added to this may be an uncomfortable studio with an unnatural *acoustic sound*[45], a *headphone mix*[46] which is not realistic, the possible frightening notion that what is being done is for posterity, an uncooperative *producer*[47] or other musician, plus one's individual problems from both the artistic and personal contexts. It becomes clear that optimum performance in the studio can be quite a challenge.

The attitude should be as natural as possible; that everything is the best it can be, while at the same time the attempt is made to correct any problems. But a musician should not lose sight that he's there to make music for the public and conditions must be secondary to the creative impulse. When the green light goes on the artist must be ready to go all out. Because of the difficult conditions there may be a tendency to rely on what is tried and tested. A conservative approach to recording compared to live performance can be beneficial as long as the line between spontaneity and stiffness is drawn so that it doesn't appear as if an improviser isn't really attempting to do what he is there for, which is to truly improvise.

Recording: The Mix

Upon leaving the studio, it is very valuable for the artist to take with him *rough mixes*[47] so that he can manipulate takes if necessary to get the best version. Also, it is almost impossible to be objective about a specific performance in the studio itself. A little space and distance really helps the artist listen to the quality of the music unencumbered by the studio environment. Depending upon the album, there is nothing sacrosanct about *splicing*[48] or editing good parts of one take to another. If the record concept was meant to be a loose, free-wheeling blowing session, then splicing might seem to be a bit dishonest artistically. On the other hand, many of the jazz albums produced in the 1970's and 1980's were concept types, employing extensive overdubbing techniques; a case where splicing may be crucial. This should be a personal and artistic decision based on the goal of the artist, but of course in reality there may be outside commercial pressures which affect how artistically pure the recording can be from the outset.

Suffice to say, that the *mixing*[49] process is crucial and can make or break the final outcome. Factors such as the *EQ*[50], *panning*[51] and the relative volumes for all the participants can make a performance sound very different from what was played. Fortunately, in recordings where art takes precedence over commercial considerations,

---

44 *acoustic sound* – the sound of instruments when heard without amplification and/or microphones; also refers to the sound heard as a result of the room shape, sound properties of the material used in construction, etc.

45 *headphone mix* – in recording, the relative sound and volume of the instruments heard by each musician in his headset.

46 *producer* – in a recording session, the person who oversees the technical aspects of the recording along with the engineer as well as coordinating the musical aspects in conjunction with the recording artist.

47 *rough mix* – in recording, a quick version of the recorded music with relative volume and e.q. present; used for reference towards the final mix.

48 *splicing* – the connecting of parts of songs or solos together in the final editing process of recording.

49 *mixing* – in recording, the process of combining the various tracks into a whole.

50 *EQ* – equalization; concerns the proportion of treble, mid-range and bass frequencies for a tone; especially crucial in mixing a recording.

51 *panning* – the placement of instruments location-wise in a stereo scenario from left to right.

mixing is a matter of attempting to best represent the musical and aesthetic goals of the artist.

After the mix, there are decisions concerning *sequencing*[52] and *editing*[53] which again can greatly affect the final outcome. Here is where the artist must make his concept final, because the listener does not know what is behind the thinking which the artist takes for granted. Objectivity here is the key and this is where a producer can be very helpful. His job in this case is to be the public's ear and at the same time also understand the artist's concept.

The producer or anybody functioning close to that role is usually the man responsible to the record company. In the session itself, he must see that the engineer is doing a good job and also be sensitive to the performers in the studio. Timing of events in the studio greatly affects the artistic sensibilities and temperament of the performers. Decisions concerning whether to try another take of a song, take a break, or when to end the session are greatly influenced by the supposed objective ear of the producer. The artist and other musicians should be thinking about the music. Ideally, an experienced producer is one who appreciates the artistic vision and can find a balance between it and the business aspects of making records.

Record companies provide several necessary services for the artist. They bankroll projects with the obvious intention of gaining a return on their investment. In order to facilitate this goal, they provide the functions of promotion and distribution so that the public will be aware of and able to purchase the product. Due to the necessity of profit making, there often exists the potential of a natural antagonism between artistic and business goals. To be sure, there are times when both parties are in agreement and then the process is one of facilitation.

But more often the case is that record companies traditionally have considered jazz too difficult for the average listener. Therefore, the promotion necessary for it to be known is rarely satisfactory except in unusual cases. The pop-jazz or *fusion style*[54] has slipped through the commercial boundary because the rhythm and sound are close enough to pop music, presenting the possibility of mass popularity. It must be mentioned that there have been freak successes both commercially and artistically as in the cases of Keith Jarrett, Wynton Marsalis and a few others.

All artists would rather be successful than not, if only because they can then afford to continue recording and working on their own music in various ways. Money buys freedom and freedom should mean time to work and experiment. However, the artist who for whatever reason remains as pure as possible can really only record in two ways: either with a small, independent company or by

---

52 *sequencing* – in an album or program of music, the order of songs.

53 *editing* – artistically refers to shortening musical ideas in order to achieve conciseness of thought; in recording, the process of removing extraneous material such as speaking or instrument sounds from before or after a take; also the final process of organizing the master tape.

Recording: The Business End

54 *fusion* – the mixing of distinctive stylistic elements from different musical genres; in recent jazz, it is specifically the use of rock 'n roll rhythms and sound with jazz harmony and improvisational techniques.

self-production of the recording, promotion and distribution of the record itself.

The small company has been the life blood of jazz for decades with occasional forays by major labels into jazz. The independents can maintain their own selective catalogue and through them jazz has remained an art form rather than another arm of the entertainment business. But with the increasing centralization of the distribution process, more and more small companies find it nearly impossible to make their products available. The budget of a small company is by necessity limited which directly affects the extent of recording, mixing, hiring musicians, etc. This sad fact means that the jazz artist is always working under pressure outside the demands of the art itself. The reality is that many jazz records become no more than recorded jam sessions or first rehearsals.

To withstand this pressure and still get one's art out to those interested ears is the challenge of playing jazz in our time. For the artist, recording is the only true way of documenting his work and evolution. Once music is recorded, the artist can move on and continue his creative evolution[55].

[55] For an in depth discussion of recording refer to *The Art of Recording* (Aebersold Publications)

The Role of the Bandleader – Overall Responsibilities

Being in charge of any organization usually means that the person's responsibilities are split among several groups of people. For a musician leading a group, the obligations are first to himself as an artist, in his ability to find artistic satisfaction through the music played. The next responsibility is to his sidemen because they too must be both artistically and financially secure to do their creative best. Finally, the leader is responsible for the business, which consists of promoters, agents, recording companies, etc., all of whom provide necessary functions so that the art is available and heard. In many ways a bandleader is like the director of a play or coach of a team. He has to create by using real people as his tools. And further, he must deal directly with the public as well as take an active role in the creating itself.

Business

On a basic level, this responsibility has to do with the usual criteria of doing good business: honesty in relationships and keeping contractual agreements as well as making sure that the best efforts have been made to present the group's music for an audience's enjoyment. As simple as this sounds, the business of running a band requires talents other than creative ones. The experience of a traveling unit means that there are timetables to meet and the necessity of dealing with people functioning as clerks, waiters, ticket counter personnel, porters, stewardesses, customs, immigration, etc. And since jazz is usually such a marginal business as far as profits are concerned, most of the truly comfortable ways of traveling have to be minimized. Add to this the phone calls, faxes and e-mail in order to facilitate prearranging of tickets, arrival times, contracts, equipment rentals and more. All of this means that the bandleader will spend a lot of time taking care of necessary business and this distraction can be very dangerous to the creative side if not kept in balance. Although there are so-called "managers" in jazz, many jazz musicians do everything themselves. The sophistication and acumen gained through such experiences are invaluable for dealing with life as most ordinary people do daily; somehow this experience finds its way into the positive challenge of relating one's art to real life and people.

The Audience

Of course, the leader is not alone. He must instill a kind of *esprit de corps* in the group so that there's a feeling of mutual responsibility, much like there should be during the actual playing. The group's responsibility to the audience is to do their job on the highest level possible. If the understood goal is to play creative, high-level music, then one need not be overly concerned about whether the audience will fully comprehend it or not. The main goal should be to do the creative task at hand. In this way the public will have been, in a sense, entertained.

Obviously, if for whatever reasons, a particular audience has come with different expectations or a group is playing a venue that is not suitable or accustomed to such music, there is little that can be done. The leader's obligation is to have prepared the group so that within the context of their presentation, the musicians will reveal an awareness that they are playing for a paying audience. On stage, the leader must create a psychological environment suitable to the needs of the group so that their best abilities can surface. For example, simply introducing the members to the audience and giving them a sense of their importance helps this goal. Finally, exhibiting good manners and respect for the audience is crucial. The way this is accomplished varies for each leader and ranges from bantering with the people, to simply saying hello, goodbye and thank you.

Sometimes, musicians become so sensitive to the response of the audience that they will try to do what they feel gains approval. To my mind, if serious art is presented, it should be with dignity and a feeling on stage which is commensurate with the music. Commercial art and music is meant for everyone – deep, sophisticated art may not be and the two shouldn't be confused.

The intimacy of a club usually means the presentation can be looser and less formal than in a large hall or stadium, where the challenge is to create a bond with so many people. Also, festivals or concerts where several groups are playing usually dictates that the energy and excitement level is very high. There is also quite a difference in how an audience greets a group if they are the main attraction as compared to being an opening act for the performers that the audience primarily came to see. A bandleader must be glib enough to handle all these situations in relation to the audience as well as setting the other musicians at ease.

Sidemen: Contemporaries vs. Young Musicians

In jazz, there is a definite traditional view of the need to be an apprentice to a great musician. This means that having worked and traveled on the road with a master, a young musician has "paid his dues" and in a sense becomes accredited in the jazz world. There is a respect quotient given to such a musician by the jazz business community who are the promoters and entrepeneurs producing jazz around the world over the years. The jazz community is very small and everybody is quickly recognized. To become a bandleader who will be responsible for hiring sidemen and organizing a body of music, there is no substitution for learning on the job. (This situation of course is less available in our present period; more about this in "Ruminations…").

Once a musician has the opportunity to choose a group, there are two possible ways of accomplishing this. Although financial and business considerations may dictate which way is plausible, let us assume the leader can hire either contemporaries or younger, lesser known musicians. Financial considerations such as how much salary can be paid and the amount of expected work are important. Because of these factors and the possibility of other outside influences, there may be pressure felt towards hiring musicians who already have a reputation with the public.

Playing with one's contemporaries is a very unique and challenging situation. Everyone is more or less equal in the musical sense, because being contemperaneous with someone else assumes that you went through similar experiences at the same time. Even if you've never played with a contemporary, there is the bond of a common musical language because you grew up and learned at the same time. This feeling of comraderie and commonality can make the music very strong. On the negative side is that this equality can make it difficult for one unified concept to emerge and for the members' egos to accept a situation where everyone is equal. The reality is that most of the time, one's contemporaries are interested in their own career and body of music. Except for a few recordings or other special musical gatherings, most leaders do not play with their contemporaries too often.

Playing with less experienced musicians is both difficult and a great experience. The challenge is to teach them how to do what you want and still make them feel that they're being themselves. A young artist has an extremely sensitive ego, usually more so than the experienced one. Also, being younger means a certain amount of naiveté in life's passages and realities as well as musical experiences. The bandleader becomes a sort of teacher of life in general, depending of course on the personalities involved. The beauty of this situation is that a young talent is like an empty blackboard waiting to be written upon. A more experienced artist (he need not be older chronologically) can really influence the future of the art by teaching a new talent through his own music. Obviously, the public doesn't want to witness a classroom situation, so the leader must know when and how to impart his knowledge.

Sidemen: Set Group vs. Pick-Up Unit

A musician who can command work might have the choice of whether he wants to have a set group of sidemen or employ other musicians wherever he plays. The obvious advantage of a set band is that material can be developed and communication highly evolved as a result of the amount of time spent playing together. There is no substitute for developing music on the bandstand with other musicians. As much as the idea of spontaneity is emphasized in the act of improvisation, when one can count on a certain musical response from other musicians, that confidence can generate a high quality and quick rate of personal development. When creative interaction can be counted upon, the improviser can devote his energies to a different, possibly fresh musical idea instead of wondering whether basic functions and communication are being accomplished.

On the other hand, if a musician leads many pick-up groups, he can become very clear and strong about his own direction. He learns how to quickly get to the heart of his playing; how to make material and musical directions concise and clear; how to best relate on a high artistic level to mostly strangers. This is a valuable learning experience. And although there may be situations where amazing strength of musical direction is required because of very weak sidemen, there can be times of unexpected magic and spontaneity with unfamiliar musicians.

Sidemen: Treatment (Ethics)

When I was a sideman, I sometimes resented the leader's directions especially in relationship to limitations placed on my soloing; for example, when and how long to solo or what material I was required to play. But as a leader, I realized that decisions of timing, sequencing, etc., were among the most important made on the bandstand. Therefore, sometimes necessity meant cutting another musician off or editing his solo. This intrusion can be very touchy, which brings up the whole psychological area of how to treat sidemen. A band is not like a factory where the boss can demand productivity. Therefore, the dynamics of interpersonal relationships are quite intense in a creative endeavor like playing and performing music.

A jazz group is a showcase for how people relate to each other. The actual situation is in theory like a democratic government. Everybody is supposedly free to have their say, meaning that the quality of vibrations among a group of artists cannot help but be reflected in performance.

A musician has to be made to feel that he is respected by the leader and appears in a positive light to the audience. A younger sideman also needs to feel that his ambitions can be satisfied by playing in the group because he has his entire career ahead. So the leader is confronted with balancing his own artistic and psychological needs with those of his sidemen. Often, conflict of egos, especially when critics or the audience continually single out one musician (maybe not the leader) can occur. Deciding whether to fire a sideman can create tension as may a musician's decision to go on his own.

But tension in a performing group can be positive for the music. Frustration due to bad traveling and performing conditions, being physically run down or emotionally unsettled can energize a musician to great results. However, this is not always the case; every personality is different. But a leader can be sure of one thing; there will be some bad times experienced by any group of people placed together because of what they do, rather than how they feel personally about each other. For example, there is no guarantee that in a marriage, the bride or groom will be able to relate to the in-laws for any reason other than the necessary mutual relationship put upon them. In a band, the musicians need not love each other in all ways to make great music. As long as professional respect is exhibited, the group controlled by a strong leader can make art together. More often than not, time spent together means constant improvement of communication, a common purpose and a shared history, resulting in a positive feeling between group members.

Sidemen Chosen as a Consequence of Specific Material

Although this situation is more common for recording rather than a working group, a leader may choose his sidemen based on the requirements of the music to be played. If time is available he may hire musicians whom he feels can learn and contribute to whatever concept he has in mind. If he is reasonably flexible, the evidence of a promising musical chemistry can make the music take its own unique direction over time. The leader may have to alter his original concept because as the sidemen contribute, the music may change. On the other hand, if the leader has a strong commitment to a certain sound in his head, he may do better to audition and search for those musicians best suited for the specific style he has in mind. Usually through music circles, reputations are well known. In any case, the process makes the leader more knowledgeable about his own direction and how to best fulfill it.

Choosing a Set

The final responsibility in live performance and recording is the choice of the set to be played. A large part of the musical and communicative success of a performance is the sequence of tunes. By his knowledge of the general mood which a particular piece usually evokes, the bandleader is programming the emotional climate of the set both for the other musicians and by association, the audience. There are several key elements to be considered.

Of great importance are the first and last songs because the former sets a mood while the latter leaves a lasting impression. For this last reason, it is customary to end the entire performance with what may be called a "flag waver", usually a high energy dramatic showcase for all the musicians. More often than not, a drum solo will come at this time.

Since the situation may call for two or possibly three sets, the timing of the entire evening is a large consideration. Some groups leave an audience at the end of the first set or even the entire evening feeling like they want more, because of a certain timing in the music which has peaks of intensity in the beginning or middle of the evening rather than only at the end.

Another important compositional decision is where to place a ballad or other dramatic pieces. This selection is usually very effective in terms of the audience because slower (and possibly softer) improvisation is easier to follow and emotionally dramatic, especially if the material is not familiar. Finally, where to play recognizable songs from familiar albums by the group or a standard that is well known will have an important effect on the entire set. All in all, any verbal communication with the audience should be handled by the group's leader or in a cooperative band, by the musician who is most glib. The banter on stage or the dropping of a few key comments between the musicians themselves can be important in either increasing or relaxing tension. Those moments on stage are very special and unlike any other. If the energy is harnessed in a positive fashion, an audience will have been fully "edutained."

Club in Germany, early '80s (© Hans Gruber)

Musical Autobiography 3

The next chapter in this book is called "The Basis of My Art", in which I describe my aesthetic and creative principles. In order to give the reader an understanding of where I've come from musically, this present chapter is devoted to portraying my journey from its beginnings to the present. Besides the major events, I've tried to relate who and what my influences were and how they affected me.

In life, we are to a great extent the products of our teachers, whether they serve officially in that capacity or as friends, parents and acquaintances. In an art form, the apprenticeship system works to the extent that we try to emulate our masters. As the years pass, I've realized more and more what exactly it was and from whom I learned. These are lessons not contained in books – they are passed on through the *oral*[1]/*aural tradition*[2].

One's masters provide the inspiration in early attempts to test oneself in the field. They pass on not only specific knowledge of the craft, but through their example, they demonstrate the mental, emotional and physical attributes necessary to survive and contribute to the world as an artist. They give the student a sense of confidence in his own creative abilities.

Even now, when I see older artists still on the road bringing their energies and art to the people, I feel a combination of pride, respect and inspiration. Above all, I'm humbled to think of how many hotels, airports and dressing rooms these man have seen!

My art is also the sum of other influences both in and outside of music. The late twentieth century has made everything available to us at our fingertips. One immediate result of this incredible wave of fast communication is the ability to experience many areas of life that would have been out of reach fifty years ago to all but a few. We are in an age of eclecticism and multi-layered influences from every source. I am a product of this phenomenon.

I have been influenced by the music and thoughts of Western Europe, India, Brazil, Africa, Cuba, Bulgaria, Israel, Harlem, Brooklyn, etc. Also, I have observed the arts, philosophy, politics and basically everything that I found useful. The second section called "The Influence of Other Idioms," is descriptive of some of these factors.

---

1 *oral tradition* – the legacy passed on verbally and by example.
2 *aural tradition* – hearing as the main source and transmitter information.

Formative Years

I was born on September 4, 1946 under the sign of Virgo. My parents were teachers in the public schools of Brooklyn, New York where I grew up. My earliest musical memories are of my mother playing piano, particularly the Spanish theme called *The Breeze and I* (Andalucia); my father humming Stephen Foster's *Beautiful Dreamer* and my older brother practicing the accordian. The family was not especially musically inclined and what was heard besides radio, were some of my father's old 78's; Tchaikovsky, Brahms, Beethoven and Enrico Caruso. At nine years old I began piano lessons with a neighborhood teacher, Mrs. Luba Galprin. Taking music lessons was what a typical youngster from my environment did. We lived in a mixed Jewish/Italian middle class section called Flatbush and there were usually some cultural pursuits introduced at an early age. Fortunately, my mother and father intuitively realized that piano was a necessary tool for learning other instruments. At this time, I did not evidence either great talent or desire to play music of any sort, especially the classics Mrs. Galprin taught.

The pieces I remember for those first years were *Spinning Song*, Beethoven's *Für Elise* and other elementary compositions. It was between the ages of nine and twelve that I became a rock 'n roll fan with my favorite performer being Elvis Presley. Finally, I asked Mrs. Galprin to teach me the sheet music to *Love Me Tender* and thus, the beginning of playing chord changes.

My stack of 45's (which I still have) was my most prized possession. I would trade and barter to get a certain Jerry Lee Lewis record or maybe Gene Vincent. Slowly, I became a fan of the tenor saxophone as heard with the groups of Bill Haley, Duane Eddy, Johnny and the Hurricanes and others. Some of the first records by groups featuring saxophone which stood out were *Honky Tonk* (Bill Doggett), *Walkin' With Mr. Lee* (Lee Allan), *Topsy* (Cozy Cole) and *Tequila* (The Champs). Instrumentals were my favorites and the desire to play saxophone became strong. By age twelve, the future was beginning to be set.

I began studying saxophone by being told that I had to play the clarinet first. There was a philosophy expounded that beginning on the more difficult instrument would make it easier to learn saxophone. The premise was that every saxophonist eventually doubled on the clarinet. At Bromley Studios in Brooklyn, when I began lessons, there were dance band workshops where we learned the rudiments of playing *club dates*[3]. My parents figured that I would play in bands in the future and help support my college studies. So on Saturday mornings, I took clarinet and saxophone lessons with Nat Shapiro; piano lessons with Mr. Bromley and combo workshop with his son, Eric.

With Mr. Shapiro I went through book after book of exercises and technical studies; learned to *transpose*[4] at sight and basically how

---

[3] *club date* – the type of musical situation in which the music functions as an accompaniment to some social event such as a wedding or party; also called "general business."

[4] *transpose* – to change music from one key to another.

to get around the sax and clarinet, soon to be joined by the flute. Mr. Bromley taught me arpeggios, scales and basic harmony via the piano. But it was the combo workshop and hearing young Eric, who was a Julliard student, that marked my first awareness of improvisation. We learned standards like *I'm in the Mood for Love*, *Besame Mucho*, *Deep Purple*, cha-cha's, tangoes, Jewish songs and more. When Eric would play and improvise for fun, I was fascinated by how fast he moved his fingers and the fact that he wasn't reading any music. I began to ask questions about what he was doing and my first records were purchased: Herbie Mann, Stan Getz, Horace Silver and of course Dave Brubeck. I subscribed to *Downbeat* magazine and started becoming familiar with the names of jazz musicians.

At age 14 as a student in a large public high school (Lafayette), I met others who were into jazz. My two closest friends were pianist Mike Garson and saxophonist Steve Lipman. Mike and I formed a group called the *Impromptu Quartet* and Steve and I began going regularly to hear jazz in the city. Our quartet worked club dates and spent several summers as the house band in hotels located near New York City. The Catskill Mountains was a large resort area where many young musicians furnished the dance music and accompanied singers for shows. But more importantly was hearing and playing with so many aspiring jazz musicians in jam sessions after work. This was a great breeding ground for a whole generation of New York-based musicians.

For a while, the fact that I was wearing a tuxedo on the stage and getting paid produced an exhilarating feeling. It made me seem special and different from those around me, like a member of an elite club. By the age of sixteen, I was already realizing that playing club dates was neither creative nor special. Such a musician was a laborer, fulfilling a preconceived function: the more individual or passionate you were, the less desirable you became. To reproduce music purely for a functional purpose began to bother me increasingly and within a few years I knew that I couldn't play music in that way. The idea of making a living from real serious playing seemed quite distant. A college degree was not only expected by my parents but appeared to be a necessity. However, the club date years were valuable for learning repertoire, reading music and basic performance techniques.

In essence, it was seeing saxophonist John Coltrane performing live many times during this period (1961-67) that made everything clear to me. I had no idea what he was playing, but I realized that there was a great deal of real creativity and passion in the music. Seeing his incredibly energized group a few feet away from my table was unforgettable and made a lasting impression upon me. I'll never forget the first time I saw Coltrane's group with Elvin Jones, McCoy

Tyner, Jimmy Garrison and at that time, Eric Dolphy. It was at Birdland in New York City where underage kids were allowed to sit in the last row of tables called the "Peanut Gallery" all night for one admission. When I walked in with my date, the Bill Evans Trio with Scott LaFaro and Paul Motian were playing. I was fifteen years old and had heard of Coltrane but I had no idea of what to expect. I was incredulous when the group began playing what turned out to be *My Favorite Things* and Trane was bleeping and screaming through his horn. I couldn't believe that such musicians would play a song from a corny movie like *The Sound of Music*. But even more than that, I couldn't stand what he was doing; Coltrane sounded like he could barely play. I remember though enjoying Dolphy. Such was my initiation to John Coltrane. Of course as the years advanced and I grew musically, Coltrane's music became directly responsible for me wanting to pursue jazz as a means of expression. The beginnings of becoming serious about jazz were quite pure in motive. I never considered the possiblity of making a livelihood from it.

It is during these impressionable teenage years when most people's lives are unconsciously set upon a path because of an inspiring event. When Steve or Mike and I would leave Birdland or the Half Note jazz clubs, we would ride in silence back on the subway to Brooklyn. The nights in Manhattan were like a film depicting life on another planet. The whole atmosphere of the clubs, the music, the musicians who were mostly black, the excitement preceding the music, the calm after the storm; these impressions were indelibly printed on my psyche.

I met Coltrane very briefly during this period at the Village Vanguard as I was walking to the men's room where there is an alcove in which the musicians hang out between sets. I knew Pharoah Sanders, who was then playing with Coltrane, through my acquaintance with the *loft scene*[5] where he frequently played. At this time, (1966) both Coltrane and Pharoah were playing several woodwinds including the flute. Sanders, with Coltrane standing nearby, said hello and asked me to show him something on the flute. After a few comments and a lull, Coltrane relaxed among a group of people. A man asked, "How's it going tonight?" Coltrane replied in a soft, humble manner which I'll always recall, "It goes better at home than on the bandstand." Coltrane's humility together with his reputation for constant self-improvement and practice made a great impression on me.

During this period, I began a lifelong relationship with drummer Bob Moses. We met at a girlfriend's birthday party, jamming on *Well You Needn't*. At a young age, Moses was already familiar with the jazz scene as well as actively playing. He became my guide to the music and customs of jazz. We spent hours playing duets, listening and

---

5   *loft scene* – endemic to New York City; musicians living in former factories converted to living areas; the geographical situation and isolation from neighbors means playing hours are open ended.

discussing life. I even hired Moses to do some club dates with me. We still laugh at how I hassled him to play the merengue beat straight! With Bob I began to play at sessions with some of the musicians I would know for years to come.

One time I drove down to the Showboat, a famous club in Philadelphia, hopefully to sit in with Moses who was playing with multi-reedman Roland Kirk. When I got on the bandstand, Kirk turned around and yelled "*All the Things You Are*, first note is F♯!" Between the strange key and the fast tempo I didn't have a chance for a decent performance. After two fumbling choruses, Kirk played. The next tune was a standard that I was a bit more familiar with called *September Song*. The point was that Kirk embarrassed me on purpose and in doing so made a rather obvious point which a young musician should be aware of: don't get up to play before your time has come!

College began with a major in music education at Queens College. The first day I had a rude awakening. They handed the music majors a four year listening list of the classics beginning with Monteverdi and Palestrina working its way up to Stockhausen. Try as I could that first year, there was no way for me to catch up with the classical repertoire. Certainly not when I was trying to transcribe Coltrane solos! By my sophomore year I was settled at New York University with a major in American History, a subject that I had enjoyed and done well with in high school.

Increasingly though, during the college years I led two lives. Somehow I managed to get through school, even winning a schoolwide history essay contest that offered a cash prize. But most of my emotional and social life was tied up in seeking out places to play and listen. The first regular group of musicians I played with included Larry Coryell, Jim Pepper, Lenny White and Randy Brecker. Moses and I played for a year every Friday night in a Greenwich Village art gallery. I even persuaded the New York University student government to let me put on some concerts at the college. This was the initiation period for me. Fortunately, my musical life became more serious due to the influence of three major teachers during these years.

Through my friend Mike Garson, I was introduced to the music and eventually the teaching of Lennie Tristano. Traveling three hours roundtrip by subway for a fifteen minute lesson with Lennie was quite an experience. Although I was not particularly attracted to his style, I realized that his approach was extremely disciplined and methodical. When I arrived for my first lesson and could barely play a scale with an even sound from the bottom to the top of my horn, he told me to go home and come back with it done cleanly. In 1963-64 when I studied with Lennie, there was a lot of energy and passion in whatever I played. But I was only approximating the music and really couldn't handle chord changes. Lennie demanded fluency in basics and required his students to sing along with selected solos (Lester Young, Frank Sinatra, Billie Holiday, Charlie Parker), play melodies and improvise on them without the benefit of chord changes and play scales with the metronome. Lennie Tristano made me aware of the discipline and study required to become a jazz player.

At around this period, I also began lessons with a man considered among the top saxophone teachers in the world; Joe Allard. Most saxophonists went to Joe at one time or another, including many famous ones. For several years, I saw him regularly in Carnegie Hall studios, where he taught. After those beginning years, I still checked in with Joe periodically. And he did at times come to hear me play. His presence was always a great honor. Joe taught by metaphor; he used diagrams, placed his fingers in your mouth and recited anecdotes. He used any device to get across his fundamental point: "To blow is to breathe." It is a natural process and there shouldn't be any impediments for allowing this to proceed. When the mind is encumbered with all sorts of directions and methods, the cluttered imagination cannot operate as it should. Combining this wonderful artistic philosophy with some ingenious technical pointers and an awareness of jazz technique made Joe Allard the guru of countless saxophonists as well as a great inspiration.

Finally, one night I went to see saxophonist Charles Lloyd playing with Cannonball Adderley and directly asked him for lessons. He was an interesting Coltrane-influenced musician who was about to enjoy several years of popularity. His sidemen included at various times: Herbie Hancock, Keith Jarrett, Pete LaRoca, Tony Williams and Ron Carter. Our relationship was more of an apprentice/master rather than a formal teacher/pupil one. I would help Charles in various ways, hang out with him, and of course see him play every night. He was a direct inspiration to me in those beginning years not only in the way he played but also in his life-style. Slowly, I began to imagine that maybe there was a way to be a full-time jazz musician!

The culmination of my initiation period was a trip to Europe before my final year of college. I took my horn and a few names of musicians during that summer of 1967. The first night in London I met Dave Holland and John Surman. After three weeks of playing with London musicians, I went to Stockholm, coincidentally arriving on the day of Coltrane's death. There I did my first recording with Swedish musicians of music reminiscent of the Charles Mingus small groups. This European trip was my first taste of what it was like to live jazz every day. I commited myself to pursuing a life in this music upon graduation from college. A year later, the day after I played Coltrane's *Naima* at graduation ceremonies (from New York

University), I moved to upstate New York and spent the next six months practicing eight hours a day. This organized period was the most systematic practicing I ever did and through it I gained the basic fundamentals of playing jazz.

My adult life truly began in 1968-69 when I lived in the first of many lofts on West 19th street in Manhattan. Eventually, the other two lofts in the same building were occupied by Dave Holland and Chick Corea, both of whom were then with Miles Davis. I had graduated with a teaching degree so that I could financially exist, serving as a per diem (daily) substitute teacher in whatever school would need me, anywhere in the five boroughs. Needless to say, substitute teaching in the New York City school system is a tale in itself. But it enabled me to stop any commercial gigs, play pure jazz and pursue the life of an artist.

The three years on 19th street were like being in a laboratory. I made serious friendships with a few compatriots, delved into alternate lifestyles, Oriental philosophy, mysticism, psychedelics and above all, kept constantly playing. My place was a meeting point for literally dozens of musicians at any hour. At this time, saxophonist Steve Grossman and I were quite close friends.

Musically, we were most influenced by the late period of John Coltrane. Specifically, the format of the recording *Ascension* was a guide. The style was free form group improvisation; most often not tonally key centered or in pulse; highly energetic and long-winded. If for example there were only saxophonists at the loft, we would play together eventually splitting off onto other instruments. Many of us became quite adept at the piano and drums through this kind of activity.

An outgrowth of this learning period was a musician's co-operative we called "Free Life Communication." Collectively, we realized there was little work in the jazz field during this period when rock 'n roll, symbolized by Woodstock and hippie culture, was so dominant. And in order to grow musically we had to perform in public and develop an audience. Using the examples of the Chicago-based Association for the Advancement of Creative Music collective and several similar New York groups, we organized. At first we put on concerts in local churches until we received funding from New York State as well as a permanent home in a multi-media arts center which also housed the Alwin Nicolais/Murray Louis Ballet Companies and Joe Chaiken's *Open Theatre*. At one point we had forty dues-paying members and audiences numbering several hundred. A list of original members reads like a present day Who's Who of Jazz.

Admittedly, this was heavy stuff for all of us. We were quite young and naive with great ambition. Here we were involved in learning an art form, developing a creative lifestyle, dealing with tax returns and grant forms, lawyers, accountants and each other. And as a generation, we were all products of the 60's and all the tumultuous events of that decade. By the early 70's it was time to get on with the professional life of being a musician; to serve an apprenticeship with a master musician and eventually develop one's own body of music.

Apprenticeship

Drummer Pete LaRoca was the first jazz master I worked for. By 1969 he was highly established in jazz (Sonny Rollins, John Coltrane, Art Farmer and Paul Bley), and had a strong desire to play his own music. I was recommended by Bob Moses and the audition was at bassist Steve Swallow's house with Chick Corea on piano. After a few choruses of *Softly as in a Morning Sunrise*, Pete stopped and said, "Let's rehearse." This began a six month period where we played several clubs, almost always with different bassists and pianists. It was my first exposure to playing with great rhythm sections and it was an exciting and nerve-wracking experience for me. With an incredible ear, Pete would sing the exact phrasing he wanted for his melodies which were replete with tricky rhythmic counter lines derived from his extensive experience as a timbale player in Latin bands. His sense of phrasing and swing was (and still is when he occasionally steps out of his present career as a lawyer to play) extremely loose, flexible and devoid of clichés. He is also a rare master drum soloist. Pete is a perfectionist and idealist of the highest order who taught me a lot about music and life. It fell to him as my first employer to help me gain confidence in myself. He made me aware of how insidious an overly critical and negative attitude towards oneself is; bad thinking promotes poor performance. My biggest fear was getting lost in the form of a tune as Pete and the rhythm section would juggle everything around. His response to me was that "getting lost" is normal if you're in the heat of creativity, but recovering is what has to be developed. The point is not to dwell on the mistake, but to listen to what is going on around you and rely on your ear and intuition to point the way.

In 1970 my good friend from the Catskill days, trumpeter Steve Satten joined a band called *Ten Wheel Drive*, which was patterned after the early rock-jazz bands like *Blood, Sweat and Tears* and *Chicago*. When the group needed a reed player, I got the job which meant playing baritone, tenor and soprano saxophones as well as flute. The writing was a melange of Broadway, jazz, and rock influences with a very showy lead singer in the Janis Joplin mode, Genya Raven. The band was supported by a large record company able to employ everyone on a steady salary. For me, *Ten Wheel Drive* was the beginning of being a full-time musician, ending my teaching days in the public school system. It also began my touring life, gave me an insider's view of the rock culture and marked the beginning of playing the soprano saxophone.

After an internal squabble caused the entire horn section to leave en masse, a few of us formed a band called *Sawbuck* that was more jazz based with extensive soloing and fronted by a very strong male singer. The tunes written mostly by guitarist Link Chamberlain employed jagged rhythms and melodies. It was the loudest group I've played in except for Miles Davis. Unfortunately, I never recorded with *Sawbuck* (eventually they did on Motown Records), because I was hired by Elvin Jones in the fall of 1971 to replace Joe Farrell. Though I was having fun playing rock 'n roll and being involved in a communal rock band feeling, I was grateful to return to jazz.

with Elvin Jones in Hamburg, Germany, mid '80s (© Veronika Gruber)

Elvin was already a great spiritual influence for me because of seeing him so often with Coltrane. His ever present *triplet feeling*[6] played so behind the beat is one of the more subtle and special rhythmic feels heard in contemporary jazz. To play with this master drummer and become acquainted intimately with his indescribable feeling was the biggest thrill of my life up to that time. Elvin's time feel is to my mind the perfect combination and balance between looseness and steadiness. The story of how I was hired is a classic.

One night in January 1971, bassist Gene Perla, who had just begun working with Elvin, phoned from the lower East side club cal-

[6] *triplet feel* – underlying basis of each beat is a division of three rather than two (duple feel).

led Slug's Saloon. He said Elvin wanted me to come down and play. When I arrived there after midnight, Elvin, who was standing at the bar, said to me, "Are you ready?" We went on stage with just Elvin and Gene playing for a few people in the audience. After *Softly as in a Morning Sunrise*, Jerome Kern's *Yesterdays* and the jazz classic *A Night in Tunisia*, Elvin said he wanted me to record the next month with him. That album, *Genesis*, marked my recording debut in the professional jazz business. Within a few more months, I was a permanent member eventually playing alongside my good friend, Steve Grossman.

This was the real scene; playing three sets a night for weeks at a time in clubs as well as major overseas tours. The experience of playing continuously was a revelation. I was playing tenor, soprano and flute as well as composing some of the material. It was the jazz life all the way!

Over the years, many saxophonists have said that the album *Live at the Lighthouse* was among their all time favorites. I think that this album captures the incredible energy of this particular unit and historically documents the first wave of saxophone players molded in the Coltrane tradition, establishing his vocabulary as a standard much like musicians did with Charlie Parker's music a generation earlier.

Besides the wonderful musical and career experience gained working with Elvin, there was just the knowledge of life that you could feel by being around him. Elvin has been through a lot as a man and is not one of those people who pontificates about his hard times. He is full of warmth, generosity and great humor. His sense of duty and leadership have grown over the years as has his place in musical history. Elvin is a rare human being to whom I am thankful for having had the opportunity to be close. Playing with Elvin was THE gig for a saxophonist.

During the early 1970's, Bob Moses and I formalized our musical relationship in the *Open Sky Trio* with several bass players, but most frequently Frank Tusa. Our two records for Gene Perla's P.M. label were my first as a leader (cooperative leadership in this case) and in general was an eclectic mix of several directions including the free music of Coltrane, the free-bop of Ornette Coleman, ethnic melodies and some funk rhythms. Both Elvin's group and *Open Sky* did not use chord instruments. My approach to each was different because of the two drummers' different rhythmical awareness. With Elvin, the pulse was always being stated, whereas Moses played over and through the time more often than not. He affected the colors and shapes of my lines in a way that became a permanent part of my rhythmic approach. I did not have to be limited to only even eighth note *legato lines*[7] but could also employ *jagged asymmetric shapes*[8].

---

7 *even eighth (or sixteenth) note legato lines* – when the rhythmic feel and articulation is smooth and not accented.
8 *jagged asymmetric shapes* – melodic lines that are unevenly contoured; unpredictable in their flow; often quite pointillistic.

Moses made me play differently than anyone else, a fact that still holds true whenever we play.

My period of apprenticeship reached its culmination in the year and a half I spent with Miles Davis. I had met him over the years in a variety of settings; being in New York and part of a tight scene, eventually everyone knows everybody else. In August 1972, I took part in a recording session as part of the album *On the Corner*. This session was famous for the number of known musicians present including John McLaughlin, Herbie Hancock, Chick Corea and others. When I arrived at the studio, the recording was in progress. Miles motioned for me to take my horn out and play. I had no idea of the key or where to start conceptually. In any case within a few months, he came to the Village Vanguard where I was playing with Elvin. After a few nights of sweet-talking me to join him, I told him he had to ask Elvin. The next night when I said hello to Elvin, he hugged me and said, "If Miles wants you, then you go." My first night with Miles was at the famous Fillmore Theater in New York that week, while still working with Elvin.

The music with Miles was very heavily influenced by Sly Stone and James Brown. To my mind, there was a Sun Ra influence also. At different times during my tenure, there were three guitarists, numerous keyboardists, tablas, electric sitar as well as the basic band of Al Foster on drums, Pete Cosey and Reggie Lucas on guitars, Michael Henderson on bass and Mtume on congas. (Reggie, Michael and Mtume went on to become quite popular commercially in the R&B field). The music was wild, chaotic, disorganized, very loud as well as mysterious and exciting. Miles himself was playing for the most part through a wa-wa pedal and I too was amplified via a pick-up.

My job was the same as all the great saxophonists before and since; as a foil to Miles. In one of his abstract comments he remarked that people liked to see a saxophonist because he moves his fingers fast! Like most of his utterances, you had to read into the meaning. I interpreted this to mean that he could play slow and spacious (which of course is his trademark) as long as the saxophone was around for the fast motion. I think this was a pattern he observed in his early years with Charlie Parker.

One of Miles' strongest assets is his ability to perceive other musician's abilities. Somehow, he gets everyone to play what he wants; in fact, in many cases Miles' sidemen never play in that particular manner again. By using few words or in some cases, just nuance and force of personality he achieves his objectives, often creating an atmosphere of creative tension.

As a soloist, Miles offered an encyclopedia to learn from. His use of space, tone, dynamics and color are well known. He often didn't finish a musical cadence, seducing the listener by omission, allowing the rhythm section to fill up the space thus enabling him to be set up nicely for a new entrance. He was the most lyrical of players and even when playing on vamps in one or two keys for most of the set, he was still able to come up with fresh melodies night after night. As a horn player, to listen to Miles so closely was among the greatest lessons I ever experienced.

And of course, Miles Dewey Davis is not called the "Prince of Darkness" for nothing. He was a complex, often moody person in the years I was around him and seemed to excel in creating dramatic scenes. He would make a great actor or stage director because his sense of timing and effect were quite intense. He was also generous to those he trusted; could make a hell of a fish soup and knew a lot about people, culture and the arts. Knowing Miles was definitely a unique experience. Playing with Miles gave me worldwide exposure and entry into the arena where one can have a solo career, groups and recording contracts. Musically, I was as ready as I could be and

with Miles Davis in New York, 1981 (© Julie Coryell)

had developed enough of a relationship with a few of my contemporaries to begin my own musical search. Artistically, I could begin to hear the beginnings of my own playing, especially on the soprano saxophone. (More about Miles Davis in *Miles Davis and David Liebman – Jazz Encounters;* Edward Mellen Press)

On My Own

In the history of jazz, great music has often been made as a result of a relationship between two musicians. Examples are Billie Holiday and Lester Young, Charlie Parker and Dizzy Gillespie, Bill Evans and Scott LaFaro, Tony Williams and Ron Carter, Don Cherry and Ornette Coleman and many others. I was fortunate to have a long association with pianist Richard Beirach. We were raised only several blocks from each other in Brooklyn, but as is often the case in a city like New York, we didn't meet and begin a friendship until we were both living in Manhattan in the late 1960's.

To my mind, Richie is a great example of an artist who by his own disciplined nature arrived at a unique way of improvising. He has weeded out influences, studied his musical roots which are in the classical literature and by fusing together contemporary jazz and twentieth century modern music, arrived at his own means of expression.

Under his influence, he made me aware of harmony through the eyes of a pianist. Being a horn player, I am very dependent on how the rhythm section accompanies me. With Richie as the helmsman, a rhythm section was always alert and sensitive. My sense of spacing, melody and soloistic flow are inextricably linked with the fact that for a good number of years I had Beirach behind me taking care of business. Philosophically, we were at times in disagreement, but always with compassion and a sense of humor towards each other's views. He was a close friend and important musical compatriot.

The group *Lookout Farm* grew from our relationship along with bassist Frank Tusa, drummer Jeff Williams and for a while on tablas, Badal Roy. During off periods with Miles, I played most often with these musicians, so it was inevitable that they would comprise my group when the time came. The first album called *Lookout Farm* on ECM was very representative of the band and even more, my musical inclinations. Each of the four tunes represents a musical genre and direction which I have continued in one form or another. The music coalesced into an identifiable group sound over our three year period. After *Drum Ode* on ECM, I signed with A&M/Horizon and among the three albums I made, one was a duet with Richie which was a kind of culmination of this creative period.

With *Lookout Farm* I was able to assimilate and personalize all I had learned in my formative years. We played with tremendous energy and enthusiasm, were well received by audiences and critics worldwide and in this way it launched my own career successfully.

In 1976 we won first place in the Downbeat International Critics Poll as "Group Deserving of Wider Recognition". Most important, I became my own man without the crutch of having to lean on the strength of my former employers. I was responsible for the business, the general musical direction, inspiring and making the other musicians feel comfortable as well as working out my own individual style. It was an exciting and intense period of my life.

Lookout Farm *while recording* Sweet Hands *in 1975 (A+M/Horizon). Left to right: Don Alias, Richard Beirach, Jeff Williams, David Liebman, Frank Tusa, Badal Roy*

By 1976, I was both worn out and eager to be more successful commercially. I got together with former James Brown sideman and composer-saxophonist Pee Wee Ellis who for a time had played with me in the the *Sawbuck* band in 1970. Because I needed a change and the San Francisco area seemed more hospitable to the kind of music we would play, I moved to California. The *Ellis-Liebman Band* was an expensive, business-oriented venture which I felt could bridge the gap between a true sense of improvisation and commercial needs. Pee Wee played gutsy soulful lines that affected my playing directly in an expressive manner. I played my type of lines over the straight ahead funk rhythm. The combination was interesting but neither commercial enough nor serious enough to be popular one way or the other. This dilemma in fact has plagued much of the jazz-rock fusion genre throughout its history. For me to play in such a restrictive harmonic setting on a consistent basis proved too limiting although I learned quite a bit about blues inflections.

After the *Ellis-Liebman Band* venture, I formed a group with some young San Francisco-based jazz musicians (including Mark Isham) and played for a few months with trumpeter Eddie Henderson alongside trombonist Julian Priester. Eddie's music was a contemporary mixture of jazz and funk-based material played with a true improvisational spirit. The band was first class, but there wasn't enough of a jazz audience on the West Coast to make such a group an ongoing reality.

With the desire to get back to New York, when Chick Corea asked me to do a three month world tour playing music from several of his albums which featured a string quartet and several brass, I eagerly accepted. Being the main soloist with Chick and hearing his fine compositions on a nightly basis was a wonderful musical experience. Even more beneficial was the chance to hear and play with a string quartet, which culminated in what I feel is one of my finest albums, *Dedications*.

This album on a German label (CMP) featured two pieces that I wrote and arranged along with an arrangement of a Beirach original by the cellist-educator, Dave Baker. The group consisted of a string quartet, Richie on piano, Eddie Gomez on bass and myself on soprano and flute. It has been re-released on CD with newly recorded string-soprano duets.

This album marked the beginning of what has become an ongoing compositional and performing challenge. Since this album, recorded in 1979, I have written and published several more string, woodwind and saxophone quartets. The idea is to use the harmonies and textures of twentieth century music to offset and highlight my improvisations. This fertile field was momentarily pursued in the *Third Stream*[9] movement during the early 1960's.

Upon returning to New York in June 1978, I found the scene very active for me. There were many record dates featuring jazz, mostly for European and Japanese record labels. I wanted another group, but this time without a piano and featuring a guitar-two horn format. The compositions would be more single line oriented and a combination of vamps with chord changes as well as a few straight

9 *third stream* – the fusion of jazz and classical genres led by Gunther Schuller

ahead jazz tunes. The band formed included John Scofield, Terumasa Hino, Adam Nussbaum and Ron McClure and for a while Kenny Kirkland. The two albums recorded on the Dutch label, Timeless, and later released on MCA give a good demonstration of the diversity of color and feeling achieved by this quintet. After two years in which this group toured Europe and Australia, Richie Beirach and I decided to get together again.

In 1979 I recorded what I consider one of my most successful venture into fusion music. The album *What It Is* featured John Scofield, Kenny Kirkland, Don Alias, Marcus Miller, Steve Gadd and produced by Mike Mainieri. The challenge was to play in that format with a great rhythm section of the style but with a sense of urgency present in jazz improvising. This was one of the most comfortable and relaxed sessions of my career and though it was hardly promoted, it became fairly successful.

In 1981 Richie and I put together *Quest* with Al Foster and George Mraz. The subsequent album was a straight ahead jazz record featuring originals and our adaptations of *Softly as in a Morning Sunrise* and Ornette Coleman's *Lonely Woman*. By the late 1980's as evidenced in our recordings, *Quest II*, *Midpoint* (Storyville Records), *Natural Selection* (Evidence) and *Of One Mind* (CMP), Billy Hart and Ron McClure have become our bass-drum team. At the same time, we often did duet performances and recorded a session of standards, *Double Edge*, as well as a live album of originals, *The Duo Live*, which was accompanied by the complete transcription of the music done by Bill Dobbins.

For me the duet was a great technical challenge. Every note is heard from beginning to end and ideas are more exposed than is the case with drums and bass accompanying. The duo music evolved from the very tonal, romantic beginnings of *Forgotten Fantasy* to more contemporary atonal musings as heard on or last recording *Chant* (CMP). *Quest* took the duet a step further to include the power of the bass and drums, but still dealing with the language of the duet.

The years between 1982 and 1985 saw me playing and recording more than previously with pick-up bands around the U.S. and in Europe. This was a financial necessity because of the difficulty of steady work for a set group. I find that there are good players everywhere and some of these spontaneous sessions are magical and have resulted in close relationships between myself and these musicians. Of course, there is no substitute for an organized group, but this kind of traveling and playing is like that of the ancient troubadour. You come in for the evening's work, earn your room and board, then leave the next day. I felt good about working in what I call "the trenches." This is not meant in a perjorative sense, because it is on the grass roots level that jazz survives. In local situations across the world, jazz is alive and available for the community, small as it may be.

During the 80's I made several solo albums. On *Memories, Dreams and Reflections* and *Picture Show* I played horns, keyboards and drums. *Memories* consisted of compositions with simple improvising formats. *Picture Show* was all improvised based on the musical feeling of each of the various idioms I have been interested in. The *Loneliness of a Long Distance Runner* on CMP was performed completely on the soprano saxophone and represented a very tight combination of composition and improvisation based around two themes depicting the runner as a metaphor for all human beings who try to go the distance in their own way. In a sense this is my most personal and deepest recording.

By 1990 and with the recording of the CMP *Of One Mind* which was a kind of free association session based on those musical settings we enjoyed, but completely improvised on for this CD, I decided that *Quest* could go no further. I wanted to move more into the rhythmical realm employing odd meter, sectional writing, occasional use of synths, a guitar as a front line "horn" and a very eclectic sound.

The Dave Liebman Group *with Vic Juris (guitar), Tony Marino (bass) and Jamey Haddad (drums); early '90s (Private collection)*

Putting together the *Dave Liebman Group* in 1991, I decided to use the most versatile musicians I could find who would be able to play many of the idioms I liked. As of this writing our recordings range from electric/acoustic *(Voyage, Turn It Around)*, to acoustic *(Songs For My Daughter)*, jazz *(Return Of The Tenor)*, Brazilian influence *(New Vista)* and a live performance from New York of Coltrane's *Meditations Suite*. The members are Jamey Haddad on drums/precussion, Vic Juris on guitar, Phil Markowitz on piano, and keyboards, Tony Marino on electric and acoustic bass.

The Influence of Other Idioms

As mentioned in the introduction to this chapter, I have been widely influenced by many aspects of art and culture besides music itself. I have always felt that the vastness of life's choices should be enjoyed to the utmost. Of course, during the evolution of any artist, there are times when it is necessary to specialize in order to gain control of one particular area and master it. But in the end, it's the broadness and inclusiveness of an artist's vision embracing many aspects which can help create a universal and rewarding art.

Pop Music

My first musical influence was the rock 'n roll of the 1950's which featured oddly enough, quite a lot of saxophone playing. In the 1960's and 1970's guitar and keyboards became more dominant, but in recent years the sax is again being heard in pop music. And although this was the direct inspiration for me to play saxophone, I never tried to imitate the honking, staccato style as exemplified by people like King Curtis, Junior Walker and other recorded saxophonists. I didn't feel comfortable with what appeared to me to be a rather bright sound in combination with such preponderance of staccato phrasing. Almost from the beginning of my awareness of jazz saxophone, I favored a smooth, more legato approach to articulation as well as a brighter tone. And as I became more experienced as a listener to the great horn players and familiar with the actual equipment needed to play (mouthpieces, reeds, etc.), I slowly evolved my concept of tone towards a rich sound which underplayed any tendency towards shrillness. So funk and rhythm and blues were not directly influential upon my playing as they have been on some of my contemporaries.

But there were other factors stemming from my listening to pop music over the years which have had effect on my musical development. The rhythmical steadiness underlying all pop music is a necessity because of the fact that the most important element in this music is that people dance to it. The predominance of the *back beat*[10] placed either squarely in the center of the *pulse*[11] or in some cases slightly behind, is an element that stands out. Also, the endless rhythmical permutations of bass lines and drum beats, mostly in 4/4 time has been a source and even direct inspiration for some compositions in my repertoire.

---

10 *back beat* – the emphasis on the second and fourth beat of a 4/4 measure; a major characteristic of pop and dance music in general.
11 *pulse* – the actual placement of each beat.

The blues scale is the main source of melodic and harmonic content in pop, especially soul and funk music. My favorite artists in this genre were Sly Stone, James Brown and Earth, Wind and Fire. The influence of the blues is pervasive throughout the history of jazz. Although my playing is not heavily blues based, several aspects of this style have had strong effects upon me.

Quest. *From left to right: David Liebman, Richard Beirach, Billy Hart, Ron McClure, Germany, 1988 (© Hans Gruber)*

The twelve bar blues is a tight, recognizable form in which all the signposts are a known quantity: the placement of the three chords, tonic (I7), subdominant (IV7), and dominant (V7) as well as the basic melodic pitches to be used which make up the blues scale. In accord with the idea of musical *slack*[12], the blues improviser becomes freer with other musical aspects such as rhythm variations of the available pitches, harmonic shadings within the basic chord structure and most important, great use of expression to enhance the emotional content of the melodic line. The blues feeling is primarily vocally based and represents the universal cry of life. Musically it is available in one form or another to every culture. No intellectual underpinnings are necessary to convey the message. There is an entire tradition of blues playing in the United States which began to

12 *slack* – when one element of music is emphasized, another may be simplified.

take shape over 100 years ago and is now part and parcel of what is called pop music.

Basically, it is complexity disguised as simplicity which makes the blues so fascinating. The three chords represent the entire history of Western harmonic thought in terms of tension and release. The blues scale is inherently an emotionally dynamic melodic pattern which contains a high degree of lyricism. The clarity and simplicity of expression makes it able to absorb a great deal of feeling. This conciseness of feeling and emotion can be viewed as an aesthetic goal to be conveyed in all music, especially jazz which is so historically tied to the blues tradition

On a more personal level, the rhythm and blues players definitely affected my own use of expressive devices such as smears, *bends*[13], *shouts*[14] and other vocal colorations. After working with Miles, I realized how much of the blues was present in his playing even when he was not specifically playing blues notes per se. The feeling of the blues is present in most of the great jazz musicians. Besides the musical value it provides a continuum with the entire legacy of jazz and pre-jazz.

Vocalists have likewise been influential for me because of the way the voice can inflect a note in such a variety of ways. Since the voice doesn't have the fluidity and technical potential of a horn, this limitation usually means economy of expression. When Lennie Tristano required me to sing along with Billie Holiday and Frank Sinatra, I could perceive the rhythmical value of the exercise as well as the more obvious aspects of expressive devices. Both Holiday and Sinatra, as well as other vocalists, have a very relaxed, swinging approach to rhythm. They seem to phrase effortlessly without straining at all. As any instumentalist knows, it is a true technical and physical challenge to input the required air or other forms of energy into the instrument in question without tension so that the musical results sound and feel relaxed. The voice is more easily capable of doing this natural act and instrumentalists can realize this more readily when they listen and try to imitate vocal phrasing.

One other aspect of pop music concerns itself with form. In this case, it is the songwriters such as Stevie Wonder, Paul Simon, Lennon and McCartney and others going back to Gershwin, Porter, Kern and numerous Tin Pan Alley composer-lyricists. They are masters of the *short form*[15]. By short form, I mean a compact format as in *AABA*, but not necessarily limited to that. Underlying the short form is that apart from the ending where there often is an ongoing vamp, every section has a predetermined bar length. In other words, the song is *through composed*[16]. In jazz, for the most part and especially in Coltrane's music, the prevalent form is long, meaning open and up to decisions made in the moment. Short form teaches con-

---

13 *bends* – a nuance achieved by playing around with the sharpness and flatness of a pitch.
14 *shouts* – one of the vocal-like effects produced on a wind instrument as a coloristic device; others are growls, buzzes, humming, etc.
15 *short form* – an improvisation or composition of short duration, found most often in pop music.
16 *through composed* – everything written with no space for improvisation.

ciseness and the idea of getting to the point. For jazz improvisers, there may easily be a natural tendency to over extend oneself and thereby lose the point or message. An interesting guideline might be: if you can't accomplish what you want in 8 bars as well as 8 minutes, then it may not be worth saying!

And finally, there is the sheer exuberance and positive energy of most pop music where the message is quite simply to enjoy oneself. Rock 'n roll was an integral part of my growing process via Elvis, the Beatles, Jimi Hendrix and others. For a while when I was getting more heavily into jazz, I turned my back on pop music because I considered it too unsophisticated to merit any of my attention. However, once I got past the attitude that because music is simpler it is less valid, I realized that the message of any music should be to satisfy people spiritually and emotionally.

My love of pop music in general has helped me to combat a common tendency in jazz or any serious music to be pedantic and overly intellectual. When music is centered upon one simple idea, a great deal of subtlety can be achieved. Consider how many songs have been written using the blues or a typical Tin Pan Alley progression, and yet many are distinctly different from each other. In fact, American pop music as a whole provides history with a great example of the extensive use of basic theme and variation principles.

World Music (non-European Based)

In world music there is little or no harmony present and the form is essentially quite simple. This leaves the elements of melody, rhythm and color quite exposed and therefore very useful for study purposes.

Indian classical music is my favorite of all world music for several reasons: it is a rich and spiritually meaningful tradition; the melodies are highly expressive using nuances such as the bending of pitches and *glissandos*[17] to an extraordinary degree; the rhythms are extremely sophisticated and often in *compound* and *odd meter*[18]; it is an aural tradition passed on for 5000 years mostly by face-to-face encounter and the imitative process between master and student.

Indian music is very similar to our blues because they have in common the same directness of communication as a main priority. Both musics use scales (Indians call it ragas) for melodic material and a similarly wide range of nuance and expression to present these modes. In both Indian music and the blues, there is emphasis upon singable and lyrical melodies. The source for both idioms is not instrumental, but vocal. The Indian instrumentalist is required to sing for years before being taught an instrument. Another common element with the blues is the frequent use of the call and response technique of improvisation, whereby a phrase is repeated by another instrumentalist, possibly with slight variation.

17 *glissandos* – an aspect of phrasing whereby notes are connected by a fast run that creates a sliding effect.
18 *compound/odd meter* – metrical division of rhythm made up of any combination of two and three beats as in five, seven, nine, etc.; a characteristic often found in ethnic music such as Greek, Turkish, Indian.

The Indian tradition is actually a very sophisticated improvised music. Performances may last for hours, often with long pauses between ideas for both the audience and performers to catch their breath and prepare their concentration for the next sequence. The underlying fact of Indian music is that a raga is a musical portrayal of something specific, be it the time of day, a holiday or a song in praise of a deity or natural force of the universe. This specificity and high spiritual idealism of the music gives the content great depth and emotion. My favorite Indian performers are: sitarist Vilayet Khan, flautist Panallal Ghosh, shenai master Bismillah Khan, sarodist Ali Akbar Khan and a vocal duo, the Ali Brothers.

Indian music offers colors provided by a wide variety of bowed, wind and percussive instruments. The nuances achieved by breath control, finger tapping and other subtleties can be of value for Western instrumentalists to learn from. Of all the characteristics most admired by Western musicians, the rhythmical intensity and permutations have had the largest effect. For myself, it has been primarily through listening and studying this music that I have any understanding of how to conceive of, let alone play in compound meters. The rhythmical concept of Indian music could easily be a lifelong study.

The other major area of world music that has interested me has been connected with drums and rhythm; especially African and Latin American music. Much has been written about the influence of both these musical traditions upon jazz. Direct traces of African rhythmic patterns can be found throughout jazz history. The bossa nova beat is a famous example of the use of a Brazilian samba rhythm which was fused with jazz harmonies. My interest is in the manner in which drummers play with each other using rhythmic patterns as one would use melody. When I hear the music of many Cuban or Haitian drummers together, like *guanganco* for example, I imagine melodies to be played over the rhythms. I try to hear where I would place these melodies in direct relationship to the rhythms. I feel that this imaginative journey has added to my rhythmic flexibility when playing jazz. Also, once again as in pop music, the rhythms are meant for dancing and ceremony so the sheer physicality and naturalness of the music attracts and effects me in a positive manner.

One other area of world music which I consider more ethnic-oriented, is the use of flute-like instruments throughout the world as evidenced in much of the folk music heard in various cultures. In Iran it is called the ney; in Yugoslavia there is the double flute; in Africa, the nose flute. As a reed player, I am always curious about phrasing and breathing as well as the variety of specific musical *nuances*[19] and expressive devices heard on similar instruments. Although these exotic sounds may not reveal themselves directly in

---

19 *nuances* – expressive devices employed on one note especially.

my actual playing, they enter the subconcious and in some way might exert an influence at some time, even if for only one phrase of a lifetime's worth of music. Sounds that enter into the unconscious are very important because they mix together with other elements. In combination with one's studies, ideas and emotions, these sounds will be unrecognizable from their origins by the time the individual actually plays or uses them in some way. This is one of the ways that the reservoir of creativity never runs dry.

Classical Music

I never had much affinity for classical music in the sense of the traditional repertoire. Like most young people, I didn't have the concentration required to seriously appreciate the classics. As I became acquainted with the elements of music, I realized that it was the rather stultifying rhythms which were probably most responsible for my not having empathy with the baroque, classical and romantic periods in particular. Fortunately, twentieth century music always appealed to me.

But as I became increasingly interested in composition, I realized the necessity of studying some of the basic classical harmony and literature. As my style developed towards a more chromatic, polytonal

with Richie Beirach, late '80s (© Joan Powers)

approach, twentieth century music became a specific source for harmonic ideas. Further interest in writing for strings and woodwinds has led me to the study of specific scores to hear the colors and ranges of these instruments.

Richard Beirach made me aware of how much can be seen and heard in the slow movements of classical music. When the stiff rhythmic approach which forms a strait jacket around the melody and harmony is lifted, real connections between these two musical elements can be more easily discerned. My favorite slow movements are from Mahler's Fifth Symphony, Beethoven's *String Quartet Op. 131* in C♯ Minor, the beginning of Schubert's *Quintet in C*, *The Unanswered Question* of Charles Ives, Toro Takemitsu's *Requiem*, the slow movements of Bartók's *Concerto for Orchestra* and Debussy's *String Quartet*. Classical music is a genre that I feel will become more and more attractive to me with time.

Pre-Be-Bop Jazz

Be-bop is the major category of jazz since the 1940's. Other idioms alongside be-bop are modalism, chromaticism (or polytonality) and *atonalism*[29] These are mostly harmonic designations. In the rhythmic context, be-bop connotes a straight-ahead jazz feeling. Other rhythmic idioms are broken *eighth note*[21], *sixteenth note feel*[22], odd meters and *a-rhythmic*[23] or *free pulse*[24] The mastering of the be-bop idiom in particular will always remain a challenge because like older classical music, every note is accounted for harmonically in the theoretical sense. This form of musical mathematics has to do with the ability to understand *cadences*[25]. Also integral for comprehending jazz is the rhythmic feel called swing. As a product of a later period, the 1960's, my natural inclination and ability lies in modalism, because that is what I grew up hearing, be it rock 'n roll blues progressions (which can be seen as modal because of the blues scale) or the music played by John Coltrane's quartet which made such an indelible impression upon me.

But even more difficult for me to play, let alone listen to, was jazz before the 1940's. This included Louis Armstrong, Coleman Hawkins, even Lester Young, as modern as he was when he first began in the 1930's. I just felt no empathy with the very plain diatonicism and stiff 4/4 beat being chugged out by the older rhythm sections. Because I knew that I was missing some vital information which was necessary for my knowledge, I tried to listen for other things, shutting my ear off to those aspects which distracted me. I began to notice the individual instrumentalist's technique, melodic approach and time feel. As I listened for these aspects, I would in my mind's ear substitute modern notes and chords. Soon I began to appreciate the obvious: the same elements of phrasing, flexibility, *soloistic flow*[26], time feel, etc., were there in the great old masters.

---

20 *atonalism* – when the harmony is without an established key center.

21 *broken eighth note feel* – a rhythmic manner of playing in which even eighth notes are the underlying basis, but by omitting some of them occasionally suggesting a spacious and open texture.

22 *sixteenth note feel* – when the rhythmic basis is such and subdivisions derive from it.

23 *a-rhythmic* – (also called rubato and free pulse); indicating rhythms that are not metrically even.

24 *free pulse* – an important aspect of most free jazz; no established or steady pulse; rubato also.

25 *cadence* – a resting place after ongoing tension, a resolution.

26 *soloistic flow* – the continuity of ideas in a solo.

My awakening concerning soprano saxophonist Sidney Bechet was really amazing. If you replaced the notes of his arpeggios with more chromatic tones, the results would be a lot like Coltrane. Clarinetist Barney Bigard with Duke Ellington's Orchestra was another great "discovery." Also, how Miles was related to Armstrong's phraseology.

Eventually, I was able to get past *stylization*[27]. Each period developed a way of playing the rhythm or chords that became the standard of that era in musical history. A way of phrasing in the swing period evolved from the Dixieland style and so forth. Once I could appreciate the historical perspective, I was able to enjoy the music and furthermore, even try to use some of these older devices in my own playing. This could give my music more breadth by mixing aspects of the present and past.

In general, listening to all kinds of music, even an idiom as distant as country music can almost always show an artist something valuable. Even if an insight shows only what not to do or what to avoid, then the time has not been wasted. I feel that for an artist to have a broad vision, he should be at the least familiar with as much of the entire spectrum of music as possible.

[27] *stylization* – a musician's way of playing which is identifiable from a particular era.

Other Extra-Musical Influences

Earlier in the "Artistic Process," I made several allusions to the difference between a "musician" and "artist", my point being that the artist includes all aspects of life in his vision and reflects upon these matters through his chosen field of expertise. His message goes beyond merely the art itself. In order to gain worldly wisdom, an artist must be dedicated to learning as much as he can about everything, especially how other thinkers and creators have viewed life.

Thus the serious artist evokes an interest in fields other than his own as well as in the men and women who worked in these areas. Biographies, collections of diaries, letters and journals are a great source for this information. There is inspiration readily available upon reading about how someone else felt as they went through life and the creative process. There may even be some concepts applicable to the artist's own work. Historical treatises and current events show us that everything we witness has happened before somewhere and sometime. The recognition of historical cycles and their relationship to the present can be illuminating for an artist to observe where culture has placed him in the scheme of things. Psychology obviously can lead to more inner knowledge. Mysticism and the occult may set the imagination aflight into areas otherwise not noticed. The great epics of literature give one a sense of compassion and sympatico with how people feel and relate to each other as well as real images to fuel the creative mind. The sciences, philosophy, and mechanical arts keep the intellect alive through analysis and attempting to comprehend technical matters. Whatever specifically interests an artist is unimportant as long as it serves to stimulate him. Along with this, the artist like everyone must stay physically fit and emotionally well. In total, the life of an artist should be one of continually searching for knowledge in all walks of life; past, present and future. In the end, there are no new ideas, only different manifestations of certain basic themes.

Flute with wooden joint. Tübingen, Germany, 1988 (© Hans Gruber)

The Basis of My Art

Every artist has a system of thought which is applied to the creative process. In this chapter describing mine, all the judgments and opinions are unequivocally subjective; the patterns of thought are based on over twenty-five years of personal experience. The reader who is familiar with my work and career will be at an advantage. But even to the initiate, the ideas espoused should be of interest and stimulating.

Intuition comes first. The intellectualization and verbalization of my music has evolved after the fact. I did not have these ideas and concepts before the process of hearing, feeling and experimenting. When an artist sees consistent results in any given area, he assumes that this regularity is due to thinking in a certain way. This is what I attempt to reveal in this section.

I follow the basic pattern of the earlier chapter, "Creating the Music." Each of the five elements of music are described separately. How I have conceived of the elements from the beginning of my artistic life through the present is written chronologically. In general, the section on "Improvisational Style" is in answer to the often asked question: "What am I thinking about while improvising?" "The Act of Playing" is descriptive of a variety of related areas, some of which have been described earlier from an objective and generalized standpoint.

My sole concern about melody in earlier years was of course to play the written notes. And if it was a known melody, such as a standard, to interpret it loosely by using the usual methods of melodic variation and expression *(syncopation[1], augmentation[2], diminution[3],* etc.). I think that my period with Miles Davis, observing how he played simple lines with so much variety repeatedly, influenced me a few years later. Even though the music Miles played during my tenure seemed so different from his other stylistic periods, I was still able to transfer his approach to other musical vehicles in my mind's ear. Since Miles' music over the years was so familiar to me and so dominant as an influence for all improvisers, it made me understand more about the entire basis of modern jazz improvisation. Melody is of course the result of harmonic movement, but more important, it is higher in priority than I believed at first.

The idea of *running changes*[4] or scales, was so much a part of the challenge of be-bop, that I was slow to realize how important the

Improvisational Style: Melody

---

1 *syncopation* – rhythms resulting from a mixture of upbeats and downbeats.
2 *augmentation* – enlarging a melodic phrase by adding auxillary pitches and/or longer rhythmic durations.
3 *diminution* – the shortening of a rhythmic or melodic phrase to achieve variety; opposite of augmentation.
4 *running changes* – playing in a vertical, arpeggiated manner primarily, resulting in clear outlines of the harmony.

melody of the improvised line is in creating the entire musical story. Of course, this doesn't preclude playing with either harmonic or rhythmic emphasis at times to achieve variety and balance. But the function and importance of melody can easily be overlooked in the pursuit of these other elements.

The notion of lyricism or "singability" began to influence me several years after working for Miles, and also after my first group, *Lookout Farm*. By 1977-79, I could hear a more lyrical sense beginning to occur on tunes I had played for years, like *Stella by Starlight* and *On Green Dolphin Street*. Tunes with a familiar syntax are always good as a measure of the growth of one's playing. They're like old friends who understand you, allowing you to be very open in your attitude towards them. I could feel a sense of space around my lines; like punctuation in writing. The pauses were stopoff points between either a new or possibly complimentary melody line. And most important, my choice of intervals was becoming more lyrical.

I realized that if a given line is composed of intervals, the choices of distance between them was a crucial factor in the overall effect of a melody. The question was how does each interval sound to me in the sense of what I wish to express? A simplistic way of understanding this is the traditional pairing of the minor third interval as sad, while the major third is assumed to be happy. As a melodicist, the point was to somehow be able to be both objective and subjective about the expressive powers of each of the intervals. I had to know for my own way of thinking which sound corresponded to what emotion or picture I was imagining. Of course, this could never be truly calculated or expressed in words, but every artist does have his own method or private vocabulary to define the materials he deals with. Drummer Elvin Jones once stated at a *teaching clinic*[5] that he sees the *ride cymbal*[6] changing colors as he plays. For myself, musical sound is realized in shapes consisting of all types of lines: straight, broken, curved, wave-like, figure-eights, etc. The rise and fall of a line resembles a geometric pattern of one sort or another. And of course, a musical thought also evokes a physical and/or emotional feeling as well. Somehow all of this combined has given me a kind of system of relative aesthetic values which I employ.

Lyrical melodies are primarily made up of major and minor seconds and thirds which appear smooth and round in shape. Fourths and fifths often end and begin lyrical phrases, and if strung together consecutively create a very open symetrical feeling with an angular shape. Major and minor sixths are just *mirrors*[7] of thirds, and similar to them in expressive content, whereas sevenths and ninths create more severe angularity and a system of shapes similar to the ups and downs of a hill and valley landscape. Another way of organizing intervals is in the following classifications: close (2nds,

---

5 *teaching clinic* – a music seminar usually involving direct instrumental coaching.
6 *ride cymbal* – the main cymbal of a drum set used for marking time.
7 *mirror intervals* – major thirds and minor sixths; minor thirds and major sixths; perfect fourths and perfect fifths; they all sound the same notes.

3rds, 6ths), pentatonic/cadential (4ths and 5ths), and wide (7ths and 9ths).

It is the juggling together of the intervals and their corollary effects and colors which I use to create the mood of a specific line. This same concept guides how I make my choices when dealing with the other elements of music as well.

Harmony

All harmony can be reduced to a general scheme of three possibilities. A chord either functions as a tension leading somewhere (the V chord), a preparation to or from a tension (the IV chord), or a resolution (the I chord). No matter whether a chord is replete with *dissonances*[8] or *consonances*[9], the expressive as well as the actual function of a chord depends on what comes before and after it. Therefore, if I could perceive harmonic colors through some sort of graduating scale of tension that was in agreement with my expressive impulses, I could treat harmony more as changing textures rather than only groups of notes put together in a variety of voicings. This scale of relative values is subjectively based and built up over years of listening to harmonies ranging from the ancient Gregorian chants to Beethoven to pianist Cecil Taylor and other sources. After hearing the same twelve notes rearranged just so many ways and getting accustomed to these sounds, a personal value system is inevitable and once understood, extremely useful.

A chord voicing in itself tells you what the specific notes contained in a scale will sound like, either as a tension, release or preparation before even hearing them. It serves as a guide for making melodic choices in order to aid the goal of expression. Once you're aware of how these choices will ordinarily be heard in context, you can choose according to what you wish to express. The chord and its corollary scale are not dogma. This is the awareness I acquired after so many years of playing countless chord changes. In any given style, for example be-bop, this means that the choices of pitches in relation to the chord produce certain expected cadences and tensions expressing that specific harmonic style and its syntax. The innovative music of Coltrane's quartet was derived from a different standpoint than be-bop, but still a related harmonic basis, called modalism. Melodically, Coltrane's modalism derived much of its material from *pentatonic patterns*[10]. This leads to a different set of note choices than in be-bop. This pattern of thinking can be discerned in any analyzable style. The main point is that no matter what context you deal in harmonically, chords are no more than textural or coloristic changes.

To accompany this overall concept of dealing with harmony, I figured a general way of classifying the complex chords I became interested in. (The following is solely an overview. Refer to *A*

8 *dissonance* – the opposite of consonance meaning instability and tension.
9 *consonance* – relative to dissonance connotating stability and rest; usually refers to the harmonic element.
10 *pentatonic patterns* – consistent and unbroken sequences which follow the pentatonic scale.

Chromatic Approach to Jazz Melody and Harmony, Advance Music). The first priority was to spell the sounds of contemporary music in the simplest way possible. After years of confusion, I realized that you could either name a chord in relation to the bass note as in the standard diatonic system, or you could break it down into its simplest components. The value of the second method was that by seeing and conceptualizing a sound in an unusual way, I was more likely to hear and play different melodic shapes. I believe this is due in part to how terminology triggers the intellect.

A simple example is the chord consisting of the following pitches ascending: F, G♯, B, E. Calling this an F minor, major 7th, flat 5, suggests the F diminished scale beginning with a whole step. On the other hand, naming this a "slash" chord, E/F (E triad over F bass note) suggests two tonal centers, that of the keys of E and F. Although the E tonality seems to outweigh the F by sheer number of notes in its part of the chord, the fact that F is in the bass compensates for its lack of several tones. Thinking of the two keys simultaneously yields different melodies than those derived from solely perceiving in F diminished. One guide to creating melodies in two keys at once is to play no more than three notes consecutively in either key before shifting to the other. Preferably, the consecutive number of notes in either key will vary endlessly and not fall into a pattern.

in a Paris photostudio, early '90s (© Mephisto)

Another important aspect to bear in mind when speaking about the key of E, is that I don't specify major, minor, augmented, dominant or diminished scale quality. It is in my terms, "E-ish" or in the realm of an E tonal center regardless of quality. This means that the shape of my lines lead in direction to that key center via a wide variety of passing tones. This places a high priority on melodic shapes that clearly outline one note as a tonal center rather than a scale or chord.

A basic principle which underlies my harmonic concept is *superimposition*[11]. In be-bop, the placement of common tritone substitute chords (D♭7 for G7) over the regular changes, is a simple example of superimposition. Going further, I may place the substitute chord alongside the known one. This means that when I see a G7 to C major cadential pattern, I can also play a D♭7 in the same bar as the G7 in any of many choices of harmonic rhythm: 2 1/2 beats for G7, 1 beat for D♭7 and back to 1/2 beat of G7 for that bar. If you go further and use the usual accompanying II chords (in any *quality*[12]) and their *tritones*[13] (A♭, D), even more variations on a normal V-I progression can occur. The melodic possibilities over these moving colors gives an elusiveness to what is an expected resolution.

In modal or pedal point harmony, for example, playing in a dorian scale or on F♯ pedal as the basis for improvisation, I might superimpose a progression over the stationary tonal center. Although the progression may not be expected or reacted to in a very literal and exact sense, the result will be that the lines and melodies based on the superimposition should reflect this different movement in contrast to the stationary key center. The result is melodic lines that although they have a dissonant chromatic coloration, still evidence a logical sense of motion and expression.

The most important aspect that I always keep in mind is that an harmonic ordering being used is learned in order to be in a sense, forgotten. In the end, *lines*[14] are made up of intervals and their expressive facets, no matter what the underlying sources or guiding principles may be for discovering what they are.

One last area is chord voicings. My concept of voicings is an extension of how I described melodies. Since a voicing is no more than a few intervals (therefore melodic fragments) put together, the principles are similar. There are cluster voicings consisting of mostly 2nds, 3rds, pentatonic voicings based on 4ths and 5ths, triadic voicings based on consecutive major and minor 3rds, wide interval voicings in which 7ths and 9ths predominate. The *tension and release*[15] values of a voicing are very relevant when accompanying the melody instrument. Obviously, the kind of voicing will have such a crucial effect upon whatever melody I play, that unless the musician who is functioning in this role (the comper) and to a lesser extent

11 *superimposition* – the placement of one harmony over another, resulting in bi- or polytonality; same analogy for rhythm and melody.
12 *quality* – in chords; major, minor, dominant, augmented or diminished.
13 *tritone* – an important interval between the perfect fourth and perfect fifth which is the midway point of the twelve chromatic tones; the tritone substitute is a common chord altering/reharmonization technique (D♭7 for G7).
14 *lines/line playing* – in a manner which emphasizes long melodic thoughts played mostly in eighth notes.
15 *tension and release* – the basic metaphysical as well as physical premise underlying art.

the bassist are familiar with this language, it is usually better to play without a chording instrument. Often an inexperienced comper will try to *second guess*[16] the melodicist or worse, force him into a strait jacket by overly anticipating the solo line.

Playing in this described chromatic manner should not degenerate into an ear training test or a game of second-guessing between the players. They should listen, leave space when very unsure and use their instinct when only slightly unsure. Emphasis should be placed on the overall tension-release color of what is being played, not on the specific notes. In any case, knowledge of the keyboard and analysis of other harmonic *idioms*[17] with their respective set of chord voicings is mandatory for this way of playing.

16 *second guess* – slang for trying to decipher an improviser's thought process.
17 *idioms* – various styles and genres of music.

Rhythm

Of course, the major challenge in jazz is rhythmic. The feeling of swing is personal and subjective, but definitely needs to be addressed by any musician purporting to play jazz. The important factors of *articulation*[18], beat placement, dynamics and nuance have been described in an earlier chapter. In short, *transcribing solos*[19] (see "Education") with exact imitation of phrasing as the primary goal, was how I went about this pursuit. This must be combined with analysis and of course trial and error through actual playing. Ultimately, an improviser's time feel should be as individual as his tone and soloistic concept.

Once this mountain was satisfactorily climbed, I wanted to incorporate one of the major facets I learned from playing free, group improvisations earlier in my development. That was attempting to apply the multi-noted, uneven rhythmical flurries and permutations which are an integral part of free music. To play pulse-oriented music using these rhythmic lines over and against the steady pulse became a major challenge. Again, as in harmony, the principle is superimposition.

To do this, I had to be able to feel the pulse without the necessity of regularly marking off the eighth notes in a symmetrical manner. Of course, at any instant, I should be able to return to the established pulse and clearly demonstrate where it is. But once the confidence to do this was gained, I felt the freedom to play around the basic pulse.

Playing the drums was as much an aid to facilitating these rhythmic goals as was the piano for learning harmony. A drummer deals with these principles in a very physical way. As one limb does a single pattern, another may be working independently. Also, the use of a metronome for practicing rhythmic superimposition is quite useful.

The idea is to make rhythm as flexible as melody and harmony; to not be limited to one way of feeling time. When I discussed the idea of playing "free" with Pete LaRoca, he said to me, "I'm free in 4/4

18 *articulation* – the manner in which a note is attacked ranging from smooth (legato) to percussive (staccato).
19 *transcribing* – the process of writing down an improvisation from a recording.

time and swinging, too!" In fact, it was LaRoca who taught me the important principle of both beginning and ending phrases on the "and" of the fourth beat, or on the four itself when playing normal 4/4 time. This is quite common in Latin rhythms. Basically, it's a matter of perspective and having a wide variety of choices at your disposal while improvising.

Color

Previously I alluded to the fact that I made a study of both blues players and singers as well as straight jazz vocalists. My objective was to emulate the subtle nuances which are so readily available to the voice. In addition, I also listened very carefully to ballads by the great interpreters, Miles, Coltrane, Bill Evans, Charlie Parker and others. Through these studies, I realized that every note should have its own particular inflection or nuance. Of course, much of the time in playing, it would be too difficult for this to occur on every single note as in a run, for example. In that case, nuances should be apparent for every group of notes.

At the same time in my development (late 1970's), the major tone production principles taught by my teacher Joe Allard finally began to be clear in my playing. I realized that one of his exercises, specifically the overtone-matching practice was a key to achieving this feeling of vocalization I was searching for. In short, you could produce the overtone of a fundamental pitch without changing to the regular fingering for that particular tone. To facilitate this, I had to use my larynx or voice box to a great degree. The physical sensation felt in my throat was similar to what occurs if I sang a note. Extending this feeling throughout the range of the horn and making this sensation felt at all times, not only for the exercise, results in a richer, darker tone. Also more expressive nuances became available for coloring. Finally, I felt as if the horn was really an extension of my body.

Form

I will discuss how I use form technically in the composition section. But the overall form of my improvisations has evolved through the years. The curve of my solos formerly would build up in intensity and then finish by dramatically lowering the level of energy. Once again, Miles made me to be aware of another choice for the *soloistic curve*[20]. He said to me, "Finish before you're done." I took this short epigram to mean that a solo need not necessarily have a climactic end. Musical entrances and exits are not bound to be at the beginning or end of the form every time. In other words, attempt to be unpredictable with this aspect of soloing: entering and exiting in places other than expected. This achieves two basic results. It gives the rhythm section more space in order that they can respond as well as initiate ideas for the soloist. It also raises the attention level of the band because they now become more than just a backdrop for

20 *soloistic curve* – the highs and lows in terms of energy and excitement of a given solo.

a soloist, but become an integral part of the improviser's game plan. Leaving a solo with a sense of surprise gives the listener a feeling of wanting more. The next soloist has a chance to either quickly continue the last train of thought, providing him with some focus for the beginning of his solo, or he can leave the space open and collect his thoughts before beginning.

Overall, I'm attracted to two extremes of playing. That is the lyrical/reflective and the intense/energetic. Both extremes bring out parts of my personality that I feel comfortable with emotionally and creatively. The ability to be sensitive and subtle means sophistication, finesse and discipline which are hallmarks of great performers. Conversely, the pure work aspect of energy-playing attracts me in the physical sense. I like to feel that I have sweated after playing. The challenge in intense playing is to be musical also. It is not difficult or particularly artistic to be crass and ponderous, especially when playing with a lot of energy. The balance between these extremes is what the general form and emotional content of my music revolves around.

The Act of Playing: Considerations During Actual Soloing

The process of hearing beforehand what I am about to play is slightly mysterious. If I were stopped in my tracks and asked to sing the exact line about to be played, a great deal of the time I wouldn't be able to produce it exactly pitch by pitch. But what I am sure of intuitively is the beginning of the line in terms of the pitch area, the general melodic contour, rhythmic shape and expressive setting (including dynamics, articulation and nuances). As the line is revealed, instantaneous response to the accompaniment leads to constant revision and reinterpretation. After the outset, a line becomes truly spontaneous meaning that where it will end is also unpredictable. This is particularly true for the longer lines played.

At other junctures, I may be thinking of different conceptual approaches because of the need to balance what has preceded or to prepare for what is to follow. An example would be a specific rhythmic phrase in order to propel the rhythm section off into what I hope will be the response I'm seeking from them. Another idea would be holding a tone for some duration in order that the chording instrument can hear a proper voicing under my lead note. At the same time, there is also ample opportunity for another musician to offer me some rhythmical ideas to proceed upon. The idea of leaving space between phrases is very useful in order to achieve these kinds of effects. Playing a one or two note percussive rhythm surrounded by space is an invitation for response and initiation from the rhythm section, in particular the drummer.

When playing modal music, I think intervalically in terms of tension and release notes. In even more chromatic playing, it is the overall shape of the groups of intervals which give the harmony color, rather than each specific note per se.

If I'm playing familiar chord changes, I may alternate between actually referring to them as they occur in the form and displacing them, trusting my ear and instinct. Rhythmically, the placement of my eighth note feel is handled in a similar manner. At times I purposely lay back or push the pulse, mixing this together with the awareness of where in the rhythmic phrase I may play *multi-noted flurries*[21]. Added to this is my intention to be over or against the pulse. At this point the shape of the line follows its own spontaneous course as to where it will end and assumes a more important priority than the actual pitches.

At times, the use of a softer dynamic level is intentional in order to temporarily lower the rhythm section's momentum. The goal may be for dramatic effect or to collect the group's energies for an even stronger surge to come. The form of an improvisation is something I figure out according to the melodic and harmonic phrases, but in some cases where the route may be deceptive, I may have to count bars or in some way keep track of sections. Among the elements of music, form and rhythm are the most quickly internalized.

Even in a cooperative group, the audience usually focuses its attention on the horn player. This is because he is physically the most visible by being in front, fairly mobile and is almost always playing the melody. Because of these factors, he is the obvious choice for communicating verbally with the listener.

My onstage attitude does reflect who I am playing with. If the other musicians are peers, I may announce the tunes and names of the players but in a very matter of fact, direct manner, trying to blend in with my contemporaries and basically allowing the music to speak for itself. On the other hand, when I am performing with a pick-up group or students, I usually convey a more relaxed attitude and banter with the audience. The main thrust of the onstage demeanor should be judged in terms of making the band feel at ease. A great deal depends upon whether my relationship to the other musicians is as peer or leader.

The sequence of songs in the set depends on circumstances discussed in "Creating the Music." Suffice to say, the choice of material must be geared towards the effect desired from the audience. A set is like one piece framed in time that can never be repeated exactly because of the spontaneous nature of improvising. I like to catch the immediate interest of the audience by playing an exciting piece or two in the beginning, use the reflective, milder moods near the end, and conclude with the most intense piece in the repertoire.

When I first was leading *Lookout Farm*, I called entirely different

---

21 *multi-noted flurries* – melodic lines consisting of close intervals; often played at a fast speed to create a dense texture.

Leading a Band

tunes every night. In fact, my attitude was so extreme that I tried not to repeat any tunes for at least three sets of playing. This was probably a reaction to the time spent with both Elvin Jones and Miles Davis. They would play the same tunes repeatedly. At that stage of my playing I found it difficult not to become bored with the music. But over the years, I have realized that familiarity with a song can lead to deeper insights into what is possible. I remember Elvin telling me that he played *My Favorite Things* with Coltrane probably 1000 times! Elvin also made me aware of the fact that even if you no longer can relate to a song emotionally in the present, part of the interpretive challenge is to relive the memory of whatever feelings may have once been experienced. This should be accomplished so convincingly that the listener sees it as completely fresh. Repetition is in reality virtually impossible by the nature of what improvisation is as well as the changing dynamics of group interplay. An individual also reflects his daily psychological and emotional state in a performance, which can rarely be the same consecutively. Finally, there are many musical devices available which are useful for initiating different patterns; changing the tempo, solo order or form of a composition are a few.

with Steve Lacy at a duet performance in the late '80s, Florence, Italy (© Caris Visentin Liebman)

The Soprano Saxophone

I began on the tenor saxophone after preliminary clarinet and several years of piano studies. For over ten years I played only the tenor and related to it as my main instrument. When I quickly added the flute, it became useful for certain types of material which helped to achieve variety in the music. But the tenor was the vehicle through which I became familiar with Coltrane's music and did the major portion of my transcribing solos, memorization of tunes, chords, etc., and most important, used to play all the time. The soprano saxophone entered my arsenal in 1970 as part of playing the reed parts in *Ten Wheel Drive*. With Elvin and Miles I played all three, but mostly the soprano for several reasons. My partner, Steve Grossman, enjoyed and sounded so good playing tenor, that I consented to soprano on most of the material with Elvin. The nature of Miles' music made the tenor very difficult to hear, even electrified with 700 watts of power behind me. Its generally lower range was swallowed up by the funky rhythm section, while the soprano, because of its being an octave higher cut through the cacophony. Miles seemed to favor the soprano in remarks like he wished the trumpet could play as fast as the soprano; (to which I would reply that I wished I could take my time and play as slowly as he did!)

By the time of *Lookout Farm* and my first major recordings as a leader, I had a formula for the three horns. If the tune was eighth note or fusion style, I used the soprano. If the material was ethnic or classical-like, then the flute. For jazz ballads and intense *burns*[22] it was the tenor. For a few years, this was artistically a very neat and satisfying package until the late 1970's.

It finally became apparent to me that switching between instruments meant severe changes of embouchure, concepts and even how my body actually felt. Also, in an evening's program, I was only playing each horn in real time for only a few minutes. How could I become one with all of these horns and make the kind of creative breakthroughs that occur when an instrument begins to feel increasingly like an extension of the body? I needed to center on one instrument and with great personal trepidation (would I be in demand without the tenor?), but with encouragement from my associate, Richie Beirach, I opted for the soprano.

My decision to center in on the soprano rather than the tenor was based on several reasons at the outset. Being as objective as possible, I could hear in my own playing that for some reason, my soprano style had more seeds of originality in it. The tenor was definitely more derivative of Coltrane and Rollins, probably because I practiced and played that music so much on the big horn. There was a good chance that with the soprano, I could possibly make more of an individual contribution to the world of jazz. If I found my own voice on it, the rewards would be more satisfying than just being

22 *burns* – slang expression for intense, usually fast idiom of jazz improvisation.

part of the crowd. Also, besides Sidney Bechet, Johnny Hodges, Coltrane, Steve Lacy and Wayne Shorter, there wasn't nearly as much of a deep legacy as on tenor at the time (1980). Careerwise, I would be one of a few, which couldn't hurt. And finally, a lot of the tenor players around seemed to be basically copying the kinds of lines Steve Grossman and myself had developed through absorption of Coltrane's music. After a while, I could see that allowing for human nature, I could easily become a mimic of myself.

The new regime began in 1980. Of course, I missed the tenor for its power and deep sound. Fortunately, the musicians with whom I work do not play alongside an instrument, but with a human being who happens to express himself through one or another vehicle. In fact, there were times near the beginning when someone I recorded or played with reacted like drummer Peter Donald, "I didn't even notice that there was no tenor after the first note!" As of this writing I am returning to tenor on occasion (see "The Return of the Tenor" in the Appendix), but my decision was probably the best one I ever made artistically up to that point in my evolution.

By now, I can assess the results musically. Playing the soprano has added several elements to my style as well as insights into a wide variety of other musical factors. My hearing seems to be sharper with the soprano, possibly because it is one octave higher than the tenor and sounds in the actual octave where it is written. The blend with the acoustic piano is very harmonious because of this reason. The soprano offers a mellow bottom register contrasted with a brilliant and at times shrieky color in the high register, especially the *altissimo*[23]. The smallness of the horn physically gives me a very light and transparent color in my lines. Also, the compactness in both horn and mouthpiece size means that tonguing is articulated with less effort and a wider range of variety than I had on the tenor. Physically, the soprano is more suitable to my physique, which on occasion groans under the weight and general largeness of the tenor. The upper torso is involved when playing soprano with most of the effort concentrated in the neck and head area, whereas the tenor necessitates the whole body. The result is that with soprano, my lower torso feels more anchored and freer to feel the music. With the aid of the best equipment I can find, I have been able to obtain my own sound, and for the most part, tame the usual intonation problems of the "fish-horn". The truth is that at times while playing the soprano, I feel like it is a trumpet and in fact there has been some grafting of trumpet conception in my style.

Finally, I have noticed that at times my soprano playing evidences a sort of cry or wail, seemingly reminiscent of a sound found in the music of the Middle East. It is possible that my Semitic-Jewish ancestral roots (via Eastern Europe) have found a way to be expressed

---

23 *altissimo* – the range of notes above the normal range of the saxophone.

through my instrument. Is not one's art a reflection of where he has been, as far back as ancestral roots, as well as where he may be going?

Composing

My early impetus for composing began as a natural outgrowth of learning the repertoire. As a student, it is inevitable that compositions in the beginning stages will directly reflect the material under study. In fact, my first recorded composition, *Slumber* (Elvin Jones' *Genesis*), was basically a copy of Wayne Shorter's *Speak No Evil*, both in the beginning chord sequence as well as in the time feel (coincidentally played by Elvin Jones). And in those first years, there were many Coltrane-type modal compositions. During this period, events that occurred in my life as well as reactions to people I knew and places I traveled to were immediate sources of inspiration. In a sense, inspiration as well as titles for compositions were rather easy because the process of reflecting my personal feelings musically was fresh and new.

As I grew musically and began to study composition including some classical music, my methods of composing evolved along with the material. Titles began to reflect more than autobiographical happenings. Instead of being about myself in relation to the world, I was able to increasingly reflect upon society and the environment around me. The scenario is that in older age, one reflects upon the eternal verities and matters of the cosmos.

Titles reflect thoughts and feelings which translate to musical sounds for me. Of course, there are many compositions which do not necessarily deal with any programmatic material or feelings, only purely musical ideas. But for me to begin with an extra-musical thought has always made the initial melody, harmony or rhythm appear quickly and clearly. One of my major compositional premises is that the initial musical idea coming from the intuition should basically be sacrosanct. I accept this beginning idea as coming from my subconcious and try not to tamper with it too much even in terms of key choice. When one composes, the main task is to sort through the countless possibilities available as to notes, chords and other elements. In the case of the original idea, I accept it as more or less final. All the remaining composing or decision making makes up the real work and is always open to constant revision.

I have described in "Creating the Music" how the compositional process evolves in general. This scheme of problem solving, choosing among the various methods of handling the elements of music, arranging, re-arranging after hearing, orchestrating and copying is for me an organized process which necessitates that I have the physical time. When I've decided to compose in the past years, I clear a week or two and take out the sketches one by one trying to get them to completion, meaning they are ready to play. The actual playing of a new tune may not occur for a while, but when it does, I will then take note and make the necessary changes pretty much on the spot. Whenever possible, a composition proceeds to the recording or live performance stage and probably undergoes more revisions. As already stated, a composition is never truly finished and complete in jazz, because once a tune is at the performance level, my viewpoint shifts to how it feels to actually play it live. This is constantly changing, as my playing evolves, so a tune is almost always "in progress."

Obviously, not all of my tunes undergo this lengthy process or such scrutiny. Some compositions are written in a flash, a sort of stream of consciousness action with ease of performance being the priority. Conversely, with compositions in the contemporary classical vein, there are some pieces that are completely written out from beginning to end with little improvisation.

I think that most composers would agree with the observation that in essence any composition has its antecedents in a prior work. An artist's vision can be only so large, therefore he is always writing and rewriting the same tune(s). In my body of work, there are several general idioms which I've been involved in. If I consider the nearly 300 compositions, most of them could be categorized under several broad areas.

There is the jazz idiom consisting of tunes with chord changes, modal or pedal point harmony. Under this heading are also melodies that are supported only by bass lines or stand alone, with no harmonic accompaniment. In this category the presence or absence of direct harmony along with the choices of rhythmic feels (either *open eighth note*[24] or straight ahead jazz feel) are the main prerequisites. I compose these tunes primarily at the piano except for those where harmony is absent; they are done on the horn and checked with the bass line at the piano.

Another idiom is more rhythmically based. These compositions evolve from either a bass line alone or in conjunction with a drum beat. These are usually even sixteenth or eighth note based rhythms and mostly intended to be played with electric bass, guitar and/or keyboards, whereas the jazz tunes are almost always conceived for acoustic instruments. Some of these kinds of tunes fall into the fusion category.

The last group of compositions are more atonal harmonically and may involve contrapuntal lines. The rhythm is often rubato or freely interpreted and the melodies possibly more jagged than other tunes. These were mostly written with the kind of pianist who knows contemporary classical music in mind. I know that I can write a voicing which portrays a given feeling and that when we rehearse, the pianist may find other notes but remain close to my original expressive intention. When we do this, the words used for

24 *open eighth feel* – by use of pauses and held rhythms, this rhythmic basis of playing creates a spacious, open atmosphere, based on eighth note divisions.

describing aesthetic objectives are "bright, dark, jagged, smooth, lyrical, jumbled, curved, squared off, thin, thick", etc. These compositions are definitely in the twentieth century contemporary vein.

As I have mentioned, the purpose of composition for me is as a vehicle to improvise on. Some tunes are meant to be cameos or short mood pieces which may be useful as transitional colors on recordings or during a set. When I consider form, a paramount determination is that if there will be more than one soloist, each section that an improviser will solo on should be different from one another. Therefore, many of my tunes will have a section of vamping which is somehow extracted from the main body of the tune. It may be one motif or the last few bars of the song. This means that one soloist will deal with the structure or content of the main section as a vehicle for soloing, while the other player uses the looser vamp format. This gives the music more contrast and freshness rather than each soloist having to deal with repetition of what came before.

To compose is to frame a single idea or expression forever. It is a mysterious process and quite personal. Writers who use lyrics are at a great advantage since the verbal message helps clarify the composer's feelings. I envy songwriters for this advantage in expressing thoughts. On the other hand, instrumental music can challenge the imagination of the listener to a larger extent, because even with a programmatic title or storyline, the interpretations of a musical sound are as varied and numerous as the number of people listening. When I sit down to write, I picture my idea and somehow translate it into a musical shape using melody, harmony and rhythm as the integral elements with color and form as the frame around them. When a clear picture of the shape is present, I experiment over and over with each of the elements until it seems that for that moment of time, I have discovered the clearest means to express my idea. Composing is endlessly challenging and very deep in its psychological implications. A composer is constantly facing himself in the mirror of self-awareness.

Recording

As described earlier, the act of recording is an entirely different challenge than any other for the jazz musician. To feel relaxed and confident is primary and can only be obtained by experience. It took me several dozen sessions to finally feel comfortable in the studio. The goal is to balance an intellectual and logical understanding of the purpose of recording with the spontaneous and creative aspects of improvisation.

Having previously discussed the actual process, one can observe the frustrating conditions for jazz recordings and how the odds are often stacked against true creativity. There is usually little preparation time with the group; the money is so scarce that recording time is short and in some cases, the studios themselves are not functioning up to par. A reputation for speed and creative repair work is a main prerequisite for an engineer to be in demand for jazz recordings, because often the equipment places him in a position where with little time, he must patch things together. On the business end, some of the few small existing companies that record authentic jazz enter into contracts that are one sided away from the interests of the artists. These agreements often include keeping the publishing and artistic royalties to a minimum, if granted at all. The problems of distribution, promotion and airplay are staggering. But in the end, the greatest artistic frustration is that after finally having the chance to document one's work under whatever conditions exist, the artist may just have an off day with no second chance.

There are several things that with nearly 200 recordings I have learned in relation particularly to my own 80 albums as leader or co-leader. Depending on the taste of the company (and producer as their representative), I try to balance their natural desire for a successful commercial project, limited as it may be, with my artistic needs and goals. If there is any possibility of a common ground, I will attempt to compromise accordingly. I'm sympathetic to the requirements of running any successful business. After all, I run a business called David Liebman. Of course, I hope that the producer is capable of understanding something about the technical and aesthetic nature of what I record, so that the very necessary feedback in the recording session itself has some real meaning.

I try to be as prepared as possible in relation to individual or group rehearsals and furnish clearly written out parts if needed. I try to set an agenda for the session with what I would like to accomplish, but also I am constantly aware of time limitations. In the session itself, my antennae are turned up so that decisions and directions can be made quickly. As a leader, usually there is no time to think about your own playing, so you must trust your instincts and past playing experience. Also, I am constantly open to seizing upon a new idea or opportunity that will provide a spontaneous happening and energize the session. I attempt to make everyone as comfortable as possible, but insist upon discipline and the musicians' acceptance of whatever the technical situation may be. I can't stand it when musicians get too distracted in trying to get the correct headphone mix, for example. Often, this is just nervous energy running out of control.

Mixing and sequencing are of course crucial and I do the best I can in these areas. But my basic attitude is that the music will speak for itself in true jazz when played by top performers. (Other kinds of music often need surgery after the recording). Once I have completed recording, my enthusiasm and excitement are sapped. The music is forever in the air and I know I've done my best. For me, recording puts me at the top of my game and does more for my growth as an artist than any other aspect. My best album is usually the last one! It is a way of documenting one's music and providing a mechanism for continued growth.

My Own Practicing

I have not seriously practiced since I graduated college at 22 years of age and spent six months living in upstate New York. At that time I transcribed solos and did a lot of basic work already outlined. That period formed the foundation of my next ten years of playing until the late 1970's when my own concepts became clearer. I'm not proud of this dearth of practice, but there is an explanation of how I feel this has been compensated for.

An improviser must put his practice into reality. The act of improvising is one of acquiring habits and reactions to musical stimuli that in time become intuitive after they have been intellectualized through hard practice. Playing under the "best of circumstances" equals practice in this music. The best of circumstances means that as often as possible one plays with better musicians because they raise the level of the individual's own playing. In fact, a lot of younger musicians, as intimidated as they may be of playing with superior musicians, will find it easier rather than more difficult when the musicians are on a higher level.

Since the beginning of my professional career in 1970, I have made it my top priority to play as much as possible. When the year ends and I look back, one measure of a successful period is how many days or nights I physically played the horn. The sheer amount of hours spent on my instrument became the primary way of practicing. For me, I had to play to improve. I would get very nervous if I had too much time off and was continually amazed at how Pete LaRoca, Elvin Jones and Miles Davis could just sit down and within a few sets, be at the top of their form.

Of course, these musicians and in time I too, have played so much that the whole process becomes second nature. I have discovered in the last few years that I can spend time away from actual playing and do constructive things both with music and away from it. The truth is that for the artist, there is no such thing as time off, because every thing is geared towards the acts of creation, even seemingly non-related areas of life. In fact, as I've matured, activities that I formerly regarded as non-productive have revealed new insights about myself and in this way have been valuable. Personal relationships and dealing with family ties is a necessary part of one's development also.

The body must feel good for any creative, or for that matter, non-creative work to be accomplished. When I'm away from a work schedule, I do my best to ease up on my diet after eating out for weeks on end. I also do some light exercise to get in shape. Both Elvin and Miles seemed to be completely rejuvenated when I would see them after a few weeks off.

I try to pursue my interests in reading periodicals and following the news, especially because I travel so much and have ties to places and events away from home. Occasionally, I will go to a museum or an event that is involved in the other arts. I remember seeing a major Picasso retrospective in the early 1980's at the Museum of Modern Art in New York. After several floors of his work, there was one little room with Picasso's renditions of the classics like Rembrandt's *Nightwatch* and Van Gogh's *Sunflowers*. Underneath each painting they had a photo of the original. I was very impressed with how Picasso interpreted the original. It was like what improvisers do with standards. I'm always trying to correlate a concept from another art or artist to my own field.

Then there is running a business which is what an artist must also do. It's no different than owning a store or factory, except that you have no employees. But you still have multiple functions to perform: public relations and promotion, business meetings, phone calls, airlines, travel and hotel timetables, keeping your compositions, arrangements and instruments organized, supplies in stock. The conducting of business is time consuming and basically not related to the creation of the art, except that without it, there is no income or more crucial, no chance to play.

Also important for me is the fact that I feel teaching is a necessity for an artist, so there are students from everywhere. Although I see very few on a regular basis because of my schedule, there is never a shortage of interested youngsters. Having traveled so much, I have made friends with literally hundreds of people throughout the world, many of whom I speak and write to. Of course, there are neighbors and old friends to stay in contact with. Finally, my journalistic interests in writing record reviews, liner notes and books like this present one are a part of my artistic output.

So there is little chance to find the consistent practice time which is the best way to acquire new material. There has to be at least a few weeks of hammering away daily at an idea for it to have a chance of finding its way to the actual improvising stage. This doesn't mean that daily rudiments or musical calisthenics shouldn't be included in the every day regimen. This is a good habit to develop early. On instruments like the trumpet, it's almost a necessity to do a variety of standard exercises if only because otherwise, the physical toll of getting back in shape is awesome. Even Miles Davis had to practice long tones when he returned to playing after his sojourn of 1975-80.

Nonetheless, I do follow a certain musical routine when I'm off the road and have spent the necessary two week period taking care of home and personal affairs. During this initial period, I don't listen to much music or play at all, except possibly some background pop or world music that doesn't demand much attention. In truth I can't listen to music and do anything else simultaneously including eating. I marvel at musicians who can fall asleep to music because my mind is automatically involved.

Finally, I begin to listen to tapes of the recent tour or new recordings to review them. I don't listen over and over but enough to take notice of what occurred. No longer do I criticize my work in detail as I did when I was younger. I accept a performance as one glimpse into myself and nothing more than that. I have learned over the years not to make self judgments too often because in the end, it is the cumulative weight of my artistic output which concerns me. Listening time is also spent on tapes and records from musicians or students of their work which are sent to me. I am complimented by this as well as curious to what they're involved in and take it as a responsibility.

Listening finally becomes more centered on whatever influence I intend to use in either my playing or impending compositions. For example, if my next piece is planned for woodwinds, I find a few key pieces along with the score and try to expose myself to the overall sound. Or it might be a composition rooted in an ethnic or jazz idiom that I am curious about. The idea is to surround myself with the feeling of the music, not to try to copy it.

Musically, I use my time to play the piano. It should be obvious to anyone interested in music that it is through the keyboard that a musician can truly understand musical complexities, especially as a composer, orchestrator or arranger. I may sit at the piano at first playing both jazz tunes and some easy Bach inventions, chorales or similar classics. After this warm up of a few days, I begin to study from a contemporary music book, scores, piano music or jazz transcription. Then I will begin to write and work on whatever project I'm involved in. I try to set up goals for myself as well as projects to be completed so that when this period of a week or so is over, I have accomplished some real, practical work adding to my repertoire.

When I'm about to return to steady work, I begin the calisthenics of playing the horn. This includes some technical books with exercises, play-along records or sight reading transcriptions. I avoid practicing lines or material that I actually might play because one of the great feelings of beginning to play again is the freshness of being involved in the act of improvisation. Of course, I review the music to be played if I know what it will be.

The above regimen often eludes me in recent years because of the personal schedule that comes with a family and home. But when I actually do play the concentration and energy are higher than previously. Of course, in my dreams I look forward to a "Sonny Rollins on the bridge" type scenario. Maybe in the next lifetime!

The first meeting of the International Association of Schools of Jazz (1989) held in the office of Advance Music, Germany (© Hans Gruber)

Education 5

In a sense this entire book is an educational treatise. I have accepted the responsibility to teach this art form as best I can and have spent much time discussing, doing and writing about the educational process. In fact, in the early 1980's, after a crisis of sorts and a half-hearted attempt to change professions (law), it was the positive value of teaching which brought me back to jazz with renewed vigor. This chapter begins with some general considerations and then moves on to the specifics of jazz education.

An Overview

For the majority of man's history on the planet, art as well as other skills were passed on through generations by the oral tradition. Whether it was from the father to the son, mother to daughter or teacher to apprentice, this time-worn tradition of passing on knowledge was the only way to educate. The advantage of such a method is that the student is not as likely to be overwhelmed with material when he hasn't yet absorbed what came before. Intellectual overkill is cut to a minimum. But as times changed and the necessary information multiplied, the end of the oral tradition as the major educative tool was inevitable.

The teacher became a professional addressing hundreds of students over a period of time. A system became a necessity and one of the areas to suffer most was the teaching of art. Because real artistic talent is a rarity and the gaining of proficiency in an art form is a slow, evolving process, the concept of educating an artist is more complicated than other subjects. One major aspect is that the teacher must be able to demonstrate the facts he is discussing because in learning an art form, imitation is the first important stage. But before discussing the specifics of teaching improvisation, there are some general guidelines to be aware of when doing any educating.

General Concepts

Teaching a very specific skill or idea as well as providing inspiration are the apparent goals of instruction. But more important than the specifics is to teach a student how to learn. If a youngster can leave his formal education with both the desire and skills to continue learning, the main objective has been reached. After all, no teacher or course of study can purport to show a student all there is to know. No matter how many years a student stays with a master, there will be a time of going it alone. The newly educated person will begin to find out what areas of the field interest him most and want to learn more about them. He should be able to analyze and inculcate new material. This system of self-education varies from person to person, but the teacher's responsibility is to set the individual's own system of disciplined learning into motion. This is especially true for the artist who is constantly seeking new horizons and inspiration. I will discuss this more towards the end of this chapter.

In accordance with establishing positive lifelong learning habits in a student, the teacher must be sure that no matter how mundane the specific material being worked upon, its role in the context of what the overall study is should be clear to the student. In music, the drudgery of practicing exercises, scales, patterns, etc., should always be done with a clear sense of musicality as if those notes were a piece in itself. The student must not be allowed to fall into bad musical habits or sloppiness because of the simple and boring nature of what he is practicing. Specifically, the expressive element should always be addressed: phrasing, articulation, dynamics, intonation and a sense of pulse need to be pointed out and discussed. Every time the student plays his instrument, he should strive for feeling and expression as well as technically accurate music. In this way, even a beginning student will see change and most often, quick improvement in the overall musicality of what he is doing. Positive reinforcement of this kind is essential to become inspired and want to accomplish the work necessary to be a true artist.

Describing the Learning Process

There are several distinct stages in any learning process. Primarily, it is up to the teacher to be able to verbalize how and what he thinks of when actually creating. The obligation is to find those words, concepts, expressions or whatever is needed to get across how the teacher thinks to each student in terms they can understand. If the student body is large in number, this individual communication is obviously more difficult than in private or small group instruction. Once a concept is well explained, repetition becomes necessary as an essential tool for teaching. With repetition must come examples and a method of practicing for the student so he can absorb the concept.

For the majority of students, most often intellectual understanding will precede the intuitive. Of course, some of the information at one time or another will feel natural to every student without knowing why. Whichever route the knowledge takes, the process of habitualizing new information and the ability to duplicate it without thinking is the goal. In an art form, the ability to duplicate techniques and concepts is a real measure of how well something has been learned. In improvisation, the process from intellectual understanding and memorization, through practice, and finally the ability to spontaneously play a new idea is a fact of artistic growth. The length of this stage of development is different for each musician depending on aspects like practice, the strength of commitment and the opportunity to try new material in actual playing situations. Using the intellect to figure ideas out is a major tool for hearing and feeling more. Playing well is not something that descends from the heavens full blown and ready to go.

As stated above, learning to learn is something that should be taught. I insist on several things before I even present any material. I urge the students to take notes and not depend upon a cassette recording of the class because the chances are small that they will listen in detail to a tape in the future, if only because the immediacy is gone. They should ask questions in order that they understand the points made. Encouraging questions is important because of the natural shyness and fear of being spotlighted amongst student peers. When they leave, they should at the least understand intellectually the material in words that are meaningful to them personally. Also they should realize that the questions they may be reluctant to ask are probably on the other student's minds also. It is necessary to give them a specific tool to practice what has been presented. They must leave with a clear method of reinforcing the material after the session. If it's not clear, encourage them to ask. I don't use too many handouts of prepared material because there is the tendency to listen less attentively when the student feels that the information has been organized for them on paper. I might give them these sheets in the future. Also, in my case with several books and videos available, I try not to redo the book in class but attempt to go more deeply into one area or a general overview. The books are not a substitute for me, but an adjunct. In any case, the truly serious student will probably have read my book previously or shortly after he sees a class. Concerning the plethora of books in general, with so many out there explaining and re-explaining the same thing repeatedly, I try to de-emphasize their value (including my own). Having so much material available poses a real danger of inundation and mass confusion. I might recommend something specific, but overall they all pretty much do the same job. Of course, the potential of CD-ROM interactive material is great, but I can't help but wondering how many students will really use them. It remains to be seen.

It is important that the teacher lay down an important ground rule to the students. In terms of a metaphor, a student is like a sponge – absorbing material without opinion as to its value up to the point of comprehension. It can be quite unnerving to get into an argument with a student as to the value of what is being presented. This is the teacher's area and his judgement should be respected. There is a reason, possibly in the long run, why he is presenting something. If the material is either too far advanced or elementary, this should of course be brought to the teacher's attention.

Pedagogy – General Comments

There are several attitudinal aspects that make up a good teacher. These include what to notice in an individual student as well as specific techniques which help get the material across. Following is a summary of what I have learned from teaching in order to be more effective.

Observing an individual's needs is central to good teaching, especially in the one to one situation we often encounter in music. Combining experienced observation of a student's abilities, talents and deficits along with the student's own descriptions is of course essential. But there are nuances to observation. Every person is unique in how they learn. Discerning various learning capacities according to several categories can be helpful. These are aural, visual, tactile, intellectual, and even philosophical. Every individual possesses one of these aspects in a greater degree than another and it is the teacher's responsibility to try and discover this. In musical pedagogy it is often that one can observe the student who is more ear oriented or tactile (meaning technical) or intellectually oriented as their primary mode of learning. This constitutes basic psychology: how best to present material to an individual in order to maximize his chances of learning.

Basic to absorbing new material is understanding the difference between what is relative and what is absolute. Of course, these judgements in themselves are very subjective according to whom is presenting the material, but a teacher should be able to say that what he is presenting is either related in some way to other pertinent information, or is in itself absolutely the final say in the matter at hand. Most of the time when we teach something, we are reluctant to say that "In my opinion, this is the best way to do this", because we're not confident about taking such a strong position. So we use the relative scenario, saying that are many ways to see this, etc. I think there are times depending upon the information, when it is important that a student feels the teacher is absolutely sure of what he is saying and clearly states such.

It is very important that early on a student be told that mistakes are fine. Most young people naturally fear being wrong and singled out among their peers. The desire to blend in is seemingly universal among young people. But especially in art, it is crucial that a student be given the "green light" for experimenting and possibly faltering. In fact, as artistic development continues through the years, it is often in the mistakes that one sees the seeds of change. In the improvisational process itself, one can hardly predict the results. Admission of error and constant adjustment are essential components of an improviser's vocabulary. At the same time, it is necessary to make the student aware of how to evaluate his own playing. The teacher must point out that the reaction of an audience consisting of friends, family, critics and peers to one's playing is biased in one way or the other. To be purely objective is impossible, but the young artist should see as an overall goal the need to balance external and internal judgements. After all, who knows better what one was trying to play than the artist himself?

Workshop 1984 in Tübingen, Germany (© Hans Gruber)

There are several other aspects of teaching which should be highlighted. A teacher may need to exaggerate something in order to get a point across. Along with exaggeration, there is the perpetual role of devil's advocate. Even if the teacher's convictions lie elsewhere, a good instructor may find it necessary to challenge a point just for the sake of stimulating dialogue. Part of being an effective teacher is the ability to perform in order to dramatize points. Also, a teacher sometimes has to give the students assignments in areas that he may not have done to completion himself. A teacher should tell the student what should be done. In other words, the teacher must tell the students what should be done. Finally, the teacher must envision himself as an interpreter of what came before. Teaching is a constant re-interpretation of past information. It is up to the teacher to constantly re-evaluate his sources and depending upon the situation, explain them in a suitable light, even if they contradict long held views.

It is crucial that a teacher exhibit a willingness to offer the student material in areas which he himself may not personally admire or respect. Beyond his judgement as to what is necessary to learn, the instructor should be able to rise above personal taste and be open to other concepts for the sake of the student when it is appropriate. This does not mean hiding one's opinions or not admitting a lack of knowledge in an area. One of the great challenges in teaching is how to balance a student's personal desires with what in the long run is absolutely necessary for the proper kind of education. A teacher's ego and maturity will constantly be put to the test.

Jazz Education

The teaching of jazz in a formal, classroom situation is relatively new. After all, jazz itself is not very old, so it took a few decades for enough information to be codified and organized. Jazz education should not have as its main goal the producing of young soloists who will pursue a professional career as improvisers. There is no realistic correlation between supply and demand at present, and I don't think the situation will alter greatly at any time in the future. The right combination of great talent, perserverance and fortunate timing is and was always a rarity.

On the most basic level, a student educated in any art form becomes the eventual audience for the actual performers. Serious art needs an educated public and the person who has taken part in the art himself will be just that. The effect felt in society as a whole will be to raise the level of appreciation and naturally provide more opportunity for the work to be seen and heard.

More specifically, learning the art of improvisation in the late twentieth century is to become aware of the basic musical foundation of our time. A century ago and before, "the three B's" (Beethoven, Bach and Brahms) was a phrase connoting general knowledge of Western classical music and its rules. For hundreds of years, these concepts were the basis of all music heard in the Western world.

But the twentieth century marked an explosion of change in the arts and because of the communication age, it was dramatic, rapid and ultimately worldwide. The music that is most universal is pop-oriented and descends directly from the *Tin Pan Alley*[1] and Broadway composers like Irving Berlin, George Gershwin, Cole Porter through to Lennon, McCartney and Stevie Wonder. This music is all based on melodies over chord changes. In jazz this same material is the mainstay of be-bop and its predecessors, swing and dixieland.

As jazz developed into a real art form divorced from the entertainment wing of music, it became more complex in all the elements of music and slowly, parts of the jazz literature showed similarities to contemporary twentieth century classical music (Schoenberg, Bartók, Stravinsky, etc.). Once again, the material of another idiom

---

1 *Tin Pan Alley* – was an actual street in the first half of the 20th century in New York City where pop songwriters turned out songs; loosely refers to standards.

became a source for jazz styles: modalism, free-form, and other modern styles of jazz.

Adding the recent trends of the crossing over of ethnic and world music into improvisation, jazz as a whole embraces the music of the twentieth century. In sum, the student interested in musical thought for whatever reasons, whether they be in or out of the music field, can see the entire contemporary music picture by learning the basics of jazz improvisation.

The three major areas are basic instrumental and musical skills, improvisation and artistic development. In outline form:

Outline of Material

A *Instrumental and Musical Skills*
Tone production: breath control and embouchure for winds; manual technique for others; use of voice to sing what one hears; digital dexterity, etc.
Reading, writing, hearing music: the language of all western music; including knowledge of the keyboard which is indispensible for all musicians because of the ease of visualizing harmony; also ear training and sight reading.

B *Improvisation*
The mathematics of music: chords, scales, basic melodic patterns, common harmonic cycles, rules of tension and release; all information must be intellectually absorbed as well as able to be duplicated on the instrument (voice and piano to a lesser degree); eventually, required composition.
Phraseology: the analysis and ability to duplicate the legacy through playing and study of transcribed solos from the literature; duplication must be exact in terms of obvious features such as pitches and rhythm as well as nuances and expressive devices, time feel and articulation.
Playing in real situations: learning the customs and repertoire of live improvisation.

C *Artistic Development*
Knowledge of jazz legacy: includes predominant features of styles, important artists and recordings, basic historical trends.
General knowledge of all idioms: improvisation in other legacies; the classical tradition; all music worldwide from past, present and future.
Cultural development: knowledge of other arts, history, spiritual, general philosophy, science; anything that makes the artist more emotionally alive and psychologically aware so the level and content of communication to others continues to grow and deepen.

My Own Pedagogy

Generally, my value as a teacher is to students who already have the basics fairly well together. I truly respect those teachers who are involved with fundamentals on a daily basis. It takes great skill and above all patience. The advantage of studying with a player who is actively performing is that he is involved every day with the artistic process. This means that this artist demonstrates a consistency of method and discipline which, when combined with a talent for verbalizing concepts, can be tremendously inspiring for a youngster. I personally can contribute to the growth of a young artist's own conception by helping him comprehend the legacy and develop individuality.

There is one major psychological aspect to be aware of when teaching. That is to make the student realize that the teacher also struggled, made mistakes and is only human. A great artist does not appear full blown from birth.

When I hear anyone play, professionals included, my judgment about their playing is based upon several criteria. My first reaction is to the tone which emanates from their instrument. If it is balanced between bright and dark with resonance as well as clarity, I am aesthetically pleased. A musician's sound combines with expression and nuance to create a personal identity. I try to see whether there is flexibility in these aspects rather than a one way or rigid approach. I try to discern whether the colors, articulations and phrasing vary with any regularity. Added to this is the basic eighth note feel of the musician's lines. Flexibility concerning beat placement is crucial for me to be convinced that the artist is really feeling the music on the spot and not merely playing on automatic pilot. Finally, in the case of a professional, I listen for consistency of quality and what feels to be real commitment gathered over repeated listening to an artist.

Obviously, a student will not have all of the above together or he needn't come for lessons. Within a few minutes of playing either drums or piano along with a new student, I can hear where the deficiencies are in these described areas. That is where I begin: to make what the student is already playing sound better. Usually at the outset, there will be a discussion of sound production, regardless of what instrument the student plays. We may discuss the sound that recognized musicians get and what these characteristics are. I have found that an important concept to convey is the ability to identify what one is hearing and in some way, verbally describe it. When the student can do this, it registers mentally and change can be more readily affected. Clarity of thought is an essential discipline. The rationale that a student likes something but can't identify what it is does not hold with me.

After tone production, the basics of phrasing including the most important aspect, articulation, are discussed. The observation of what the pupil is doing incorrectly can usually be shown by playing back a tape of the student's own phrasing. This is followed by demonstration and in-depth discussion of what parts of the body are involved (depending on the instrument) in the actual articulation.

Subject Specifics

Instrumental training is basic with virtuosity as the implied goal. Each instrument's technique is specific but no matter the tool, the goal is the same. That is for the student to feel that his instrument is an extension of the body with all the flexibility of sound and expressive devices possible. Because of the spontaneous nature of jazz improvisation we aren't aware of what we're going to play. Of course, we do have a lot of automatic responses under our fingers, but the way something will be played is up to the moment. Therefore the implication is that the instrumentalist has to be ready at any point to translate his impulses and feelings through the instrument. The goal is that what one hears-feels-thinks can be channeled immediately through the instrument without thought as to the mechanics of production. In sum, the instrument should feel like your hand!! It is the personalization of tone and expression that separate players to the ordinary ear. If one thinks of a note like the picture of a fish, it is very clear. The head is the attack; the body is the colorization of a note; the tail is the decay or how the note goes from one to another. At each of these junctures, there is ample opportunity for an individual's own musical personality to surface.

To my mind, after tone, the main essential in jazz is the eighth note rhythmic feel which is also referred to as the dotted triplet figure. No matter what idiom one may eventually play in, the basic currency of jazz comes down to good, swinging eighth notes set within a series of chord changes with the goal of constructing melodies spontaneously that have emotion and shape. What can be taught is the best way to articulate the eighth notes (depending upon the instrument) and the use of inflection, nuance, dynamics and other personalized expressive devices to enhance their presentation. But it is only through the transcription process and its usefulness as an imitative tool, that a student who is having trouble with this rhythmic feel can begin to do it. After imitation, the individual will naturally phrase the eighth notes in his own manner, if he really desires to.

Transcription

In short, transcription represents the clearest and quickest way for a student to be able to phrase in a convincing manner within any given stylistic context. There are several benefits to transcribing:
1. *Ear training* – The student must transcribe the solo off the recording himself. This may necessitate slowing down the tape in order to sing the phrases at first, before going to the instrument

to find actual pitches. Following this, the rhythm has to be figured out. The value is pitch and rhythmical dictation as well as jazz solfege. Eventually the solo should be notated.

2. *Exact duplication* – This is how the phrasing is learned. By duplicating every nuance, dynamic change, pause, *ghost note*[2], smear, bend, glissandi, etc., alongside the actual notes and correct rhythms, the student is internalizing the proper syntax. This takes countless repetitions to accomplish and when it is done to satisfaction, the student playing along with the original should sound exactly simultaneous, given the range or octave and timbral differences that may be present between the different instruments. The student who accomplishes this will feel great satisfaction and probably be quite inspired to do more transcribing.

3. *Analysis* – Just as in the case of a classical composer analyzing scores, the young jazz artist does the equivalent with the solo he has transcribed. Particular lines should be isolated with an attempt to second guess the improviser. Questions concerning what the musician may have been thinking are good to discuss, because just this process alone is stimulating and can lead to further insights. The very idea that a solo can be analyzed and isn't just some mysterious creation isolated on record in history can be more illuminating than one may imagine.

4. *Practical use* – The solo can be played with a rhythm section or play-along record. Since most of the transcribed material should be familiar tunes, blues or rhythm changes, this should not be a problem. The solo can be used creatively as a point of departure to improvise on, with the student beginning at some section of the solo and then playing on his own. He may refer back to the transcription when he encounters problems. Also, lines that are exceptionally well crafted should be isolated and practiced on the appropriate chord change(s) in every key using the basic principles of thematic and rhythmical variation that are common: augmentation, *displacement*[3], diminutions, *alternate pitch sequences*[4], leaving rests and still fitting the line in some way, changing eighth notes to triplets, etc. Finally, the student writes out his own lines following the basic structure of the original.

In this way, a transcription becomes a major tool for internalizing the subtle, difficult to verbalize concepts of phrasing as well as some specific musical facts, practical material and valuable artistic disciplines. A few transcriptions wisely chosen over a year or two will begin to reap real benefits in the student's playing. The idea that imitation is a dishonest method of inspiring and teaching because it destroys originality is false in my opinion. There's nothing wrong with a student sounding good, maybe like Coltrane or Parker on a tune or two for some period of time. The inspirational effect of

---

2 *ghost note* – an intentionally soft, almost inaudible note used for expressive purposes.
3 *displacement* – an unexpected rhythmic positioning and use of melody or harmony achieving an effect of surprise.
4 *alternate pitch sequences* – changing the sequence of pitches as a method of achieving variety.

being able to sound like the records being admired will spur the youngster on to find his own individuality. In time, the personality of any musician will manifest itself as he grows to musical maturity. Meanwhile, there is substance and a foundation being laid down for the future.

One last word on transcription is that I am very specific as to which solo the student should work on. Depending on the student's weakness, I may recommend one musician for study in a given time period. Or if the purpose is not correcting mistakes, but creative, meaning for the student to discover a different direction, I may lead him to an artist he is not familiar with. For example, on a basic level when *playing time*[5] is a problem, I suggest blues as performed by Miles Davis in the 1950's, a simple Charlie Parker blues solo, maybe Dexter Gordon, Hank Mobley or Lester Young in some cases. If the problem is flexibility and looseness of nuance, I suggest Sonny Rollins in the mid 1950's because his use of expressive devices is so creative. To evolve conceptually on chord changes, I refer to the Coltrane period of *Moment's Notice* and *Giant Steps*, which would precede the modal *Impressions* period and so on.

Not every solo played by a musician in any given period is worth the time spent. I urge the student not to find a solo that is filled with clichéd phrases which are overly simplistic and basic. (Although in some cases, simple classic blues clichés are necessary to get an idea of basic phrasing). I say to them, "Find a solo that is a little challenging, but not too difficult; one that you would like to sound like and want to know what it is being played!" (For a complete description of the transcription process refer to "The Improviser's Guide To Transcription" video from Caris Music Services.)

5 *playing time* – slang for when an improviser is marking the pulse off in an obvious manner.

Be-bop Harmony

Theory takes care of itself by mechanical, rote practice and there is little to do except show the student what the main facts are. This is mathematical memorization of digital patterns which involves little talent – just sheer work and discipline. Scales and chords are the alphabet of jazz and they need to be memorized just as language is. Here is where the art of practicing which I will discuss below should be addressed. Make clear that there are multiple names for the same scales and voicings depending upon the source and confusion should be avoided ("superlocrian" and "diminished" for example).

Being able to deal with chord changes is basic for a student before the fine points of individual conception can be approached. While changes are being mastered, some overall conceptual and compositional tools valid for all harmonic styles will also be learned, but the priority should be the ability to play in a convincing manner over changes. It is a fact that the be-bop tradition is part of history, though some of its greatest and original practitioners are still alive.

But how can I expect a student to identify in any meaningful personal way with *Ornithology* or even *Giant Steps*? The youngster wasn't even a thought at that time! In my development, I realized that I could never sound as fresh as the masters did because that style belongs to another historical and cultural period. It took me awhile to escape the clutches of the legacy, especially Coltrane. It sounded so good to me that I only wanted to play in that way. For about a year, I stopped listening to any Coltrane and didn't play tunes in that style. Of course, I was only being impatient because the process of time takes its own course no matter what one does. Each person's individual personality will be heard soon enough. But in relation to teaching, I am very clear in instructing a student how far he must go in pursuit of the past. Interestingly enough I have found myself often returning to the legacy to either check on my progress, use an older technique in a new context (grafting), or just to have fun with something familiar.

In essence the mathematics of be-bop demands strict discipline and training. There are wrong notes in this music, though they are not so much wrong as inappropriately placed. There is choice in be-bop but it operates in a very logical way. It is similar to the rules of counterpoint and voice leading as taught for hundreds of years in classical conservatories. This is how the jazz student learns to walk before he runs!

Be-bop is over fifty years old now and well documented as well as organized methodically by educators like David Baker, Jerry Coker and Jamey Aebersold. Many universities offer this education and in my opinion it should be mandatory for all music education majors, classical and musicology students. Playing be-bop necessitates instrumental technique, theoretical knowledge, a good fluent rhythmic feel and training of the ear. It is the calisthenics of jazz improvisation no matter what idiom.

Building Individual Conception

The eventual goal of teaching is to bring out the student's own creative impulses, make them recognizable to him and help shape their future course. On the playing level, the student must develop his own individual set of expressive nuances. As stated I try to make the young artist sensitive to what nuance is through transcription and objective listening to others. When listening to the student play I do my best to notice any signs of individuality. Examples of what I look for are: how a note is attacked and ended; a particular coloring on certain tones; maybe a different articulation that occurs only in certain spots; or a unique rhythmic concept. Usually, these aspects are not noticed harmonically, but with melody, rhythm and color. (For a composition student, the harmonic and form elements may evidence traces of individuality). It has been said in many ways by great artists that it is in the mistakes where one may find seeds of originality. In any case, this process of pinpointing idiosynchratic methods of execution and concept is crucial for developing a unique sound.

If such a discovery can be objectively defined, I ask the student to write exercises emphasizing this specific element. Composition is a very important aspect of my method because it is a way of isolating an element of music in order to develop further within it. I ask the less advanced students to write melodies on a mode for example. This makes them aware of the kind of thinking that goes on in improvising from a melodic standpoint. Composition per se is a separate discipline that I require from the advanced students. Composing an exercise or short tune based on one idea is a favorite tool of mine.

Developing concept requires a lot of discussion between myself and the student about other musicians, important recordings and what it is to be an artist. Philosophy and questions concerning all aspects of life are openly discussed. I want the student to feel comfortable with me and express himself as well as hearing my feelings on these subjects. The intellectual and emotional sides of a young artist are quite possibly more important in the long run than the immediate musical training. The world can survive without another artist, but humanity benefits by one more intelligent, sensitive human being contributing in any positive manner to man's condition. In the future I envision the development of an academy where all these subjects are taught and discussed as well as the arts themselves, all interrelated.

With more advanced students I expect them to be interested in my own playing and become familiar with my concepts of playing. By revealing my thought patterns to the student, hopefully I will stimulate their own ideas and at the same time point the young artist towards what I feel are useful ways to conceptualize, based on the success of these concepts for my own work.

Finally, as part of my belief that there is a great artistic advantage in possessing knowledge of other idioms, I direct my students towards having the ability to roughly duplicate many musical genres. In fact I play a game with them at the piano (advanced students must be able to play the keyboard sufficiently). I select different genres and ask them to try this "test of idioms". A partial list includes musical styles from every source: Bartókian folk rhythms, Bach chorales and fugues, Indian drones and ragas, Slavic odd meter dance rhythms, Latin beats, James Brown funk, Stevie Wonder pop harmonies, Schoenberg atonalism, Cecil Taylor style of percussive pianistics, dixieland, ragtime, and so on. The idea is to make the student aware of all that is going on, so his future creative impulses are inclusive and open to all types of stimuli.

It goes without saying that group playing, repertoire, keyboard, playing some form of drums or percussion and of course being familiar with the legacy are necessary and inevitable for the serious student. I often use the metaphor of a tree as a good device for learning the history. Using the roots, trunk, limbs, branches, twigs and leaves as pictorial representations for the placement of historic individuals and movements is a wonderful tool. The tree metaphor can be used for an instrument's genealogy also.

In summary:

ROOTS: Pre-sources, without which there would be nothing to build upon.

TRUNK: Those who codified the root information and made it more readily available.

LIMBS: Major stylists who conceived entire ways of approaching and executing the music in question.

BRANCHES Important individualists who evolved completely unique paths.

TWIGS: Those who are spawned from individual approaches.

LEAVES: Contemporary stylists who change like the seasons.

with Richie Beirach and Chick Corea, backstage in Japan; mid '80s (Private collection)

As the student advances past these basics, composition becomes important because it is a method for bringing all the mechanics together as well as encouraging performance (and all of its extensions such as rehearsing, leading, organizing, calligraphy, recording, touring, etc.). It often begins the process of finding oneself and developing an individual approach to improvisation. Because composing is basically a slowed down version of improvising with its accompanying challenges of problem solving and choosing among options, its affect upon honing the improviser's mind is powerful. Finally, the motivational aspect of original composition is very valuable for any student.

The last area of pedagogy is usually reserved for the serious student who wants to make a life out of jazz. Depending upon my perception of the student's strengths in combination with their personality, I may make suggestions. But in any case, I make it clear that there is fierce competition and the supply of jazz musicians is way out of balance with the demand. Although it may appear that in the mid-1990's as I write there is a lot of jazz happening, in reality the opportunities for playing are shrinking. Therefore, I try to emphasize to my students that to make a living they will have to wear many hats meaning the ability to function in a variety of roles. Hopefully, these functions are related but may not be directly involved with the pure form of jazz improvisation as such, even though that may have been what inspired them to play in the first place.

There are the other areas of arranging, movies and T.V. work, the music industry, involvement with funding, instruments, management, recording, booking, etc. More specifically, for those who are highly motivated to play only, I underscore that after mastery comes content. In other words, once you can play, what do you want to say? As outlined in the appropriate area of the original manuscript, artistic development is continual and necessary for those who MUST express themselves. The student should look around him at other areas of art and life for experiences and motivation. The artist must have something of worth to tell us.

I always try to remind students that every once in awhile they should remember what it was that made them want to play jazz in the first place. Was it a home influence, seeing a performer live, a teacher in school? Can they remember that first time when they were hooked on the magic of jazz and the feeling from that experience? On the path to mastery, one can easily forget the joy and the spiritual essence of the music. It's important to remind oneself sometimes.

General Guidelines: Primary Sources

When a student is studying the history of an art form, he must be made aware of the need to know the *primary sources*[6] of a style, not only the secondary ones. Most of the time, the inspiration to learn jazz comes from seeing or hearing a contemporary artist who is well exposed to the public and playing in the popular style of the day. The youngster naturally tries to play like his idol. This is good temporarily because the student can relate to a living, breathing musician who may be considered important to the music of the present period. But for real in-depth analysis, the student should be made aware of the sources of his idol's style. Everyone comes from somewhere in the sense that there is never really anything new, just re-arrangement. Finding the root or earliest source will make everything clearer, because there is great comfort and knowledge in being able to discern a straight evolutionary line in an art form. It makes the art appear not to be some mystical, unreachable goal for the student. The earlier metaphor of a tree can be useful.

6 *primary sources* – the original innovator or concept rather than succeeding generations.

Objectivity

By objectivity, I mean that the student becomes very clear about his likes and dislikes when he is listening to music. This takes some years to develop and a teacher should guide the student by showing the various possibilities of any given musical element under examination. This means that upon hearing a piece, attention is placed on one specific, for example the tone of an instrument. A student should be able to verbalize what the sound is and his opinion about it. This ability to use words to describe sound is very difficult, but in the long run it will benefit the developing artist because somehow it sheds new light and clarity on these subtleties. The smallest details are sometimes never expressed and therefore can be weaknesses later on in an artist's makeup. When one makes a judgment about something and can back it up with sound reasoning, he is ready to change behavior and move on to the next step. Of course, background experiences, emotional depth and maturity affect judgment. It is up to the teacher to try to even out these personal factors to develop better objectivity in the student.

Grafting

Much of art consists of *grafting*[7] from one source to another. It could be across artistic boundaries as in the Romantic period of the nineteenth century when painters, writers and musicians borrowed often from each other. In jazz improvisation, there is a difference between fusion of styles and grafting. Fusion refers to combining elements of several idioms together like classical harmony with jazz (called *Third Stream* in the 1960's); or rock rhythms with jazz harmony and melody as in the *fusion* style of the 1970's. Grafting is more specific and has to do with instrumental techniques. For example, as a soprano saxophonist, I often try to play in what I consider a trumpet style. Another example are guitarists who consciously try to adopt the legato phrasing of a saxophonist. The possibility of grafting should be in the artist's mind because the process can help lead to an individual instrumental approach.

7 *grafting* – applying a method or technique used on one instrument to another, quite possibly from a distant instrumental family; or from one musical idiom to another.

Creating the Illusion

The artist is the master of deception. By centering upon one aspect he creates the illusion of more or less happening than is the reality. How subtly he accomplishes this is a measure of his skill. This can be developed in improvising so that in the spontaneous moment it is more likely to occur. The main objective is to learn how to balance both the obvious and unobvious. When playing a rhythm or pattern, if the conclusion or cadence can be easily predicted, an attempt should be made to disguise this at times. It's a matter of taking the obvious and by a slight musical alteration, shifting it around. In all of the elements of music, this is plausible: harmonically, by the use of a different chord quality than is expected; melodically, by a change of direction; rhythmically, by displacing the pattern by a beat; coloristically, by dramatic changes in dynamics; form, by leaving something out at a given point when it usually comes. Practicing and conceptualizing in this way adds flexibility to the act of improvisation so that the art is never easily predictable.

Life as Practice

Finally, practicing the music and instrument represents half the battle of being an artist. The art of living assumes equal importance after the initial years of gaining technique. Worldly knowledge gained through life's passages becomes a major source of the creative impulse. One's relationships with other human beings gains in importance as maturity occurs. Awareness of the world's diversity, inter-relationships, cultural patterns and history all add to the artist's reservoir of knowledge and feelings. If the commitment to beauty and truth through creativity is sincere, every moment of life is in a sense practice.

Practicing

This outline is predicated on certain assumptions, the foremost being that learning the art of improvisation and living the life of an artist are synonymous; that one's life is dedicated towards self-expression and creativity; once a commitment is made, the majority of the person's energies will go towards these goals. To accomplish these tasks, the most important ingredient is disciplined practice or ritual.

The function of ritual is to bring one closer to the activity being done so that there are mental, emotional, spiritual and direct musical benefits. As rapport with an instrument grows, a musician begins to hear more and more of himself coming through in the music. For awhile, the greatest improvement is in terms of sound and other disciplines related to playing the instrument. As familiarity with the language occurs and begins to be practically applied, the growing musician gets more inspired and realizes that he is improving and fulfilling the dream of playing. A oneness grows with both the instrument and tools of music. The artist is finally beginning to express himself. From this point, a few special artists will go further on to be fully individual and creative with something of value to say.

Although I touched upon practicing earlier, I want to develop it a bit more. I am a strong believer in leaving the students with very clear methods of duplicating and reinforcing new material. It can be counterproductive to offer new material without a suitable framework towards helping the student acquire the information on his own. Therefore, the methodology of practice becomes important. The goal of any practice is to instill new behaviour and/or modify the old. Repetition results in habitualization. It is repetition which solders the connection between an auditory sensation and an actual physiological motor response. The success of the connection depends upon the clarity of the intended response in combination with the individual's psychological makeup and the difficulty of the task at hand. Here are some general guidelines to good practicing:

1. *Ritual:* As mentioned avove, it is the constancy of practice which is the key. It has to be a necessary part of one's daily life to be effective. It cannot be done intensively one day a week.
2. *Objectivity:* Practicing is not good or bad – it just is. One shouldn't feel elated or depressed about or during practice. The main thing is to just do it!!
3. *Organization:* This is an area where the teacher should advise the student as to how to divide up whatever time is available. Blocks of time should be ideally 45 minutes to one hour on a given subject.
4. *Priority:* It is impossible to practice everything needed every day. With a teacher's advice, the student should address his most glaring deficiencies first for a period of at least few months, depending upon the material. Basic instrumental warmups should probably be daily, again depending upon the level of the student.
5. *Singularity:* This means being very specific about what and why you are practicing a given exercise. If there are more than one major and maybe a minor point trying to be accomplished, the results can be confused.
6. *Attitude:* Patience, consistency and total concentration are the key attitudes which need to be present for a student to accomplish his goals. These traits are not easy to learn in the short term. Practicing is an art itself, which like learning how to learn, takes time. Keeping a journal of intended short and long term goals, reactions and accomplishments is an excellent idea. Things that may have been overlooked or left incomplete can be recalled and there is a sense of satisfaction when a student looks back upon his work. One's playing may get worse before improvement is seen.
7. *Practical:* The practice area should ideally be isolated from other

ears, well lit and ventilated. Taking breaks every hour is advisable and a student should try to do the rote type of daily exercises early in the day like sound production, scales, repertoire, etc. Leave the more creative aspects like composition, playing, and focused listening for later in the day. By the way, listening to learn is different than for enjoyment. It means listening to a track repeatedly to discover everything that is going on, not only with the soloists who are up front.

Practicing a piece for performance with Carina Raschèr in Rottenburg, Germany; late '80s
(© Hans Gruber)

Team Teaching

I have one suggestion which hopefully can be tried in a school situation some time. It is the team teaching approach similar to what doctors in hospitals as well as groups of people in industry regularly do when working on a project. They get together to discuss a students work and each participant brings his own expertise, progress report, etc. to share. I would like to see monthly meetings where the various teachers in a jazz department communicate about a student's progress and/or problems. For example, the harmony departmant along with the ensemble and instrumental teacher should work together to unify all the material. Whenever possible, wouldn't it be beneficial if a student could be working on the same harmonic material in the repertoire and on the major instrument? More important than commonality, attitude or personal problems could be spotted and addressed at such meetings avoiding future misunderstandings. Opening the lines of communication between the teachers would in itself provide positive results.

Teaching Situations

Jazz teaching exists on three broad levels of interaction. First of all, there is the bona fide formal school of jazz, be it a high school where there may be a big band playing jazz – like material all the way up to a conservatory situation similar to the traditional classical schools. Then there is the workshop, seminar, clinic, lecture or demonstration situation which can range from one hour to several weeks. And of course there is the private lesson. Pedagogically, they all differ in their emphasis and how to effectively present the material.

Obviously, in the school setting there is room for thoughtful and organized teaching with details, follow up and reinforcement. Possibly some visible mastery is evidenced over a period of several months. The prerequisite here from the instructor's standpoint is organized, step by step unfolding of the material with a clear beginning and end. This is the most obvious level of teaching because of the length of commitment which the students have to make. They have to do the work or they fail the course and the powers of coercion evident here can quickly separate the serious from the merely interested.

With slight differences of emphasis apparent from the category names themselves, the clinic/seminar/workshop/lecture/master class/demonstration format should be an intense period with maximum concentration on the points of learning how to learn and inspiration described earlier. Because of the shorter teaching period, an effective instructor can really make a dramatic impression on interested students. The danger here is that one encounters dilletantes or less than serious students because the time commitment is minimal and there is a certain show business aspect to these situations. But this can be useful depending upon the teacher. You have to gauge the audience and attempt to include them while getting your point across. It's a tricky balance and in my case, it is the area where I have done most of my teaching worldwide. One has to be careful in expecting the students to ask questions to fill the time. A good teacher should be ready to make a point, then entertain questions.

Finally, the private one on one lesson is of course the most personal and demands a great deal of skill, both pedagogically and psychologically. Depending upon the level and need, a private lesson can range from the real nuts and bolts of how to play the instrument itself to a near psychotherapy session. In the other teaching situations, an exact reading of a student's problems is not realistic, but it is in the private lesson that the material should be tailor made towards each person's needs and special problems. With the experience of encountering many students, a teacher can get really proficient at this task and be a tremendous and direct force for good upon a young person.

No matter what teaching situation, one thing is for sure and it is more true now than ever. If you're not up to doing the job right, no matter who you are, the students will know. Years ago when it was new, maybe they weren't as aware, but now they realize the differences. And just as in playing, the reputation grows quickly.

The Artist as Teacher

For most great artists allowing for a few exceptions, their most effective teaching is done through their works. What they play and how they accomplish it provides the information and inspiration for anyone interested. In music and other performing acts, students can learn directly by performing and apprenticing with their teachers. This is the most direct way of teaching an art form.

But to my mind, an artist has a larger obligation to reach students other than only by example. A person who can satisfy his material and creative needs at the same time, i.e., the successful artist, is in a very envious position compared to most people. On the practical side, he lives by his own schedule as far as work, study and play are concerned. An artist is very much his own boss whether he is in a band or displayed in an art gallery. Spiritually, he is free to enjoy and use the mysteries of life directly in his work. He can live a sort of fantasy life in his mind, no matter what environment or conditions exist. He is in a sense given license to report back to the real world on what he has observed and felt about beauty, truth and other deep matters. This is truly an elite life style and a privilege that should be appreciated by sharing this knowledge with serious, interested young people. Teaching provides a real balance to the often self-indulgent and necessarily egocentric world of the artist.

Having to explain one's art repeatedly can be educational. Verbalization of what and how one does something may lead to new insights, especially if the effort of communicating it to different personalities requires the artist/teacher to describe his work in multiple definitions. The inherent dangers are loss of interest and a frozen view of the art and its process. The teacher side can be so adept at organizing and explaining material, that the artist side may lose sight of the ceaseless dynamism and potential for change in the art itself. Balancing these aspects is the main challenge for the artist/teacher.

The essence of teaching is to spread the spiritual qualities inherent in any great art: love and compassion.

The Teacher's Responsibility

As my peers and I become the next wave of living masters and our teachers move on, the responsibility towards succeeding generations increases. If only because many of us by the age of 50 have children who are entering the world, there would be a natural desire to share one's accumulated wisdom. Jazz education as a business with its many tributaries (schools, publishing, periodicals, workshops, associations) has increased in visibility and even major jazz stars do some lecturing or teaching. In fact, it is often tied directly to the performance itself and mandatory for an artist to participate.

Therefore, musicians have become more proficient in explaining the intricacies of the art form. It is a far cry from my period of learning when musicians were still arguing about whether jazz could or should be taught. The situation is similar to the aphorism that you can lead a horse to water, but not make it drink. I can reveal my way of learning or the path I took meaning the gathering of theory, methods of practicing all the material, knowing the inspiring recordings and concepts of playing in a group, the compositional process and certainly specific instrumental techniques. But I can't teach someone to be creative – I can only show them how I did it. This is true of all the art forms and poses a paradox in teaching any art. Furthermore, more and more of the material is available in books, videos and now on CD-ROMs. What then is the teacher's role?

I always return to what I see as the main functions of teaching which are twofold. One is very pragmatic while the other is more subtle. My first goal is to show the student how to learn. Revealing the mechanism by which one gathers insights, practices and learns them until they become habitual, then uses the information as a springboard for continual and hopefully personal growth is a primary function which anyone purporting to instruct is responsible for. This goes far beyond the more obvious (and necessary) presentation of material, facts and real skills that are usable. The ability to succeed in this first function depends upon the teacher's verbal and organizational prowess, but with a little thought, time and of course, experience, it is not too difficult. By doing this, a teacher is giving a student a tool for life which will always be useful.

To inspire is a more different and subtle matter because it is so personal in nature. Having charisma helps the teacher of course, as does reputation, but when students see an energetic and disciplined, yet loose approach combined with the ability to musically demonstrate the concepts, they are usually quite inspired. Such a teacher is after all a direct example of what the student is striving for and there are no books which can replace that influence upon a young person.

There is a deeper reason that it is our duty to teach this art form. Not all of the students will become musicians and very few will be true artists. But by showing them the magic and spiritual power combined with the great discipline present in jazz, you are providing them with a very positive life example. As these youngsters enter life's mainstream and the very complicated as well as increasingly precarious world we live in, there is a good chance that they will remember the beauty, depth of feeling , the twin goal of balancing individual and group needs as well as the incredible freedom to express oneself experienced through this music which is not widely available elsewhere. From a practical standpoint, teaching helps to create an audience equipped with some of the necessary and sophisticated skills needed to understand the subtleties of great jazz. Also, there is always the chance that a former student will become useful in helping the artist and/or the art form in real concrete ways later in life. But more important than these real life possibilities is the fact that they have had a glimpse of the spiritual values inherent in an art form which stresses beauty and truth. All of these attributes and more are the gift of jazz to the world at large.

For us, the teachers, we should hopefully feel the positive satisfaction of knowing that we are involved in an activity which does not harm; doesn't pollute the planet; doesn't add to the violence or decadence; doesn't enrich those aspects of life which are destructive; and in fact adds a positive light into the world.

Montmarte, Copenhagen, Denmark; early '80s (© Hans Gruber)

Ruminations on Jazz 6

This chapter is a potpourri of thoughts on a variety of subjects, all directly related to the field of jazz. These are my personal feelings about past, present and possible future events. The areas covered include the categorization of jazz artists in relation to the content of their work; parallels between jazz and classical music; the life of a jazz musician in society; the question of audiences, critics and the current state of the jazz scene both musically and in terms of work opportunities.

Types of Jazz Artists: The Professional

The main feature that makes a musician truly a professional is a consistently high level of performance. Rarely does the professional fall below a certain minimum level of inspiration, energy and musicianship. On occasion there are leaps into greatness. This artist has total control of his instrument commensurate with his musical conception. He has the ability to make ideas flow smoothly and through a wide range of moods and musical styles. He knows how to tackle new challenges in an orderly and methodical fashion. His commitment to the art and constant self improvement is beyond reproach. He sees himself as part of the entire jazz legacy and realizes the need to carry the message to whomever and wherever he can. Jazz professionals can be further looked upon in terms of their improvisational concepts.

The Classic Improviser

This is the artist who has perfected his style and continues to improve within it. By and large, he sticks to the language he feels most comfortable with, even to some extent the same material. Remaining with his basic style, this musician will usually ignore current trends around him. Change for him means redefining or perfecting some aspect of his playing. Sidemen accompanying this type of musician are almost interchangeable because their roles are fairly well set beforehand. Most of the musicians from the be-bop era who are still alive fall into this category. The term "classic" even bears some connection to the classical musician, in the sense of reproducing the essence of what was and perpetuating the legacy.

Innovators

In jazz improvisation and to some extent in other art forms, innovation is at first recognizable as an instrumental breakthrough from a technical standpoint. This development is usually inextricably linked to a definite fresh musical approach. When new technique and innovative concepts combine, they become quickly adapted and are considered common and required knowledge from that time forward. In jazz, the examples abound: Louis Armstrong extended the usable range of the trumpet and with it set the standard for jazz rhythmical phrasing; Charlie Parker doubled the speed of saxophone playing while at the same time employing more complex harmonies; John Coltrane added another octave to the saxophone's range as well as a whole compendium of musical developments; Art Tatum, Cecil Taylor, John McLaughlin, Tony Williams and Elvin Jones, all pushed technique and in some cases, musical ideas further on their respective instruments.

A truly major innovator like Charlie Parker effected all music and instruments besides his own. Parker changed the way harmony and rhythm were thought of in jazz, as well as freeing the rhythm section. Great innovations take years to be widely felt because of the normal time lag between creation and absorption by other artists in the field. It is a rarity for an artist to develop multiple innovations in his life. John Coltrane continued to change in his short career and of course Miles Davis exemplified constant new discovery.

Innovations can be seen as original insights into an old way of doing things or the grafting from one idiom to another. In jazz, many of the harmonic developments were already widely used in twentieth century classical music for decades, but never with the jazz rhythmic approach or spontaneity of improvisation. The innovator is the artist who arrives on the scene at the right time when many diverse elements are coinciding and through a combination of intuition, courage, luck and hard work tries something different. To be sure, the great innovations were not easily arrived at.

Instrumental Stylists Because of the nature of improvisation, a jazz musician deals primarily with his instrument as the vehicle to convey musical ideas. This differs from classical music and other forms where interpretation of the music takes precedence. Therefore, the instrumental style of an improviser may exert an historical effect similar to that of an innovator but limited to the instrument itself. In jazz, there are numerous examples of musicians who have contributed in ways that stem directly from their own unique style of playing and expressing themselves. And in this way, they were quite influential. Some examples are pianist Bill Evans, trumpeter Clifford Brown, bassist Scott LaFaro and saxophonist Albert Ayler. If a young musician plays these instruments, at one time or another he will probably absorb some of the characteristics of these stylists.

Musical Stylists A musical stylist is one who exerts an immediate influence in the present because his manner of playing reflects contemporary values and trends. Of course, even an innovator begins as a stylist in general, but with time moves beyond the common vernacular of the day. The contemporary stylist is usually quite popular and known for a particular song or genre of tunes that the public favors. Whether he can move beyond this category is a real challenge, for commercial success can breed complacency.

Parallels Between Classical and Jazz

It's interesting to see how jazz has followed a similar path to the evolution of classical music. Of course, jazz is not even one century old while the classical tradition can be traced nearly five hundred years. In that short period, jazz has paralleled many of the same developments, especially harmonically. One possible explanation is that by the advent of jazz around 1900, a musician had the benefit of hundreds of years of musical thought and analysis. An advanced musician could quickly absorb the information and equipped with this knowledge, compose spontaneously (improvise). In any case, the similarities between classical stylistic periods and those of jazz are fascinating.

The dixieland style is very similar to baroque music with its weaving contrapuntal lines. Swing music, especially in the big band format bears similarities in formal techniques to the classical period, particularly in the concept of soloist accompanied by an orchestra (concerto). Be-bop shares some of the artistic attitudes of the romantic era (art for art's sake) and musically corresponds in extending diatonic harmony. Finally, twentieth century music has greatly affected jazz harmony of the past few decades as well as common usage of avant garde compositional and serial techniques. The following examples of jazz pianists reflect direct harmonic similarities: Debussy/Bill Evans; Scriabin/McCoy Tyner; Bartók/Chick Corea (selected periods).

I don't imagine that in any of the eras mentioned above, a particular jazz musician sat down and calculated ways of incorporating classical music. It just seems that both forms followed a sort of prescribed journey from simplicity to complexity. Also, Western classical music was the first world music which extensively developed in the harmonic realm. This added intellectual aspect made the possibilities quite vast, especially when mixed together with rhythmical concepts from other cultures as became the case in jazz.

The Jazz Life

The jazz subculture has been one of the great tales of the twentieth century, written about and even commercialized in the "hipster" image. The movie "Round Midnight" is a prime example. Both the sound of the music and the life style of the musicians have contributed to the feeling of being apart from worldly woes, or being "cool." The speed of the notes, elusive rhythms and harmonies combined with the appearance of little overt effort on the part of the musicians helped create this image. Added to this personna is the language spoken by jazz musicians which evolved from the black tradition of double meanings. The very notion of being cool means not showing how intense one's feelings might actually be. The word "bad" actually means good and so on.

This jazz image is hopelessly out of date in the late twentieth century. Most young musicians see the past through clear eyes and are interested only in the music and what they can learn from it. But the folklore of jazz is important in keeping a tradition alive. Jazz is music made by living and breathing individuals, not machines. The image of a jazz subculture may be an anachronism now, but its significance has made it an important part of twentieth century Western culture and folklore.

One cannot divorce jazz history and culture from the plight of black people in America. There can be little argument that most of the roots and early evolution of jazz were accomplished by blacks. Being oppressed and kept out of the white (and to some extent black) mainstream had incalculable effect on those who made the music. At first jazz was the popular music of the day, played for both black and white audiences, usually separately. By the time jazz was in middle age the be-boppers declared it an art form. They made music for themselves without concern about its acceptance into the larger white culture. This attitude lasted for a few decades, but increasingly jazz is now considered by many musicians and media alike as an arm of the entertainment-music complex. The relevant point is that a good deal of the history of the music and musicians who played it (especially after the 1930's), was greatly shaped by its being in a renegade relationship to the dominant culture and the more popular musical forms of the ensuing periods.

Jazz and the Audience

In any serious art, the level of the audience's sophistication and the depth of the work presented should be equal for maximum effect. It isn't fair to place serious, complex and abstract art in front of people who are not educated. That's why in the case of jazz, with some exceptions, the nightclub setting is musically precarious. There are too many distractions for great art to be properly presented. Unfortunately, when serious jazz is performed in such an atmosphere, many musicians will change their playing (possibly subconsciously) in order to gain approval. It is only human to want an audience to admire one's performance. A key consideration in any performing art is to be judicious concerning where and for whom one performs.

A jazz performance centers upon the process of creation. The final objective is not only the finished product, but the path and

with Phil Woods and Pat Dorian (director) at the COTA Festival; Deleware Water Gap, Pennsylvania, USA, early '90s (© Walter Bredel).

process taken towards it. The interest is created when there are challenging musical exchanges between the personalities present. An audience, is in effect, receiving a true performance when they can feel the attempt at musical communication among the performers. If the musicians come on stage and simply play the "show", even if it is done well, the true jazz lovers have not received their money's worth. They can get many records that fulfill this basic function. It is the possibility and reality of exciting exchanges which brings the real jazz audience to a performance. In a way, a jazz concert is like a bull fight; the outcome is fairly well known but there are many possible twists and turns before that conclusion is reached.

What this means is that the musicians have to play for themselves. They should be committed to the idea of spontaneity and letting things go. Of course, a performance should never fall below a minimum standard of musical and stage professionalism. Good creative energy is contagious and whether or not the audience notices the subtleties, if the musicians have truly given to each other, the performance can be considered a success. Even better, a really great performance means that the musical challenges and exchanges were well accomplished and communicated between the musicians and the audience.

Critics

Critics provide the necessary function of publicizing the music to the public. At times, their reactions and comments about the work can offer an artist some insights that may be useful. But because of their importance in making the public aware and by that, affecting the livelihood of an artist, their choices of whom and what they write about are very important. Negative criticism hurts all jazz artists, especially when it is personally directed. Criticism should be more elucidation rather than judgment, giving people background and important signposts to listen for. Instead, what some critics do is perpetuate the star system, by which a few chosen artists are openly supported while the majority are neglected.

Another disservice is the careless manner in which critics categorize styles and musicians resulting in the wrong impression. Surely, a certain style of playing can be described in both musical and non-musical language. This is necessary information which helps the listener know where to begin appreciating what he is hearing. But an overly simplistic explanation which functions as a summary of an artist's music (as in "the style of so and so") causes people to think no further and assume they can already hear what the music sounds like. These are artists, assumed to be playing what they believe in and should not be dismissed by a casual labelling of their music. The final word on critics is "buyer beware!" The interested listener should make his decisions based on multiple performances and recordings as well as considering a critic's view.

Jazz of our Time

To my mind, there is something missing in a lot of what is called jazz in recent history. The feeling of the quest for new and different ways of expression during the heat of improvisation is becoming a thing of the past. Whether it is the deadening influence of commerciality or the difficulty of holding the attention span of several T.V. generations (now video), jazz musicians seem content to put on a show and in this way feel they have really improvised. The language may be jazz-like but the spirit is not. Instead, jazz either resembles a pop show in which the musicians play directly to the audience's expectations, or perform recycled jazz without the sense of urgency and discovery that is vital to the art of improvisation. Certainly there are a few resilient and honest artists who pursue the feeling of spontaneous invention and discovery every time they play, but they are few and far between. The sad part is that some of the musicians who have demonstrated this attitude in the past have gone in the complete opposite direction in the pursuit of wider acceptance. In some of these cases, the example they set has not been very inspiring upon hearing the result. One question to ask about any music is whether you would listen to it in ten years; does it have sustaining power?

Fusion Music

The legacy of the 1970's and to some extent 80's (not withstanding the effect of Wynton Marsalis) gave us fusion music. What is meant by the term is rock-oriented rhythms and sounds with more extensive improvisation than would be ordinarily present in pop music. It also indicates the predominant use of electric instruments, especially keyboards, guitars and bass. Harmonic movement is fairly static as is the flow of the rhythm. Often, fusion melodies are composed around the rhythmic shape of the bass or drum part, rather than

with Wayne Shorter at Live Under The Sky, "Tribute to John Coltrane", Tokyo, Japan, 1987
(© Caris Visentin Liebman)

existing in their own right. The frequent use of pentatonic and blues clichés usually played at a fast speed is a major characteristic of the music. Important aspects of the rhythm revolve around groupings of sixteenth notes. Using electronic instruments and synthesizers, fusion has developed the musical element of color to a high degree; compositionally, it has contributed to frequent variations away from the more common song forms such as "AABA".

The group *Weather Report* was the standard bearer of fusion music in both form and content. They used world music, rock and jazz in a creative combinatory process for much of their work. My feeling is that their music will remain with us long after the memory of the fusion explosion of the 1970's and 1980's is gone. Fusion contributed positively to the improvement of the recording process for jazz musicians. Because the sound of rock music is crucial, jazz musicians who ventured into fusion were forced to technically upgrade their recordings. They took their cues from pop artists who are typically more attuned to the sound of the music. This has resulted in a definite overall improvement for jazz records. Also, the popularity of labels like ECM and other lesser known ones, dedicated to serious artistic music and the fusing of diverse improvisational and compositional idioms, have had a positive effect on jazz production in general.

New Music

The jazz *avant-garde*[1] is often the darling of the critics. They can tout something that until recently was confined to small, esoteric audiences and therefore cultivated an image of elitism. Also, there is a lot to write about because in some cases the mixture of styles from the past and present make this music often appear to be interesting, at least on the surface. Finally, there is an aura of serious art surrounding any avant-garde movement.

The truth is that the jazz avant-garde dates back to the late, 1950's with Cecil Taylor and Ornette Coleman. In the mid-1960's, Coltrane embraced the movement and a plethora of saxophonists became associated with so-called *free music*[2]. By the late 1970's a new generation added to the early survivors.

Free jazz is a fusion of several distinct styles and borrowings from other idioms. A partial list includes *free energy playing*[3], *free-bop*[4] ethnic melodies and exotic instruments, wide use of assorted percussion instruments, twentieth century classical serialism, polytonality, and eclectic borrowings from ragtime, blues, marches and other genres. The premise in much present day avant-garde is eclecticism and calculated surprise. The *Art Ensemble of Chicago* was the premier group in this field having dealt with this music for many years. Their sense of timing was impeccable and truly indicative of this style of improvised music.

---

1 *avant-garde* – a category of art which in its time is experimental and radical compared to the mainstream.
2 *free music* – a style of jazz improvisation generally based more on immediate reaction and free association, rather than formal structures.
3 *energy playing* – a category of free jazz in which the basic premise is high intensity in terms of volume, speed, atmosphere and emotion.
4 *free-bop* – in free jazz, the character and sound of be-bop melodies and rhythms, but loosely connected as far as the usual structures are concerned, especially in the harmony; popularized by early Ornette Coleman.

The Current Working Situation

In the 1980's and 1990's, the entire music scene found itself in an entirely new set of circumstances. Within this period a wide range of events coincided: the video explosion, cable T.V., the abundant array of synthesizers, computers, home recording equipment, the wide use of pop music permeating movies, T.V. and commercials, wide popularity of a few popstars and their being increasingly embraced and merchandised by the mainstream, the enormous rise in basic overhead costs of running a business including liability insurance, rent, utilities and heat. These are just a partial list of occurrences which have effected every facet of life in the modern world, including the performing artist.

For the jazz improviser, the situation has deteriorated due to the fewer opportunities there are for practicing the art. Because of the economics of running any kind of entertainment establishment, especially a jazz club where people come to listen and not primarily to socialize or drink, there are only a handful of places for real listening remaining in the world. And some of these few that exist do not feature jazz every night. If they do, the high level of competition and general oversupply in relation to small demand means that bands do not work for more than a few consecutive nights and then only on rare occasions throughout the year. The main forum for small group jazz has all but disappeared.

The consequences of this on the art of the improviser is incalculable. Established leaders cannot or will not try to keep a band together, opting instead to pick up musicians wherever they go or combine momentarily in all-star groups. The entire apprenticeship system which worked so well for years is gone. The audience senses a lessening of creative energies towards perpetuating a group sound so their artistic awareness and overall interest slackens. Record companies, entrepeneurs, the music press, all aspects of the music business see that there is no future in serious jazz and neglect it more than ever. The need for consistent experimentation and trial-error in order to gain necessary experience cannot be accomplished by the artists. In the end, the art form loses vitality and the legacy is weakened. Without opportunities to play, jazz improvisation is in danger of standing still and eventually dissipating.

On the positive side, there are new opportunities for musicians to produce creative art, albeit not in forms where the music itself is primary. This is in reference to movie and T.V. scores as well as creatively using the medium of video. The combining of sound and image is not new, but with all the opportunities in our time the possibilities have increased in vastness. What you hear increasingly in movie scores now is *pedal point*[5] and modal harmony, with a variety of melodic treatments ranging from rock to ethnic to *space music*[6]. The visual arts are now borrowing from the creative music of the past several

---

5 *pedal point* – constant bass figure usually in one key for a duration; harmonically it sets up a kind of drone.

6 *space music* – use of strange, weird and extra-musical effects lending other-world quality to the music; most often produced by synthesizers.

decades. In general, it takes the mainstream that long to catch up with more advanced artistic creations. *Muzak*[7] in an elevator these days derives a lot of its harmony from Charlie Parker as does some of the better compositions of Stevie Wonder and others like him. Overall, there are wider opportunities than ever for elements of the jazz improviser's music to be used, even in a hybrid form.

[7] *Muzak* – background music heard in offices, stores, elevators and other similar environments.

Technology and Music

Finally, the ease by which a musician (or anybody) can duplicate other instruments and sounds on computers and synthesizers as well as record the near equivalent of a finished product in his home must be considered. On the surface these machines might seem to hasten the end of most musician's careers and with that, the desire to practice and improve on a chosen instrument. Although this may be temporarily the case, it more dramatically effects those musicians who play in functional roles such as studios, dance music and other forms of non-creative music. But for the truly inspired young artist with the need to create, it only increases their value and functions in society. Pressing buttons or playing with floppy disks in computers does not answer the basic, eternal questions: Is the individual free enough within himself to express personal feelings? What is it that he wishes to say? How does one go about it so that the art moves people and is lasting?

There is yet another cultural trend which may be as the biggest artistic problem of our time. That is the incredibly small attention span that most people possess, particularly the young. The three-minute attention span ties in with the fallacy of instant star celebrity. Everything is flash and surface; serious art cannot survive in such an atmosphere. In our cultural education of young people, there must be a way found to reinforce the notions of patience and concentrating on a subject. These are values that are necessary for a society's continued evolution on the level of real ideas and deep feelings. Otherwise, all becomes technology and materialism.

Ruminations '95 – The Scene

I suppose it is normal that an older person will usually view the younger generation and their scene with scepticism, no matter how open he may be. After all, nothing is as good as it used to be, and this will always be true in some respects. But all of us were once part of a new or different generation at some time, so it helps to remember. The point is that there are always positive and negative currents happening simultaneously.

Much of what I wrote in "Ruminations..." ten years ago remains true today. The age of the "young lions" is fading, although the jazz media will always look for fresh faces to extol. There is definitely too much product released and one competes not only with peers and even former students but with constant reissues. Small, independent, artistically oriented companies are disappearing because the means of distributing the product has centralized into a few major companies, although with the popularity of computer-based communication and the internet maybe this will soon be circumvented by direct ordering. Many musicians are still chasing ghosts and innovation is rare. Is there anything left to do except recycle the past? Jazz sells cars, perfume and, of course, liquor (as it always did in Japan by the way). The entire easy listening, yuppefied *CD 101*[8] format has more or less taken over the air waves in the few commercial stations playing jazz, especially in the U.S. Every other person is a critic writing for some magazine. (Isn't it amazing when you think about it – even bus drivers take tests for their jobs, but there is none for an art critic!) The legends are slowly dying and retrospectives are the order of the day. To be an individual is to be a pariah as conformity abounds. Is jazz destined to be like classical music? Have we seen the end of it as a living, breathing art form?

I have one hope and predict that it will occur because of the advanced communication technology of this era and to come. I am convinced that as other parts of the world reach a certain economic plateau and with that more leisure time, some people will inevitably be drawn to jazz. For them it will be a new music which offers spontaneity and values individuality. The fact that it is by and large an American creation adds to its allure. For better or worse American culture becomes world culture. I am optimistic that just as jazz itself was a fusion of so many cultures in its beginning, so will the future see input from places far and wide, changing the very face of jazz. Already it is happening, but I see it only increasing in intensity with the passage of time. Wait until China gets a hold of this music – we'll all be touring and teaching there. And even if only one percent of that population like it (about average for jazz recording sales), that would still mean several million people!!

And then, what about *virtual reality*? Will a person be able to play Coltrane licks just by moving their fingers? The future awaits!!!

[8] *CD 101*- a trend setting radio station in New York City which has an easy-listening jazz policy.

Ruminations '95 – Personal

Having a wonderful family does change one's priorities and daily life from before. There is rarely enough time to do what is necessary, forgetting what you'd like to do. The difference in my life style now and before is immense. In the time I have I need to organize the travel and work as well as staying in communication with the many people I know. My everyday life and the music are the same in the sense that this is the work I need to and want to do. There is little time for much else and the taking care of the business side increases in intensity as the scene and my position change (getting a manager is not the answer – believe me!) I am still project oriented in that when there is an opportunity to write and organize music for an event I will use that for research and learning by doing. The days of relaxed listening, deep conversations with my peers, practicing, playing just to play are unfortunately gone from my life for now. But when your life and work become seamless, there can be a very positive effect in that when you do play, it is very meaningful and one's concentration is more intense that formerly. Can it be true that less is more?

My aesthetic has solidified in this decade, primarily because of teaching so much and having to clearly represent certain secure values to students. As I have described my musical influences and inspirations, I remain a dedicated eclectic. The recordings I have done cover the entire range of interests I always had from fusion to classical to ethnic to jazz standards. Recording for small, independent companies has meant that with tight budgets, great preparation and organization are essential. I have become an expert at turning out finished product very quickly for little money. Part of the reason has been the availability of a fine studio *(Red Rock)* near my home which had the necessary tools for low cost recording. Of course, this has meant a great deal of professionalism on the part of the musicians and myself, in that almost all of the projects are direct to *two track*[9]. But with digital editing, a lot of work goes on in post production to tidy up the product.

I decided that the name of the game is productivity. An artist must produce to move on, so I have plunged headlong into getting everything documented. Hence the large number of recordings under my leadership as well as the books and videos. Mass success has eluded me, especially in the U.S. for reasons both known and unknown. But I have followed my own personal inclinations, refraining from being associated with this or that school of playing or clique of musicians. Being individual has been the major criterion, even in the recording of standards which I have done more in this past decade than previously. Often, I would ask myself whether I would do such and such a project if I had ten million dollars in the bank!! In other words, given no need for material reward, would I still do it? The answer has unanimously been yes, I'm happy to say.

From the vantage point of the soprano sax which was my primary solo instrument from 1980 through 1995, I have emphasized flexibility and variety of tone and expression as well as loose rhythmic placement. These values are essential to everything I play and remain top priorities. Each group I have led has always had in mind a central concept. With *Quest* from 1982 through 1991, I enjoyed the pleasure of being able to solo in front of the force of a powerful and experienced rhythm section. Having had Billy Hart, Ron McClure and Richard Beirach as the set personnel from 1984, I feel like I was as close to the feeling that Coltrane and Miles may have had with their groups. The four of us came from the common musical heri-

---

9 *two-track*–as compared to multi-track recording, the music is mixed directly to left and right stereo; but more important, corrections cannot be done easily.

tage of the 1960's with the emphasis on real time improvisation and a minimum of written material. Also, with Richie Beirach, there was the accumulated rapport of years of harmonic give and take reaching its zenith with Quest and in various duo recordings over the period. After the last *Quest* CD, titled Of One Mind (CMP), I felt there was nowhere left to go at the time and I wanted to play more developed compositions as well as shifting the emphasis from harmony to rhythm. Hence, the Dave Liebman Group of the 1990's,

with Richie Beirach, Rottenburg, Germany, 1985 (© Hans Gruber)

employing guitar and keyboards with percussion, as well as acoustic piano, drums and bass. The music we have recorded reflects all of the areas I am interested in. When I am ready to move on, it may likely be back to a trio setting without a chord instrument which is where I started with the Open Sky Trio in the early 1970's. I am still tied to the need to have a steady group to further my own playing regardless of the difficulty of sustaining it. Without a group of my own I would feel an emptiness for sure. I try as much as possible to stay with the same musicians because over a period of time the rapport builds. Somehow, growth is evident even if the group only plays together a few concentrated periods per year. What is important is to record with the same musicians.

I have developed several very positive relationships with European musicians for several reasons. From the standpoint of opportunity to perform in reasonably good settings and make a living at it, Europe has traditionally provided many more chances. Musicians there appreciate someone like myself playing with them and they take care of the necessary business arrangements to facilitate it. Because of government support on both local and national levels, Europe still remains the place where many American jazz musicians spend a lot of time. The star system is less pronounced so that artists who do not have wide name recognition among the public can still get a decent audience from interested people. Also, the European musicians are rightfully claiming the scene for themselves and less American groups as such are going over, so it is more opportune to be a featured soloist. On a yearly average, I go to Europe ten to fifteen times.

But what it makes most interesting is the chance to play with such widely varied influences. Being a horn player gives me the great advantage of joining a set rhythm section and dramatically feeling the effects of a different approach. In particular, there are two rhythm sections of well known European musicians with whom I have played often. The Scandinavian trio of Jon Christensen on drums, Bobo Stenson on piano and Lars Daniellson on bass is classic because of the "Nordic" way they play, especially in the rhythmical and coloristic sense. They have a highly developed melodic approach at the same time. Overall, I would rate Scandinavian musicians as the most well rounded in Europe because of their ability to play in many styles well, yet with a singular outlook. I also play with the well known trio of Daniel Humair on drums, Jean Francois Jenny Clark on bass and Joachim Kühn on piano. They enjoy playing complicated, intervallic melodies set in fast jazz time, often without changes and with great intensity as well as quite free. Lyricism is not a priority for them. All of these mentioned musicians are from my generation and therefore we all relate to similar musical values and concepts. In Italy, I have played with bands that like a more straight ahead, chord change style. And I often get invited to take part on young musician's recordings and orchestral as well as big band settings throughout Europe. There is no doubt in my mind that more original music is going on in Europe than in the U.S. They are aware of, but less intimidated by the jazz tradition and also can't help reflecting the very rich contemporary classical music which has its roots in Europe. What is remarkable is how different the music can be in such a small geographical area and it is exhilarating for me to participate in these differences.

International Association of Schools of Jazz (IASJ)

One of my proudest accomplishments has been the founding of the IASJ, a network of jazz schools worldwide. Beginning with a letter written in 1987 (see appendix 7) which I had sent to schools where I had taught over the years, then forming in 1989 and holding yearly meetings with newsletters and a magazine ("Changes"), the organization emphasizes student to student cross-cultural communication and is growing rapidly. I envision a virtual United Nations of schools with students from all over meeting regularly throughout the world and sharing ideas and music, eventually at a center where these activities can take place. It is exciting to see young musicians put together music within a few days of meeting, never having played together previously.

Personal Reflections: Black and White

I have played, traveled and lived for periods with both black and white musicians, Europeans, Japanese, Israeli, Indian, Australians, Canadians and Latinos. Music is truly universal as I have learned first hand. But there are admittedly differences that do exist, depending on the specific music being played. There are also differences in audiences and students around the world from my observations. In jazz music there has traditionally been discussion of the differences between whites and blacks.

In the past twenty years since the late 1960's more white musicians have been involved in jazz or jazz-related music than previously. Before this period, the music almost exclusively belonged to Black people. Probably due to the fusion of jazz and rock, more middle class whites became interested while, especially in the 1970's, the young Blacks seem to have mostly gone into funk, soul and other related pop fields. The white attitude is usually grounded in a more intellectual approach due to the historical inequities in the educational system, rooted in America's racist legacy. Blacks in former times learned jazz almost solely by ear and within their subculture, which musically had antecedents in gospel music and blues. With the whites came jazz education and the notion that someone could be taught to swing (a gross simplification of the process).

To my mind, the cultural heritage of the Black people more naturally reflects a loose, flexible attitude towards life which is heard in their music. Whether this makes any Black musician more natural and therefore a better improviser than a white one is a value judgment which would be quite suspect. Suffice to say, there often has been a difference in the rhythmic feel between whites and Blacks, but with so many exceptions, even this statement is dubious.

With the popularity of fusion, there are white musicians who play truly funky, for example, altoist Dave Sanborn. In fact most of the students that I hear sound so much more convincing in this basic pop style than when they try to deal with higher sophisticated levels of playing. Needless to say, one of the greatest educational challenges in jazz still is and will always remain, how to get to a youngster who doesn't know the legacy and its vernacular to begin phrasing in a jazz manner.

Because I was attracted to jazz in the early 1960's before many whites were into it, I went through a period of trying to emulate Black culture in a physical and verbal manner. Being impressionable is part of youth and even in my period with Miles, I affected some of his mannerisms and attitudes. These affectations were not always positive or even useful, but it was a stage I had to go through. I feel that I learned a lot about Black culture and assimilated some valuable musical and attitudinal traits which have served me well. One of the greatest compliments that Miles gave me was his remark to a friend, "Dave ain't black or white, he has no color!" The point is that knowledge of other cultures can be useful for an artist's vision, and you don't gain deep insights without paying some kind of tariff to enter.

Audiences

As described above, Europe has traditionally been and still is a saving grace for jazz musicians. The expatriate American musician is a fact of European cultural life as the example of many artists in jazz history reveals. The reason is that in Europe, culture is accorded respect by the people and therefore, support by governments. Most of the work in Europe is financed in some manner by the state, be it local or national T.V. or radio. The audience spans all ages and because the broadcasting system was traditionally nationalized and noncommercial, it featured all kinds of music including jazz. The youth were not fed only one style and therefore evidenced more interest in all forms of contemporary music. Because there is the self-realization that culturally they are sophisticated, or possibly for some other reason, both the European audience and critics are extremely opinionated; maddeningly so as far as I am concerned. But as long as they continue to be interested enough to have such strong opinions in the first place, my criticism is negligible on this account. Of course, as I write in the mid 1990's governmental money is shrinking everywhere, but the tradition of support will not disappear, at least I hope not.

Remarkably enough, I have found enough differences between the various countries in Europe to make generalizations. The German audience is the most sophisticated and interested. In fact, some of the most serious European work is in Germany. Scandinavians are in general really good audiences except if they begin to drink too much and get rowdy. My definition of a good audience is one that is at least slightly educated as to whom is playing and what to expect but not so impressed that they applaud a shallow or show-off kind of performance. Also, a good audience is ready to respond with enthusiasm when the time is appropriate. As far as enthusiasm goes, the Italians and the Spanish, though late to develop, are energetic and show their approval (or disapproval) quite openly. The French audience can be very affected by what is hip or chic at the time, but this characteristic is true to some extent of all Europeans and even more, the Japanese.

Japan opened up for jazz in the 1950's probably as a direct result of the Occupation. Their love of anything American may be responsible for the popularity of jazz, but I feel that it is their artistic sense as a people which leads them to appreciate beauty and anything done with excellence. Their national arts speak for this reasoning. However, the Japanese are more faddish than Western cultures possibly because everything is new and happening so quickly to them in so many ways over the past fifty years. Therefore, the Japanese generations since the late 1970's seem to enjoy a style for two years and then discard it. I must admit that they have been inundated by American groups and culture. The truth is that I'm a bit disappointed by the lack of depth which reveals itself in their culture nowadays.

Other countries have no tradition of jazz, so when performing in Turkey, India, Asia and other Third World places, the enthusiasm is generated because the music is known as American jazz. To these people, this means everybody from Louis Armstrong to Jimi Hendrix. There will always be a small coterie of informed listeners, but nowhere near the numbers in Europe. However, going to the Third World once in a while is exotic, artistically stimulating, thought provoking (I'll never forget my first trip to India) and gratifying because from the first note, people go wild. They have no preconceived opinions or do they care what it is called. They are mainly very appreciative that you've come.

I have one prediction about China. I feel that in the near future, jazz groups will regularly be touring there and the reception will be like Japan was twenty years ago. They are the originals of the Orient; they have a long tradition of creativity and culture; they are disciplined and hard working; and possibly the individual freedom which is the core of jazz will have great relevance to a people just coming out of a very tight authoritarian grip.

My last comment on audiences concerns America. This is not the place for a diatribe about the deadening effects of aspects of American culture, particularly the emphasis upon flash, money and power through commercial success. It is sufficient to say that outside of the universities and a few people in the major cities, jazz, and in fact any serious art form does not have a home in the U.S. In the case of jazz, the irony is that the music reflects so much of the American ethos of individual freedom and is historically a product of certain facets of American's history, specifically the growth of urban life in the twentieth century.

With great sadness, I must admit that even the traditional center of jazz, New York City is suffering. To an outsider, there seems to be a lot of jazz activity and many young musicians interacting together. Of course, in proportion to elsewhere, this is true. But being a native New Yorker and although living outside of the city for some years, an active member and observer of the scene, it is in my opinion that jazz is on the wane at this juncture of history in the Big Apple. The

with Mike Stern in Tübingen, Germany, early '80s (© Hans Gruber)

economics of running clubs which were more evident in New York than elsewhere has finally affected their viability. To hear a set of music is a minimum of twenty-five dollars per person with no relief in sight. The real traditional jazz audience made up of musicians, students and intellectuals cannot afford this price. What's left is the tourist from Japan or Europe who often think they must go to a jazz club while in New York, in the same way they go to the Empire State Building. It's a place to go, to be able to say that you went to a New York jazz club as part of the trip. I particularly dislike the fact that food is served while the music is played. The sets are timed to turn over the audience. There is no sweat and guts and the music is underplayed which results in the loss of its urgency. So why even play original compositions or rehearse a group? What you hear for the most part in New York is the overworked standard repertoire or on the other hand, music being touted as great art but devoid of real depth. There are unspoken restrictions on spontaneity and the club scene has become just another gig, rather than the major forum of this art form. This is truly an upsetting development for all New York based musicians.

So the best place remeining to play is the clinic/workshop setting where the students are interested, enthusiastic and cannot be fooled. Students are both highly critical and desirous of being inspired. Young musicians around the world also differ in interesting ways. For example, the Japanese who have such a knack for copying are the same when it comes to jazz. As a group they are among the best of all the young musicians I meet. They know their scales, tunes and literature. Their sense of rhythm is learned by exact imitation and when crossed with their own musical tradition, the results can be very interesting as for example trumpeter Terumasa Hino, whom I had the pleasure to play with in many different circumstances over the past decades. The German students do not know the jazz syntax nor the tunes too well, but they bring a European approach to the music which is in some ways freer and more experimental than traditional jazz. The sense of improvisation is there, but in a different way. And there is a whole Scandinavian school of playing which is well documented on ECM Records; most notably in the music and sound of saxophonist Jan Garbarek. One thing common to all students everywhere is their burning desire to express themselves in some way. If they can find a way to relate to jazz as well as their own roots, interesting hybrids can occur in the future.

Competition

The reality is that any art form is a highly competitive field. The relationship between supply and demand is way out of proportion. This is especially true nowadays when more people are involved in the academic pursuit of creativity evidenced by the number of students enrolled in such programs. To my mind, competition is stimulating and very positive in jazz. It's similar to athletics where actual performance ability can be seen by everybody and in that way serves as an inspirational experience for an individual. Many of my best musician friends have been other saxophonists, contemporaneous with me. The reason is that we all understand what each of us must go through to play the instrument. The resulting friendly competition can be most stimulating.

Stardom   Everyone wants their name in lights; to be popular doing what they love. It is human nature to desire reknown and popularity. I was no different for a time until I approached thirty years old. Finally I realized that I am part of a tradition which reaches out to the soul of man, as well as the body and mind. I gained humility slowly and not without pain and remorse. I realized that fame and glory can be like an albatross around one's neck. The star system has a subtle way of making a person, especially an artist, repeat his work and cease growing. I have the greatest respect for those artists in any field who achieve fame, but because their creative mind beckons, they turn their back on the very thing that placed then at the pinnacle. In the jazz world, when John Coltrane entered his late period (1965-66), disbanding the well known quartet to play some very fierce, chaotic and at times incomprehensible music, he lost a large part of his audience. Obviously, this did not dissuade him from his artistic calling. Being an improviser places the artist in the context of a continuum from man's earliest musical attempts as part of an ongoing tradition, rather than a fad dictated by current trends.

Drugs   I'm going to be honest and not pontificate. Without going into detail, I will admit that I learned something of value from experiences with drugs. I knew myself well enough to realize that I had a good deal of self-control and discipline. I am not an abuser. But part of my personality is that of a striver, thirsting for new experience. Maybe this is why the nature of spontaneous improvisation makes jazz the most powerful addiction in my life. It is when I feel best. Drugs taught me about relaxation as did Oriental philosophy including meditation, yoga and dietary practices. For a time in my youth, I really believed drugs made me play better. Whether that was true or not is besides the point. The main thing is that when you're really good at something, you don't need any stimulation to help you.

In fact, if drugs are involved in creativity to any great degree, one will always wonder whether it could've been accomplished without them. For me, I think drugs made music feel physically better than normal, but I suspect that what was played sounded worse. "Under the influence" means you're not the master of your physical or mental body. This control is a goal that is continually sought after by the performing artist. Drugs place you at a disadvantage by distracting you from the task at hand. The goal of clear and beautiful creation is difficult enough to attain in an ordinary, controlled state. I learned a lot about myself as in any self-awareness process, but I would never recommend something so deceptive or dangerous to anyone.

Contemporary Pop Scene

Every few months I try to catch up with the contemporary commercial scene. I'll watch MTV, ask some friends and students who are informed about recent recordings and generally check out the radio to see what's happening. Sometimes I'll hear something interesting and purchase the cassette. In the case of a real mega-hit or a much discussed album, I'll automatically buy it. In years past when I listened more to pop I enjoyed the music of Earth, Wind and Fire, Stevie Wonder, Prince, Sting and Michael Jackson. Often it's the lyrics which have attracted me in these artists particularly. Sometimes it's the beat or chord progression.

   I listen to the current scene to be able to relate to what the pupils I teach are hearing as well as enjoying physically relating to a lot of it. Also, there is so much interested young talent that the level of the music and its accompanying video scene has to keep improving. Commercial music has come a long way in the past forty years from the number one tune being Eddie Fisher singing *Oh My Pa-Pa* in the mid 1950's when I first remember noticing the hit parade to the present era. It can be illuminating to know what other good artists are involved in.

Spirituality

I feel that the spiritual aspects of creating art are understood and obvious. We are mediums through which some sort of Higher Force manifests itself just as nature reflects this same power. The message is love and compassion for all living entities. I don't admire performers who evoke the name of some special diety or religious movement in connection with their performance. The spirituality of a work of art should be felt as a manifestation of good positive energy reflecting the central core of the artist's beliefs. And the artist's life should reflect a respect for that connection with the cosmos which he enjoys.

Creating the Masterpiece

I'm often asked what I think about when I hear an old album of my own. Until a few years ago, I had great difficulty enjoying myself at all because of being so critical of the playing. In time I reached a stage where I objectively could take notice of bad execution, something that is disturbing in principle. One premise of being an artist who is attempting to express himself through an instrument, (paint brush or poetry for that matter), is that one should expect of himself near flawless technique. It is enough to deal with expression and feelings. This may appear a bit idealistic, but it is a worthwhile goal.

Therefore, in the technical sense I look for good intonation, a nice time feel in relation to the accompaniment which means not rushing or dragging, clean articulation when I was attempting it and other specific elements. What disappoints me is when I try to play something and it is flawed in execution. Of course in the end, I am listening beyond technique. This means the artistic success of the overall solo, considering factors such as pacing, unexpected phrases and unique twists and turns. A major aspect to which I listen closely to is whether the expressiveness is convincing and universal enough for the average listener who is sensitive and open to receive some meaning from it.

This brings me to my primary goal in music: the creation of masterpieces. A masterpiece goes beyond style, vernacular, historical time, place and even the creator's personality, although all of these elements are certainly factors in any great work. It is a creation that is ineffable and will live forever because the depth of what it says is of the utmost sublimity. A few of the great musical works that are in that category for myself are: Beethoven's *String Quartet in C♯ Minor* (the slow movements), *The Goldberg Variations* by J.S. Bach, *Sketches of Spain* by Miles Davis, *Crescent* by John Coltrane. The creation of a piece in this category is worth a lifetime of work and truly makes a being as immortal as possible.

APPENDIX

A Conversation With David Liebman[1]

by Gunnar Mossblad

MOSSBLAD: I am sitting across the kitchen table from David Liebman, one of the most influential jazz saxophonists to date, in Stroudsburg, Pennsylvania, a resort community in the Poconos just outside of New York City that has attracted many artists to its beautiful atmosphere. This same kitchen table has been the sight of many stimulating conversations about music, business and life with Mr. Liebman. Today our conversation will be documented.

To begin with I should congratulate you on the recent award you received from the National Endowment for the Arts. I understand the grant you were awarded involves a rather musically-unique concert in New York as well as another location. Would you like to tell us about that a little bit?

LIEBMAN: It's a performance grant awarded for original, creative projects that may not otherwise have an audience – which in this case means I will give two concerts, one in New York at the Greenwich House and then out where I live in Stroudsburg, Pennsylvania at East Stroudsburg University in December. These concerts are in conjunction with a recording that I just finished which you are included on of course, which is entitled *Classique*. I recorded it for a record label called OWL Records based in France. I have done six other recordings for them. This one is a series of pieces that I wrote in the mid 80's for various quartets plus the soprano saxophone; two for saxophone quartet, two for woodwind quartet, and one for string quartet. In addition to the original string quartet, I play *Adagio for Strings* by Samuel Barber. In that case I improvise over the actual written music. I also included a few short interludes that were written just for this recording. The concerts were, when I originally applied for the grant, supposed to be a kind of rehearsal for the recording, but they ended up taking place after the recording. Also on the program, I will be including a suite writ-

[1] This interview was commissioned by *Sax Symposium* and was conducted by Gunnar Mossblad on October 27, 1991.

ten and recorded in 1985 for a solo soprano saxophone album, which I recorded using overdubs. The record and suite were called *The Loneliness of a Long-Distance Runner*. For this concert, it was arranged and orchestrated for saxophone quartet by my wife Caris Visentin. It's about a 25-30 minute piece and of course you, Gunnar, just recorded that for your last CD. It will be the main piece of the night. For these concerts I'm adding percussion just to make it something a little special, although the recording doesn't include any.

MOSSBLAD: Throughout your career you have seemed to explore a wide variety of musical genres, groups and styles while maintaining a very individual sound and style. What drives you to explore and experiment with so many kinds of music?

LIEBMAN: Well, I think it has to do with my influences. I feel that I am a child of the 60's as far as my main learning period was musically as well as in many other ways also. I was very influenced at that time by people who were listening to all kinds of music. I was originally exposed to pop and rock 'n' roll because I liked that before I ever knew of jazz. As far as classical, ethnic and world music, especially Indian and African music, this was kind of in the air at that time. It was the first time you really had recordings widely available of music from all over the world. I think my generation was really exposed to that. You just liked everything beyond category. In other words, I loved jazz, the music of John Coltrane particularly in the 60's which inspired me to play, but I equally loved the music of Panallal Ghosh, the Indian flutist or Vilayet Khan on sitar, and of course Jimi Hendrix and even Stravinsky. These were influences that were really an inescapable part of me. It just seemed to me that the idea was to make music that you loved and form your own mode of expression within different kinds of music, not just jazz. The root was the improvisational aspect and the way one played; one's personal style of playing would be the common thread throughout. I always felt it was important to express myself in all the various musics that I loved. You know, I'm not the only one that has done this. Of course, Chick Corea was very influential in this kind of area, and Herbie Hancock; a lot of the guys who came up became very popular in the 70's doing this on a large scale. It was really a movement, but I think that probably among many of my contemporaries on the saxophone, outside of Jan Garbarek and Steve Lacy, I have done quite a bit of this kind of thing. This present project of classical influences combined with jazz improvisation is one of these kinds of projects.

MOSSBLAD: You have been one of the few people who have had success merging classical and jazz styles together in an eclectic style. Is that something that you have made a deliberate attempt to do or is it just another exploration?

LIEBMAN: It's just another exploration. Every music has particular aspects that appeal to me the most. In classical music the major aspect that is of interest and has such tremendous expressive power among other things is the harmony. The harmony is what makes Western classical music so unique, especially that of the 20th century. This harmony is something that I've been interested in for many years, especially in my music with pianist Richard Beirach. Understanding the piano is something which is a central part of my playing in many of these idioms. So with the string and woodwind quartets, one really has a chance to paint this very rich harmonic picture, over which I can improvise. That's the challenge in this particular project.

MOSSBLAD: You mentioned pianist Richie Beirach. You have had a long association with Richie. How do you describe your musical relationship with him?

LIEBMAN: I played with Richie for over twenty years in various settings. Probably the most well known would be as a duo, *Lookout Farm* and in the group *Quest* which I just concluded after ten years. We go back to learning and playing together during the late 60's and early 70's in the lofts of New York where many of the musicians who are well known now jammed and learned together. It was a very fertile period for us. Richie is extremely influenced by 20th century classical music and of course jazz. His influence was very strong upon my understanding and ability to cope with that kind of harmony. A lot of the important harmonic innovations which occurred in the 60's in jazz came from the classical world, especially heard in (McCoy) Tyner, (Herbie) Hancock, (Chick) Corea, (Wayne) Shorter, and (John) Coltrane. When we are together in a group situation, Richie is a great rhythm section player which for a jazz horn player like myself is extremely important because how you are going to sound has so much to do with how the rhythm section (bass, drums, and piano) are reacting behind you. This creates the excitement and setting over which one improvises. I am very sensitive to this, especially after having played with Miles Davis for a few years in the 70's; a man who was very attuned to how to use the rhythm section. Beirach can really get the drums and bass to gel together. We had a very good relationship that way. We recorded 30-40 records together all those years.

MOSSBLAD: Working with Richie in a duo setting is a common classical instrumentation for solo literature ... that is, an instrument and piano; however, the way you function and interact in this setting must be different. What are some of the differences in the way you two function in that setting as compared to, let's say, the equivalent in classical music?

LIEBMAN: If we put all the music together that we played over the last twenty years, about ten percent of it was actually written on paper. We really didn't write much for each other in that respect. The goal of jazz is to be able to improvise. When you have great musicians who also have great empathy as Richie and myself, you really don't need to write much. In fact, I just got a note which is interesting from a friend, who is an acquaintance of the great oboist, Heinz Holliger from Switzerland. He is probably the premiere oboist of our time and is interested in jazz. He got a hold of our last record which is entitled *Chant*, on the CMP label; a very classical sounding recording. It happens to sound that way, more so than some of the other records we did which are more jazz oriented. To paraphrase the essence of his comment, he wished his writing would sound like our improvisations. If you think of jazz in this respect, whereby your improvisations attempt to be the most perfect compositions, this would be the goal you always strive for.

MOSSBLAD: Instantaneous composition?

LIEBMAN: Instantaneous composition; that is to be as perfect as a composer who can sit and mull over his work for hours and refine, change and edit it. We don't have a chance to refine and edit in live improvisation. In the studio you can try another take. But in fact, as improvisers we're instant composers and the goal is to have a fantastic improvisation which is perfect in form, logic, harmony, structure and so forth. To accomplish this with two, four or more people is like chasing a rainbow. It could never be perfect, which is really desirable.

MOSSBLAD: So in essence, you write structures that you use for the actual compositions and then fill in those structures with improvisation to make a complete compositional jazz statement?

LIEBMAN: Yes. Our main goal is to improvise a perfect composition on some structure, be it harmonic, melodic, rhythmic, or only a particular color. This is what jazz musicians spend their whole life on.

MOSSBLAD: What do you do when you have reached your goal, and what methods or techniques can help to facilitate that goal?

LIEBMAN: You have to be equipped. What do you practice to be a jazz musician? Can you practice spontaneous composition? You really can't. You can't sit in your studio or wherever you practice and just say I'm going to improvise as you would in front of people, or in front of the microphone when you are recording. So much of it is based upon movement; how you feel; what you've been through; your environment. It's a very human thing, which is why I love it so much; because it puts you directly in touch with what's going on around you. But in order to execute your reactions, in order to portray them and be successful enough that people are interested in it, you have to be equipped with the tools of the jazz language. If you stand up there and say, "I'm going to improvise", and then you're groping for the alphabet ... this would be like speaking now and having to spell out every word in your mind. We would never get past the first sentence. So what you practice is the language instantly ready to speak with. It's like having a dictionary in your pocket and just turning to the page, knowing the word, its spelling as well as its meaning. Also, being able to form sentences, paragraphs, chapters and entire books with these words. That's how you prepare. Plus you do other things to prepare to be spontaneous which is learning how to relax. You have to let things enter into yourself. It's a very psychological exercise. You have to be able to receive and give forth feelings through the music. And finally, in jazz, since it's mostly group music, outside of the times when you may play a capella, you must be very good at social interactions with human beings because the success of your performance greatly depends on your empathy with your peers ... the people you play with.

MOSSBLAD: That brings up the technical side of the things. Obviously, all the saxophonists that will be reading this realize the importance of scales and technical mastery of the saxophone. When you are improvising in jazz or more eclectic idioms, is there a spiritual technique so to say?

LIEBMAN: What I take that to mean is that by spiritualism there is something beyond the reality that we have here in the everyday, physical world. All human beings have this understanding instinctively. I think that we, as artists, particularly improvising artists, are in a certain way attempting to be in tune with that spiritual force which envelopes all of us. However you describe it, whether in religious or metaphysical terms, it translates to a force that goes beyond everyday reality. If you can be in touch or attempt to be in touch with it, you are just bound to be clearer about what you are doing as well as why and how you're doing it. Everything just gets more to the point. It's like finding peace in that way. You are one with nature or with God, or whichever way you want to express it. I like the way in Star Wars they call it "the force". It really doesn't matter what you call it, but that you are really attempting to get in touch with it. So, if you are an improvising artist and you can tune into that force, you are bound to reveal a deeper statement when you play. You are likely to be more convincing, communicating more, be deeper, more expressive, etc. etc. That's the role of spiritualism in music for me. When I think about how spiritual affairs relate directly to playing, I think it's rather obvious and present all the time. As long as you feel that it's there, you will always go for it. So your spiritual and aesthetic training is to be in tune with yourself. It's really a self-exercise that enables you to reach for the outer force. The more you can achieve that, the better your art is going to get, and that is really in the end the true pursuit that you are involved in for your life. It's not to play your scale cleaner or better because technically you are always trying to improve and expand. Or to learn more craft, because that's part of your job. The greater aspect of it is the higher force around all of us. If you can go for that consistently, you'll be personally rewarded as well as busy your whole life. There will never be a boring moment and it's truly a privilege to be able to live a life where such concerns are of paramount importance, rather that only the material.

MOSSBLAD: I know, having taken some lessons with you that you stress exposure to great literature other than muscial for inspiration.

LIEBMAN: Absolutely.

MOSSBLAD: As well as for learning?

LIEBMAN: That's the whole point. To understand others who have searched in that way and have examined it.

MOSSBLAD: Do you "graft" some of those concepts to your own personal artistic identity?

LIEBMAN: We graft melodies and make them our own. We graft ideas and concepts. There is nothing new. It's just a question of how one man expressed it. One may see the color red as pink and you may perceive it as slightly off-orange, yet you've both seen the same thing. So I am interested in how so and so saw it. Especially if it's a man I respect, who did great work, who was talented and was deep into it. That's why I think it's always rewarding for a budding artist or anyone to read about, and listen to biographies of other people who were thoughtful, their journals, books, and thoughts. I know that helped me in understanding myself. It inspired me to go and find my own way of expressing things. Also, I feel that an important aspect of looking outward is understanding the other arts. In other words, comprehending how other artists approach art through their mediums. Finally, the other area besides spiritual affairs and art is understanding the world around you. By that I mean current events, history, politics, government, etc. What's going on down the street or in another part of the world? We must remember that we are playing for people. We are not playing for each other, although on a technical level I feel I do play to the other musicians because they are the only ones whom I hope are able to comprehend what I am doing as I'm doing it. But in the end, my goal is to reveal the wonderful freedom of improvisation and vastness of life for those who listen to me. This means the audience, whether it be somebody listening to a recording at home or live, which of course I favor the most. And in order to know who I am speaking to, I must know the condition under which they and we live.

So to me, an artist should be aware of what's going on around them, especially the performing artist who is out there in the real world. I like that real world aspect of it. I like the fact that I'm not a painter sitting in my garret or a writer in my room isolated from the world. I like the fact that to do what I do, not only do I have to interact with my colleagues which is already a primary level of understanding of people, but I have to relate to the world because I am out there performing in it. And the traveling aspect ties it all in. So I take that on as part of what I have to do.

That's the artist's responsibility, which is why I stress in my teaching the act of looking outward at the same time that you look inward to find your own expressive way. But neither should exclude the other.

MOSSBLAD: Is that the main goal of your art?

LIEBMAN: It's to balance the inner feelings of how you feel about what you are as well as what the human condition is in relation to what is going on around you at that time in history. Then – not one hundreds years ago; not in the future; the nowness of it. That's why I love improvisation, because if there is one thing about it, it's the truth factor. I don't care what level you play on. Some of the readers of this article might just be able to barely play a blues and others might be quite advanced. In either case there is one thing that's common to anybody who attempts to improvise from the child to the completely experienced professional and that is that they are definitely in present time. If you're not, your performance is already sabotaged. I think it's great because it focuses reality. Therefore, what I'm trying to do is be in contact with present time and with myself in relation to the cosmos and the spiritual aspects, unifying all that through the medium of this improvisational language called jazz.

MOSSBLAD: You mentioned the importance of studying great literature from other artistic disciplines as well as being aware of current affairs. I am curious about your thoughts on some of the people and places that I know have held a certain significance in your personal life. If it's alright with you, I would like to do a word association thing.

LIEBMAN: Okay. Sure.

MOSSBLAD: How about the psychoanalyst Carl Gustav Jung?

LIEBMAN: A major book in my life was *Memories, Dreams, and Reflections* which was really a diary of sorts. It was just what I was talking about a moment ago. The thing about Jung that I liked was that he identified the archetype in all human beings. In a sense we have all the memories stored in human history in each of us. We are as animals a product of natural selection, but because of our brain, we have memory and generational communication. We definitely have a recollection, if not true relics in front of us when we go to the pyramids or whatever. There is a memory seed of all that has happened before within each of us. And I think Jung was important in elucidating the archetype's role in the human psyche. Plus he was such a human, humane person. I have this interview, which you saw, of him from 1959 on the BBC, and he comes off as a warm, great guy. You could see his feeling was all inclusive, plus his written introduction to the famous *I Ching* was amazing.

MOSSBLAD: India.

LIEBMAN: When I think of India, I think of the incredible vastness of experience that country has. I've been there a few times, and the extremes of everything are striking; from amazing poverty to the deep spiritualism of the people. It's such an alive place, and of course, I must say that Indian classical music, a five thousand year tradition, is the prime example of improvised music in the world sans harmony. As far as melody and rhythm go, there is nothing more sophisticated that I know of and more full of craft, feeling, and fervor. Any people who can keep that music alive and for so long has got to have something going. A Westerner can only understand it from afar. I took some lessons on the *bansuri*, the Indian wooden flute, the long one. I did it because it was influential from a technical standpoint, especially for a jazz saxophone player to understand how to make a lot out of little. They give you the scale or raga, usually only five or six notes. By the use of pitch bending, expression, repetition and rhythm, you get enough music to play eight hour concerts which often occurs in India. That kind of depth of expression and economy of material is almost the complete opposite of what a jazz musician does, who makes so much out of everything. We play a lot!! It's the Western way you know. So for me to understand that musical extreme a little bit was great knowledge. Plus, purely from the expressive standpoint, how to bend a note and how to make something meaningful with very little movement is marvelous. This is the great value of Indian music, as well as the rhythm, which I can hardly understand anyway. So it's ever challenging to me.

MOSSBLAD: Speaking of rhythms, how about the drummer Elvin Jones?

LIEBMAN: Well, Elvin Jones was one of my gurus. First of all, he was part of the classic Coltrane group in the 1960s, consisting of McCoy Tyner and Jimmy Garrison, along with John. This group was the primary influence on me accomplishing anything musically. Watching them play live so many times was tremendously inspiring and made me really want to play jazz. And then, to have the chance to work with Elvin for nearly three years in the '70s … it was a dream come true. I was standing in Coltrane's shoes!!

MOSSBLAD: Was this your first major gig in the professional jazz scene? … What was it like for you?

LIEBMAN: Yes. It was the experience of night after night playing and being on the bandstand in a major group, as well as being around all of the jazz places, musicians and touring. But more than that it was Elvin. Even when I see him now, since we have played together a few times over these years in special concerts, he is like a reservoir of incredible wisdom and depth without advertising it as such. He is one of those kind of guys that you know is just deep. You know by the way he speaks to and treats people; the way he looks at you and what he says, without really pretending, or having a pretention to be deep. I mean, he just is that way with his entire presence, his eyes, and his whole physical being – it just oozes this wisdom. He is like a great African king, of a whole continent; not only Nigeria or one tribe, but all of it! And he brings that to you when you are with him. It's an amazing power. He is one of the most admired people I have ever known and the man has been around the block more than a few times.

MOSSBLAD: You mentioned standing in John Coltrane's shoes while in Elvin's band. What are your thoughts about Coltrane and his music?

LIEBMAN: Coltrane, as you know was top of the line. Top shelf. It doesn't get any better for me on the saxophone or as an improviser; spirituality, depth, sincerity, conviction, tenacity and technical virtuosity, of course; everything about Coltrane is superlative. Everything is the best of all. He was instrumental in my life and remains so because of his incredible power as a musician and also his humility. I was young and did not know him personally, but from the stories about him as well as the few times I saw him from afar, his complete lack of pretense about what he did was inspiring.

MOSSBLAD: For a number of years you worked with Miles Davis. Now that Miles is gone and in light of the memorial service in his honor that you were invited to, I imagine you have been asked a lot of questions about Miles and have thought about his influence on you and your music. How do you best remember Miles?

LIEBMAN: My wife and I were invited to the memorial service. They called everybody who had a part in Miles' life. There were many people there, many dignitaries: Jesse Jackson, Quincy Jones, Mayor Dinkins, Herbie Hancock representing the jazz community, George Wein, etc. They all told funny stories about Miles ... It was a very upbeat affair because the man had a great life. It was not like he was deprived or cut short. I mean if anything he might have been around too long in some respects musically, but he was active right to the end. It was a great affair, and I must say, it was a shock to hear that he died. Many of us reached out to each other. I had conversations with Jack DeJohnette, Wayne Shorter, and Bill Evans. I even saw musicians that I had not seen since the last gig I had with Miles in 1974.

But also when a man dies, you re-evaluate him, and I have had the occasion to think about it because I have had some interviews since then. The BBC called me and a French jazz magazine. I would say the main thing to remember about Miles was that he had an impeccable sense of timing. If you look at it in all aspects, from his personal life to even the way he died after doing a retrospective concert in Montreux playing all of the music he recorded with Gil Evans, his timing was uncanny. After all, he did a retrospective after years of holding out, resisting offers of great money to play the older music because it was so popular. Finally, he agrees and dies 3 months later. It's remarkable ... from the timing of that, to the timing of his various musical stages, to whom he had in his bands at the particular point of their lives, to his impeccable sense of rhythm when he played ... his middle of the beat, incredible swing and his knowing when to play and when to be silent; how to use a band; how to arrange a piece. He was the master of timing and his perception of how to use it was vast and influential to generations of musicians now and in the future.

The thing that was to me the main personal note was that all the guys who played with him, in all, maybe 30-40 players, were with Miles at a young age, which is an impressionable time as well as being our first major gig. From the first sidemen in the 50's like Coltrane to the last man who was there, we all had Miles at a certain point in our life, which was similar. In a way, it's a thing that binds all of us and that none of us can forget. This is a personal thing for those of us who knew, played, and toured with him.

When I was with Miles in the 70's, I got to know him and kept in touch with him over the years. I must say with all the ongoing debate about his personality, the mystique about him, the good and bad about him, we had a very good relationship. He had respect for me. I had a good time with him. We played a lot of music together. Incredible experiences.

MOSSBLAD: What about the visual arts? Do works of the great visual artists like say, Picasso, have an impact on your art?

LIEBMAN: Picasso is very similar to Miles Davis in a certain way, especially talking about eclecticism, Picasso was "Mr. Eclectic" of the 20th century as far as the visual arts are concerned – sculpture, drawing oils, collages – he used everything. He was voracious. Everything within his grasp was used, including people to express his art. He was one-mind minded, one-track. He had all that kind of relentless energy.

I love Picasso's work because it's there and not there at the same time. He once said a great thing which I have used as a quote when I think of what art is about. I don't have the exact wording, but it's to the extent that "art is deception". Great art is leading the listener, viewer or observer on a path that seems to be going in a certain direction but ends up somewhere else. The thing that is good about that is as the cliché goes, "You can lead a horse to water, but you can't make him drink." In other words, the artist is taking an observer down a certain path without telling them, only through suggestion. This is the way it's supposed to be. The artist presents his or her art in such a clear way that the observer only has a certain amount of options or conclusions about the art available, be it an oral or visual, written, physical or musical art form. The observer is going to be led to a certain kind of conclusion which is your goal as an artist. It's not by telling them, "that's point A, point B". It's up to them. That is how you involve your audience. Your audience is there to interpret, and this is what the communication is really about. The work gives the impression of meaning a variety of things, but it's in the basic area that the artist has described. It's that two-way street which makes art valuable. If an artist was only like some preacher as in a religion, and only got up there to reiterate a doctrine which you would have to take or leave, art wouldn't be what it is. The thing that makes art amazingly great when it comes down to it is that it involves the audience. The onlooker, the bystander is involved whether they know it or not, and that's what is deceiving about it. You think the guy painted that, but he really left it up to you. Picasso was incredible with his faces, showing noses where the ear should be and eyes under the chin. You know it's a woman or a man, but there is a guitar in the middle of the chest, etc. It's something else! He was the great juggler.

MOSSBLAD: I want to ask you about your compositions, the canvas and paints you choose to create your picture for the observer. You have a very distinctive personal writing style that seems to have a 20th century classical compositional influence. I know you have studied many composers, but who are your favorite 20th century composers?

LIEBMAN: Just from the breadth of the music I would have to say Bartók. Harmony, melody, rhythm, orchestration, everything – it's all there. Consider the large output of materials ranging from the Microcosmos piano pieces, the *Children's Pieces*, to *Concerto for Orchestra*, to the *Violin Sonatas*. I listened to the solo violin piece a couple of weeks ago and it's amazing music. The guy was incredible. A couple of others I like come to mind. I love Stravinsky's orchestration and some of Schoenberg's material; of course the Debussy string quartet, the only one he wrote is fantastic, and Ives' *The Unanswered Question* as well as a few other pieces by him. Other than that, I am drawn to specific pieces by various composers. I am no great expert on this, but I'd say that I'm most struck by Bartók's consistent output.

MOSSBLAD: It is unusual that you find a performer of your notable performing credentials and output of artistic materials, in the form of records, concerts and compositions, that takes the time to prepare and publish educational materials. In addition, you take the time to do a lot of teaching. Why all the educational activities? What's the importance?

LIEBMAN: There are two aspects to that question. One is the teaching; the other is the output of materials. Concerning the output of materials, especially in the last five years, I made an conscious effort starting in the mid 80's to organize the materials and exercises that I used to develop my art. The result thus far was the saxophone book, the videos, the book on chromaticism and of course *Self-Portrait*... which was kind of a diary of an artist's thinking.

I made an effort to do it for a variety of reasons. First of all, there is an attractive aspect of making money through royalties. Not to say that these are best sellers; we are talking about sales of hundreds, maybe a thousand or two thousand over the years. You know for a freelance artist like myself this is very nice. I don't have a steady source of income. I have a family and we really work hard at what we do as I am sure most of your readers understand. The money is never guaranteed for an artist and my music is pretty much non-commercial, and perceived by others that way. That's both positive and negative which is another discussion, but it means that I have to make a living in a variety of ways, like teaching and publishing.

It's something I thought I should do, but really that's not what would make me sit down and spend an incredible amount of hours in editing and typing. I did all the works mentioned totally handwritten and typed one page at a time. For me, that's the way I am able to best organize and quickly document my thoughts. I like to be organized. I like things in their compartments. And I hate things that are not finished. I like to have things chronicled because then I feel that I have a completed product and can move on to something else. This goes for a recording, like doing a collection of Cole Porter tunes, which was a project I always wanted to do and finally completed a few years ago. Or doing this classical project we discussed earlier. I recorded on cassettes all my interviews and lectures over the years and organized those thoughts together into a book, entitled *Self Portrait of a Jazz Artist*. The same for the saxophone book, *Developing a Personal Saxophone Sound* and *A Chromatic Approach to Jazz Melody and Harmony*. From an educational standpoint, I felt the information should be available.

I was a teacher in the school system in New York City for awhile. Although that doesn't necessarily relate, I have a good ability to verbalize and express myself in writing. Thank God I have a good education. Some people just don't verbalize that well, or don't care to, or get nervous and may not write well enough to express their thoughts. I was able to do this and felt that these were things that should be said and known about.

There are a lot of people interested who will never see me, or who will never get near from remote corners of the world where this music is now available. They should have the availability of someone who has thought about and can summarize raw information, making it clear. I felt that having that kind of talent, I had a responsibility to those who were interested to do it. So that also inspired me and propelled me to the work, and of course when you do write or report something you get feedback for the rest of your life. You never know when someone is going to read a sentence that is going to strike them. It's even more immediate in a certain way than music. Music is a spiritual thing, but when you write something on paper, a person looks at it and they are able to go over it, again and again, reading it and re-reading it. The reader may find new or additional meaning every time. I get letters from people like that all the time. It's inspiring and I'm glad I've done it.

MOSSBLAD: Where do you think this exploring, curious and organized person came from?

LIEBMAN: Probably my parents. This is stuff you get at home – like speaking clearly or expressing your thoughts in a cohesive way; getting in front of people without being afraid. These are all things that are nurtured and developed in childhood, just as having confidence and the ability to verbalize. My father was very big on language. He used to flash words in front of me for the meaning. He loved words and was a great reader. He was an intellectual kind of guy, so that was always in my life; to read and be informed and be able to speak and understand vocabulary and so on. Most of that is from my upbringing.

My parents were teachers and actually principals of schools in the system of New York City. An education was important, especially in Jewish middle class homes. You've got to be cultured. You have to go to college. It was understood!!

MOSSBLAD: Are the majority of the students who come to you saxophone players?

LIEBMAN: The majority are saxophonists; however, I do get other instrumentalists of course, but mostly saxophone students.

MOSSBLAD: What do you tell your students is the most important thing that a young jazz musician should study to learn how to play jazz?

LIEBMAN: Transcription is number one and you don't need to have a teacher for it. I have a video which addresses this issue because I think it's crucial to understand the concept. Of course, you're included in this video playing one of my solos as is my wife, Caris, who sings another of my solos. It is a description of the transcription process, which is basically imitation. You take something from a recording and copy it down, which is practical ear training; you learn to play along with it which gives you all the nuances, expressive techniques and musical devices as well as the actual notes used. So much of the performance cannot be written down on paper; the way a man bends a note or how he expresses it. You copy it exactly and mimic it.

Then there are some exercises that I recommend to take what you have learned, make it more individualistic and use it for more than just duplication. In this way, it's like a didactic thing ... you are self-teaching. You are learning through imitation, which is the standard way that most jazz musicians have learned as well as in most world musics. For example, you sit with a great master drummer – he gives you the beat and then soon you are the master drummer. In India, the pupil sits with a teacher for years learning to sing everything before touching their instrument while living with him. It's the master-apprenticeship system.

In that respect, I think that the transcription process is a way that any musician reading this article can immediately help his or her playing from the all important stand point of phrasing and rhythmic feel. Copy a solo and play along with it until you can understand what it is. Then analyze it and make some exercises out of parts of it.

MOSSBLAD: Earlier, when we were discussing your publishing and teaching activities, you made reference to the business aspects of music. Obviously, the business has little to do with the creative art form. Jazz however, it is something that all of us who support ourselves in part or full by freelancing must deal with. Do you have any words of wisdom or comments on the music business?

LIEBMAN: The music business is like any other business. It's very competitive, political, and extremely frustrating. Even if you are on top it's frustrating. You must get an attitude of relaxed attentiveness and not let the frustration take over. You are constantly hitting against the wall and especially if you are artistic, you are talking about stuff that is not for everybody. I don't go for this line that real art is meant for everybody.

MOSSBLAD: Do you feel like you march to a different drummer?

LIEBMAN: Yeah. Jazz is not for everyone. Everything is not for everyone. When a guy says that it is, I look over and think, is that so? You know it's not. I mean is Picasso for everyone? Everything should be available or accessible to everybody, but whether or not everyone is ready to accept it, I don't know.

MOSSBLAD: Could it be that not everyone is ready for everything? Or everything doesn't necessarily "touch" or interest everyone?

LIEBMAN: It's both – some things are not meant to touch everyone. The audience that Janet or Michael Jackson talks to is not the same as my audience. That's absurd. Does that make me lesser than them or vice versa? It makes me different from them for sure. So let's observe the differences. And in that respect, if you talk about the kinds of things that the people who I love and I relate to are into, you are not going to see a large audience in comparison. And if you are not going to appeal to tremendous numbers of people, business is not good. If business is not good, that means you are constantly striving to make it better; you are rejected and you are always going to be climbing up a tree. It will be that way probably to the end, or until they consider you some kind of relic and they knight you, so to say. They recognize that you've been great all these years and now you are getting rewarded, which means you got to be sixty.five years old or over. You know what I mean?

MOSSBLAD: You do a lot of work in Europe. Why?

LIEBMAN: Because Europe has more respect for contemporary, living, present day artists. It's part of the European culture. They are more culturally aware and sophisticated. There are plenty of people in Europe who are "rednecks" also; they go out, have a few beers, watch a soccer game and then bash heads or whatever. People are people in every country of the world, but there is also a large community of intelligent people that are educated and sophisticated, aware of arts, aware of culture, and don't make the distinctions between, "oh jazz, I hate jazz, but I love this other music ... " It's music; it's art. You respect it. Period. That's all there is to it. You earned your way and are respected, and can work in Europe. That's why most of my contemporaries work mostly there. Even some very well known people work much more in Europe than in America, because the level of education in America is so low. The school systems are in such bad shape and have been for such a long time that how can the average young person listen to me when they don't even know where Brazil is on the map? I mean, what are we talking about? It's beyond discussion, really. The point is of course, that we are constantly trying to be successful in our country, because it's our home. Also there's no language barrier which is really a major thing. You would like to be able to travel in your own country and be known, successful and spread the music among your people. But the truth is, it's virtually impossible here.

MOSSBLAD: Maybe there is something to the old phrase you are never a prophet in your own country?

LIEBMAN: Yeah, and you can't do anything about it, so for somebody like myself, the only way to make a living and stay true to what you're doing is to have a variety of ways to (earn) your livelihood and that's why the teaching; that's why the publishing; that's why little royalties on your own compositions; that's why you get a grant here and there. You're constantly looking for different ways of making it, because there is no one source that's going to do it. It is really a game – a constant juggling game. And it takes up more of my time than creativity does, unfortunately. This is what I don't like about it.

That's the frustrating aspect. I have to spend more time working towards taking care of the details of making a living than actually going out and doing the art, which is what I should be doing, or sitting home creating and studying.

But on the other hand, there is a positive side which is that you are out there in the real world meaning that when you play, you really mean it. You are seeing life at a very real level and not sitting in an ivory tower with your servant bringing you the money on a platter and you know that you will get taken in a limousine from the airport to the concert hall. We've got to deal and there is a reality about that which keeps us grounded, especially since once you get up in that higher echelon, you easily can forget where you came from as we all know occurs. All of us can speak personally about people that once they became known, they forgot about their friends. So I'm not so sure that being on top of the heap is great either. The only advantage being on top of the heap is that it allows you the freedom to do projects the way you want. You can call in someone and you can afford it. Being able to do things the way you want does enable you to make your art grow more. That's the thing that success brings you: freedom to create more.

And that's the one unfortunate aspect of not being really well known or really popular; you are always working under a limited budget, limited time and limited means. We record in one day direct to two-track. Many of my recordings were done in four to six hours. We have to move fast, which in the positive sense means an incredible level of musicianship, but it also means constant pressure. And you never really get it the way you want it.

MOSSBLAD: You are talking about these things and yet you are one of the top saxophone players in the world.

LIEBMAN: Thank you very much. You know everybody has an opinion and art is fashion also. Art and artists are what people love to be around. This makes them feel special. There are many hangers-on or parasites in the business aspect of it, from the agents, promoters, and managers, to the media that loves the mystique of it ... the groupie-type people in each field. There is a lot of that going on. But just like anything that can be categorized as fashion, it's going to change. So what's in fashion now will not be tomorrow and so forth. I am certainly not in fashion and never have been. What's in fashion now is a certain kind of look, a certain kind of age, a certain kind of music and so forth. Maybe it will change in ten years, maybe not. I don't know. And if you are not what is fashionable at the moment, you are constantly fighting the tide of opinion which makes everything that you do seem like that's not what's happening now.

MOSSBLAD: From your perspective are you fighting against fashion or are you fighting for your own trueness of art?

LIEBMAN: For me, I have dealt with this fashion garbage. I went through a period when I wanted to be the current fashionable thing or part of it. That's one of the good things about getting older. With maturity you realize that fashion will change, so don't try to keep up with it. Make your own fashion: Dave Liebman's fashion. Let's get away from that word. Better – you come into my world, that's all.

I would like to be more well known and have more people understand my music and get to it. Yes, that's true, but not to be the fashion at the time because this is impossible and I wouldn't want to be part of that really. Slowly over the years you realize that the surface is what most people respond to at first. To have something of real depth, it must stand the test of time. Survival is the name of the game. Survival.

MOSSBLAD: What would be your advice to the young artists reading this on how to survive?

LIEBMAN: Output. You must keep your output happening; the books, records, videos, whatever your thing is; articles, just keep it going for decade after decade and you will be established and survive.

It's respect from one's peers that matters the most to me. I always wanted to be what I am. All I ever wanted when I was young was to have the heavy guys say: "He's one of us." That's when I was 18 or 20 years old. I'd go and see Miles or Coltrane. I would think: "Man, I'd love to be up there and have all the great cats coming in and listening to me." You know when you see somebody like Sonny Rollins in the audience and you think: "It's so great being one of the top guys." What a great club to be part of. All the heavy cats are in this club together. I was 18 and would be looking from afar and saying that's what I wanted to do. So having achieved a certain amount of that, I really feel good about it. I wanted to be among those who knew and I didn't want to be around people who liked me because of a hit record; something like that. It's rare to have both real artistic success and commercial recognition. Maybe Miles did, but only after he changed his musical environment and not for awhile even playing that way.

MOSSBLAD: Let's shift the subject and talk about saxophone. I know you are always stretching the bounds of the saxophone. Why at this time do you pursue that? Why at this time in your career when you have artistic success and are one of the top guys do you pursue working on multiphonics or quarter tones, altissimo range, better tone quality, etc.?

LIEBMAN: That is another thing about maturing. You realize how little you know about everything and certainly about playing the saxophone. I know I can play a certain amount, but I sure know what I can't do. In order to find deeper levels of expression you must find deeper levels in the vehicle you are using and that vehicle for me is the soprano sax. In 1980, I finally centered it down to the soprano; got rid of the tenor and eventually the flute.

MOSSBLAD: What brought you to that?

LIEBMAN: The real thought was that I must get deeper. I cannot get there by spreading my energy amongst these various horns. It was a technical problem, let alone an emotional one. An instrument must feel like an extension of your body, especially to the spontaneous improviser. I'm not thinking about how I use my hand when I speak to you or my eye motion or my voice. It's natural and spontaneous. I have to be able to speak through my instrument that way. How many instruments can you feel that way about? How many chairs can you sit in and they feel really comfortable? Or a shirt? If I put your shirt on it's not going to feel right. So it got down to, how can I feel that way about three instruments? Who am I, superman?

This was first realized from a logical standpoint, but most important of all, it didn't feel emotionally right. I still had technical problems. I would get on the flute and there would be the problem of switching and getting used to it. The problems were compounded by reeds, mouthpieces, necks, etc. I was spending far too much energy on peripherals. I didn't have time for it and I came to that realization in my 30's. I said to myself, this is ridiculous; I must be able to center on one thing so I can get deeper. I chose the soprano because it felt the most natural and there was room to be individual, whereas the tenor was historically crowded.

Returning to your original question, it was in order to express myself on a deeper level, which is the ultimate ever-present goal. You have to get deeper into the instrument in order to manipulate it with more nuance and expression as well as facilitate the technical aspects more easily.

I remember Elvin teaching me an important lesson. I used to have a notion when I was younger, a feeling that it was necessary to constantly innovate and discover a new language or new lines, because it seemed like that's what Coltrane was doing. Elvin said to me in effect: "You got it wrong, it's not only the new. Of course, that's fine. But it's also refining. What you do today will be easier to do tomorrow in the technical sense as well as expressively." The point was obviously to keep practicing and honing one's technique.

MOSSBLAD: Do you still practice fundamentals as well as explore new ground?

LIEBMAN: Yes, constantly. As I said, it's hard to find the time. As you know, intonation is an ever-present problem. Articulation, more control of nuance and of course these quarter tone fingerings and multiphonics are constant challenges. I have such great respect for the saxophonists who play like that. Guys who can play multiphonics at dynamic levels from soft to loud and tongue so fast it makes my eyes boggle. To me it's unbelievable the things that they do. They practiced hours and hours to do it. I know that's the only way to get to that level and jazz musicians in general don't put in that kind of time on their instrument. They put in the time in different ways, but not that kind; not 8 hours for years and years and years on technical things. We don't do it and I am constantly peddling up hill against technique. Art Tatum was correct when he said that one only needs as much technique as necessary to get out what one hears. Look at the difference between Monk and Bud Powell!!

MOSSBLAD: You spoke earlier about finding your own artistic voice and talk about that with regard to your sound. Could you elaborate on that?

LIEBMAN: The goal is to be recognized. When somebody hears you, they know it's you from the first note. You know Coltrane, you know Joe Henderson, Wayne Shorter, etc., and I hope you know when you hear me on the soprano. This is really a great achievement to be able to do. There are other achievements beyond, like innovating a whole style, but the first level is individual sound. Just like your face is recognizable or your fingerprints are different from everybody else. Everything about you is unique.

Every one of the five billion people on the planet are different in that respect. There is something physically about each that's different. To translate that individuality which is yours into your art and in this case, into your horn is the goal. That is the search. Students look at you and say: "But how, how do you do this?" I have some methods or systems. In general, it consists of looking outside and inside at the same time. There are ways I think that help promote this. There is no magical cure, no pill. There is no one book or exercise that will do it. It's definitely something you must put time into. You have to sit down and say, I do not want to sound like John Coltrane anymore. I do not want to sound like Michael Brecker anymore. You must make that decision and be resolute about it; that it's all important to you, that your artistic worth is no good without it. First you make the commitment, because it's important for you to not be part of the crowd.

You see, it's very psychological. It means you are standing up for yourself. You are leaving the mainstream. You are leaving what is popular at the time and most comfortable. It's like giving up something that you're used to, but must leave. It takes courage and real confidence, as well as the belief that you can do it, that you've done enough anyway. You are validated. You've reached a criteria sounding like somebody. So once you make that decision, you must look outward and inward, both of them in a certain kind of balance to try to find your own individual voice on your instrument. Maybe it's the equipment, maybe it comes from looking at the way another guy plays another instrument. Maybe it has to do with looking at another point in the history of that instrument or particular music or the way the instrument was played in that historical time; then trying to graft it to the now. Or maybe it's turning the mouthpiece upside down, which by the way Pharoah Sanders did sometimes when playing with Coltrane.

I mean, you have to try all these things and more. And you must be organized about it. I think if you go about it slowly and incrementally, you are bound to find out more about yourself which will be reflected in your sound and maybe a new style.

MOSSBLAD: When in your career did you find that you had found your own voice?

LIEBMAN: Some people tell me that they think the tenor had a very individual voice in the '70s and I guess it did.

MOSSBLAD: I do. I have always thought so.

LIEBMAN: Maybe it did. To me, it didn't have enough. I would have to say when I went exclusively to the soprano in the early 80's. When I finally made that decision, which I had been thinking about for two or three years before, it doubled my music growth by about '82, and it was really me. The other thing that develops along with a personal voice is your personal confidence. You start to feel like you can play, and you feel good about it which is reflected in your performance and your recordings. Especially in recording, because this is still the most important form of documentation for us.

MOSSBLAD: In which recordings did you first hear this individualism?

LIEBMAN: *Dedications* on the CMP label with the string quartets. That was a very important album. The first *Quest* record, called *Quest*, with Richie, Al Foster and George Mraz was as far jazz language goes, definitely me. This all went on around the early '80s and late '70s. I also started to look at the studio as no problem anymore. In fact, I couldn't wait to get to the studio and I still can't. I mean, if you gave me the choice of what I would want to do tomorrow musically, I'd say, I'd love to have a great performance with a great band, but I would often rather go into *Red Rock Recording Studio* which is fifteen minutes from home with that band and have unlimited time for a week.

In other words, the studio is to me where you really get serious. First of all, you have to have your technical thing together as well as your artistic goals in balance with spontaneity. You make decisions in the studio you would not make elsewhere because of the documentation factor and the foreverness of it. The first ten years of recording, I was kind of a nervous wreck when I'd go to the studio.

Finally, around 1980, just by having gotten used to the studio and feeling good about my playing and myself, the studio sessions finally felt pretty much like a gig. In fact it was a super great gig, so I had everything going.

My decision about the soprano coincided with this positive feeling for recording. Also, outside of the great flashes-in-the-pans, or geniuses like 'Bird', a normal grunt like myself hits his stride in the mid '30s. You've been doing it for 20 years and for the last 10 to 15 years, you sort of know what you were doing, so it's time to get heavy!!

MOSSBLAD: What importance do you place on equipment in developing your individualism?

LIEBMAN: Let's face it, saxophone players have a lot of things going with equipment. The saxophone is an imperfect instrument and there are a lot of variables; the reeds, the mouthpiece, all the mechanicals of the instrument itself; the key heights, the kind of resonators, and of course the make of the horn. And in that respect, it's a constant search for equipment that will be make it easy and minimize the problems in getting out what you are hearing so that you don't have any hitch between concept and execution.

Therefore, you're always looking for equipment that will make that flow like water. You want a mouthpiece, reed, and horn that lets the sound come back to your ears as you hear it, not as anyone else hears it. What others hear really doesn't matter in this case, although you may ask everybody in the world their opinion of it. Does it sound right to you? You don't want to say to yourself while you are improvising: "I don't like that", because as soon as you say, "I don't like that" or "That sounds weird", you have already gone away from the path of clear thinking, which is really the goal. So you want equipment that keeps the flow unimpeded.

For example, plastic Bari reeds have been a great advantage. I know a lot of players don't like them, but for me the sound itself is better. I can do more with it. Okay. That's a matter of taste. But equally strong as the sound is the fact that the plastic reeds are non-hassle reeds; the non-thinkingness of them; get it, put it on and play. You know the reed hasn't changed. I don't have to think about it, and man, that's worth everything to me.

MOSSBLAD: I would guess that most people that hear you, if they didn't know the difference ...

LIEBMAN: They would't know.

MOSSBLAD: Probably not. So, really the plastic reeds make it easier to express what you hear.

LIEBMAN: Exactly. And it goes like my teacher Joe Allard always said. It's you that controls the instrument. The instrument is not playing you. Don't tell me it's the reed or the mouthpiece. Surely you can get something that will make it easier or better for you, but it's still you who control it. You are the master. You know, this is an instrument. The very definition of an instrument is something to be used by human beings who have control of it. I see a lot of wasted energy when I see mouthpiece and reed fanatics.

I remember when I was like that. Some people take it to such a degree that they are constantly unhappy and always spending money on it. I think it may be a lot of nervous energy about their performing and playing. How much difference is there between these things? It's you who controls it. So really you find something ... you live with it ... and you make it your own.

MOSSBLAD: How has equipment played a role in your career, and what kinds of changes have you gone through with your equipment?

LIEBMAN: The most important thing about equipment, both the horn and especially in the mouthpiece development, has always been trying to find something that had more means of expression; did not have too bright of a sound; and was able to satisfy my needs in the way of color and nuance, which is one of the main aspects of my style. I have always needed equipment that was flexible and didn't cast me in one mold. I need a sound that I can go a lot of different ways with. That always was the main thing.

MOSSBLAD: You talk about Joe Allard often, and I know you had a special relationship with him. Was he a big influence on your playing and teaching?

LIEBMAN: Yes. This year Miles and Joe died. The teachers are slowly going. Joe was a magical teacher. What I remember most about Joe was his sense of humanity. These are things that you realize best when the person is gone. It was his attitude towards the saxophone which was his attitude towards everything.

I didn't know him personally, but I knew him as a teacher and I could surmise that he was that way personally. Certainly, he appeared to be that way as a human being; following the natural way of doing things. To play is natural – no big deal. You put something in your mouth; it's an extension of your vocal cords just as when you speak and sing. You are articulating the vocal cords just as you did when you were a baby.

When you come out of the womb and cried, you're just doing the exact same thing and you are going to do it right to the day you die. So when you put this mouthpiece and the saxophone in your mouth, you're just extending that very thing that is in you already – the voice and the ability of the voice to express emotions by tone and color. That's all you have to worry about. So just put that thing in your mouth and play.

Now, of course I am simplifying. But this really was Joe's concept – instead of 'you got to do this', 'you got to do that', 'put your head here, your hands here.' His thing was to get you out of all the bad habits that you might have and to instill positive ones. He didn't even have a specific thing he wanted you to do necessarily as much as he wanted you to just flow, so he had exercises for that. He had ways of doing things with his mouth, exaggerating and assuming incredible positions. He'd demonstrate for you as a teacher should, but what you got out of it was that blowing a horn was as natural as speaking.

It's natural to blow air. The heavy thing is its simplicity. It's very Zen. In Eastern philosophy, the simplest is the deepest. The universal truths are the simplest and to Joe it was like that. It was a natural phenomenon to play this instrument. Let's take all the worry, all the craziness out of it. Let's enjoy ourselves and be natural and relaxed, and feel good about it. Let yourself speak through the horn in whatever idiom desired. It's a very simple way of looking at things which you reinforce with a variety of exercises.

There were a lot of metaphors, stories, and allusions to different things. Joe was very funny also in that respect. He was constantly reinforcing this natural thing. It was very magical and in a way, it was the simplest thing I had ever been taught, but the most deep. That was the Joe Allard experience for me.

MOSSBLAD: In closing, what would you like to say?

LIEBMAN: I've said it in a variety of ways about the artist. If you are an artist, you are ostensibly dedicated to expressing yourself through a chosen vehicle, or let's say art form. You job in life is to get as deep as possible into that means of expression in order to portray to other human beings the condition of life and what you feel about it. Hopefully, through that you will inspire them in their life and in their own way, whatever their job may be, whatever they do in life, to follow a similar path of sincerity, conviction, truthfulness, and the quest for clarity and expressing positive values.

That's really what we do. We are an example to others. That's what an artist really is in the end. He is example to others about how to go about something. We happen to do it by looking at a canvas or using a saxophone to play a G7 chord. This is the way we do it, but you know, a man who cuts trees is doing it in his work. It's a way of looking at something with clarity and dedication, and really meaning it, doing your best at it.

I think that's when you have chosen to be an artist, it becomes your life. You know it's like you are a messenger. You definitely are taking a very heavy roll. This is not a light thing and that's why you are put through the vicissitudes. How to make a living, to get recognition, fighting the horn, the constant battle, the psychological battle of knowing yourself are all part of the test.

It's not the test of a person going to war or having to fight for his life against an illness. This is different. Those are physical tests, but they're equal. It's psychological and emotional, and if you do that, you are an example to others because thank God, you found something that interests you enough to be that deeply into it. You are a lucky person, extremely lucky, and that is what you are conveying to other people on the most basic level.

Some may see an amazing aura of blue and gold or they see God come out of your music. Well, that's fantastic also, but really, I'm looking to level one. Level one is look at what I do. I love it. I'm pretty good at it because I've spent a lot of time doing it and you can do that, too. Look, I'm not harming anybody. I'm just turning out nice things. Music.

MOSSBLAD: Contributing to the world?

LIEBMAN: Contributing positive energy, which is really what we are here for. That's what it's about.

MOSSBLAD: Thanks Dave.

LIEBMAN: Okay, bro.

David Liebman: In Pursuit of Balance

by Christopher Collins

"Intensity, passion, experience, depth, balance, artistry...These were the adjectives that echoed through my mind as I prepared to interview Dave Liebman. As a saxophonist and pursuer of the jazz tradition, I had come to know Dave through years of listening, reading, and studying his musical language. I felt as though I was going to meet an old friend." – C.C.

Background

COLLINS: Give me some thoughts about your birthplace, your family background, and your initial playing experiences.

LIEBMAN: I grew up in Brooklyn, in a middle-class Jewish/Italian area. Music was in my home; my mother knew enough about music to insist that I take piano before I could choose any specific instrument. I took a little more than two years when I was ten; at twelve years old I played clarinet for one year and then finally saxophone.

Eventually I studied at a local school taught by a family in their house; the Bromley Studios in Brooklyn. I went for a piano lesson, saxophone lesson, and a combo workshop every Saturday morning. They taught you how to play dance music and helped me get a gig in the Catskills by age thirteen. I worked the Catskills my whole teenage life; weekends, April until October and the summers. There were a lot of great musicians who were playing in these show bands at hotels there. And they would have jam sessions; so this was really was my first exposure to hearing jazz.

COLLINS: When did you first hear a "name" jazz musician?

LIEBMAN: My first, really great experience with jazz was going to Birdland when I was 14. I saw Mulligan and Count Basie. But then I saw Coltrane. And that was a definite revelation, seeing him and hearing him – and then many times after that. I began to say: "Well, whatever this is, I gotta try to do it." I mean that was really the impetus and the inspiration to want to play the saxophone in that kind of way: jazz. I didn't know what "jazz" meant at that time; I had no idea what he was playing. But the power was incredible, and it took me right away. When I was 14, I was already convinced that this was a very amazing thing that was happening.

COLLINS: Many artists seem to reminisce about some turning point, some experience that propels them into their craft. Is that what you would consider it in your life?

[1] published in the *Jazz Educators Journal*, March 1995.

LIEBMAN: Definitely, by far. Seeing him many times and hearing the music. I never knew that music could be that powerful – any kind of music. I was into rock-and-roll when I was a kid, up to age twelve; my first idol was Elvis Presley. I had no idea what jazz was. So it was an education for me – and completely from feeling. There was really nowhere to go to learn jazz except your friends. I had a very good friend, a pianist in my first band named Mike Garson and we pursued it. So it was a long process to find out: trial and error, by asking.

The Saxophone

COLLINS: Could you discuss the profound effect the great master Joe Allard had on your saxophone playing?

LIEBMAN: At seventeen I went to Carnegie Hall studios, where he taught. I would take the subway and see him every Saturday for a few years and then on and off throughout the rest of his life. The main effect Joe had was talking about sax sound – it had nothing to do with style.

Blowing the saxophone is no different from the process of speaking and singing. The voice naturally adjusts to the sound that you hear in your head. This occurs below the threshold of consciousness; so all you have to do is let that work. Instead of moving this, tightening this, loosening this, his whole thing was "don't do anything and it'll be fine." I'm making it simple but that was really the thing. Now I was not mature enough to hear that message. I was the kind of student who wanted to know "#1, #2, #3" – what order of events and how to practice. I really didn't get the point until many years later when I finally wrote the book about the saxophone. Then I realized it is really that simple. You have to unlearn many bad habits.

COLLINS: In your book, *Developing A Personal Saxophone Sound*, you call them "habitualized bodily tensions" and you offer a plethora of helpful, detailed exercises that I see as ways of exploring the pallet of tonal colors available through physical self-awareness.

LIEBMAN: Right. That's well put.

COLLINS: This seems very familiar to me in other relaxation methods. Are you familiar with or utilizing the Feldenkrais technique or any similar methods?

LIEBMAN: Sure. I know Feldenkrais' assistant, now one of the heads of the movement in New York and I know general yoga and breathing techniques. Everything is basically to get your body to work the way you want it to and not to have it be encumbered by blockage – mental blockage which forms physical blockage. A lot of this is mind over matter. I mean, to get your larynx to articulate what you hear in your head is a natural, God-given thing. A baby cries and does so right away. A human's ability to vocalize emotion by tone, dynamics and all the vocal control you take for granted, as well as singing, are natural.

So don't block it by bad habits. Teachers can instill ideas that get in the way. Get back to the basics; get back to the natural. My main exercise, saxophone-wise, is to do the overtones. Do the harmonics, match the overtone sound with the natural "real" fingering. Get your larynx to sing the sound; hear it in your head before your larynx sings it. You don't have to do much in your embouchure at all. This leaves the embouchure – the lips, teeth, jaw, tongue – all open for expressiveness.

COLLINS: One of the things I like most about that book is the way you explain why you should do these exercises.

LIEBMAN: Joe gave me all of this and I didn't understand why at the time. He gave me the same lesson over and over again. I went to see him for years to try to keep getting what he really was saying. After I was with Miles, after I was with Elvin, after I was already recording, I got the point. Of course, the more mature I got as a saxophonist, the more I heard what he was saying. I started to write it down; asked him questions; started to analyze it to see the real reasons – the physics of it. I really wanted to understand which is why I wrote the book. He had his way of teaching but I felt the logic and reason for doing it could be clearer.

COLLINS: Do you recall any practicing techniques from your youth when you were really getting going, that helped you to break through and begin to understand and absorb the concepts of jazz improvisation?

LIEBMAN: Well, I always say the same thing: transcription. I'm a believer in exact duplication of a solo. I have to be clear about how exact because students will say they've trancribed. But then I play them this tape which I carry with me while teaching which has about thirty students of mine over the past many years now who have done this exact duplication. I put this tape on and you can't tell if it's Sonny Rollins or the student ... or Trane ... or Miles. And then I look at them and say: "Have you transcribed?" And they look at me and say: "No" – because most haven't done it to that degree.

COLLINS: Right.

LIEBMAN: The thing that's the most difficult to get about jazz is phrasing. You can't get it through a book. You get it through experience, first with a model to imitate. And phrasing is a big word: it means articulation, time feel, dynamics, how much spit in the sound, vibrato or non-vibrato, the attack. We're talking about ten to fifteen subtle elements that go into making it swing – making two notes come together in an eighth-note feel that is jazz.

Anyone can say: "Oh that's swinging; that's not swinging" in someone else's playing. But it's very hard to do on your own saxophone, on your trumpet, on your piano, because now you're talking

Improvisation

about getting the body to respond in a certain way to what your ear is telling you to do. That is subconscious. You can't explain it; it can only be done by imitation – I play, you play. I always talk about this. If we were in a slower society, you'd only learn by ear, not on paper. That is the way it was in ancient time. Certainly in Indian music it still exists quite a bit. You sit with the master and one day you took one phrase and that was it for two, three or four hours. Then the next day another phrase. That's exactly what we do when we transcribe in this way. We must copy it exactly to get the feeling.

Then there's this method of getting it to grow into where it becomes you. I mean, you are a combination of all you've learned. But first you have to have gone through it to such a degree that you are exactly what you've heard; not just close, but as close as possible. And you know, students can do it! That is a regimen that someone who wants to play jazz should go through. Some people object to it as parasitical; stealing or copying licks becomes a crutch. It's great that you sound like somebody. When kids who can't play do that, they sound good for one solo. They love it! They know they sound good on a couple of licks. We don't want that to be the substitute for finding some kind of direction on your own, some kind of personal way of doing things. But to start off, as long as you understand it's a means to an end, I don't see a problem.

COLLINS: And as a teacher, often finding what thing unlocks that energy, that excitement in a player is the real task. If you can get them to the level where they're excited about going to the next step, then they're on their own.

LIEBMAN: That's true, because suddenly they finally sound good and they know they sound good.

COLLINS: The methods you put together, like the chromatic approach, what about these?

LIEBMAN: It's completely from me – and from Richie Beirach and our work together. The main thing about the book, *A Chromatic Approach to Harmony and Melody*, is that after years of my playing outside of the tonality, cats would say: "How do you do it?" So I sat down and said: "What was I just doing?" Over about five years I figured it out after the fact. And then I figured I'd write a kind of workbook: a player could read this and get a sampling of many ways of thinking about that. How many ways can you talk about one thing? If you can take any one of those ways, it will hopefully lead into that kind of hearing by getting your mental process together.

I get a lot of guys that come in who are very competent, play very well in changes and want to go into chromaticism. Their problem is accepting dissonance. So I have to start them off first of all with hearing Bartók, Webern, Schoenberg, etc., and of course late Coltrane and Miles mid 1960's. After they listen to certain things, their ear accepts dissonance as being ok.

COLLINS: Your compositions cover so many areas. How do you approach the process of composing?

Composition

LIEBMAN: I compose according to a particular musical context. I have about four or five formats: a straight-ahead format (jazz changes, from complex to easy); a free context (where it's bass, horn, and drums-type thing – no chords, just bass line); a fusion context (not a jazz rhythm, more vamp-type music); the 20th-century classical context; and ethnic-type stuff (odd meters, more of an Indian thing, flutes). So I'm eclectic, and I'm proud to say it. I have a lot of musical interests and every record is different – which has been a problem attracting an audience in one way but it's been so interesting. I've really been able to delve into so many kinds of music. So for me compositon depends on the context I want. Within that I go with that particular sound in my ear.

Then I think: "What would I like to play on? Will I and the musicians who I play with be interested in and challenged by playing this tune or the particular musical problem posed by improvising on it?" Improvising is solving a musical problem. For instance, the album *The Tree* is a solo recording. It's all a metaphor of a tree's structure as compared to the evolution of an art form. So, branches equals fast, light, etc. If by confronting that problem I'm going to have to raise myself up to be at my best to do it, then that's a composition to me. That's really the basis.

I will often change something, so my writing is a building-block process. Though I didn't study formal composition in school, I did do a lot of studying of scores on my own – of course, jazz tunes – but Beethoven and everything. I've written some chamber music, so I had to study scores for the strings and the woodwinds and everything: Elliot Carter, Stravinsky, etc. I understand what came before which gives me a potpourri of many different influences, so I have tunes in many different contexts.

COLLINS: I know you have a B.A. in American History from New York University.

LIEBMAN: Yes.

COLLINS: .Did you at the same time do any formal music study?

LIEBMAN: When I was studying with Joe Allard I went to Charles Lloyd. It was a very unique and singular experience. He was playing with Cannonball Adderley and I went up to him at a club and said: "Do you teach?" I studied with him for a year, but he was not a formal teacher. It was like hanging out with one of the guys on the scene. This was 1965. That was the only jazz study I had besides a little with Lennie Tristano.

COLLINS: Any traditional study?

LIEBMAN: I studied with a contemporary composer, Ursula Mamlock who was up at the Manhattan School of Music. I traded a few lessons with David Baker many years ago. He wanted some of my chromatic ideas for which he gave me some composition lessons. In other words, along the way I got some formal bits and pieces, but from beginning to end I learned on my own through classical books and so forth.

Balance

COLLINS: In the "chromatic" book there are a couple of brief sections in which you discuss playing with a group and that interactive process. I've discussed with advanced players before the idea of pursuing things on a theoretical, almost mathematical level within a group, trying to "push that envelope" a little bit and yet not losing sort of that intimate, spontaneous, interactive thing that's so …
LIEBMAN: … passion …
COLLINS: … yeah, the group experience. People are dealing with that balance – any thoughts about that?
LIEBMAN: Well, it is THE question, because to grow is to push the envelope. That's well put. There's the physical envelope, like playing a long solo, playing fast, even playing a ballad. Harmony is a mental envelope; it's about how much the mind can think about – especially the improviser who does it on the spot.

I divide it into three things: the hand, the head, and the heart … "The 3-H Club". The hand is the technique; it's the physical skill needed to play any instrument. The head is the intellect; what we're talking about now. The heart is the passion; the soul, the emotion; and it is the cement that glues it all together. When you are a player – or even just as a person, no matter who you are or what you do – you are at given times a different balance of those three things. Sometimes you're using the brain more than you're using the technique and sometimes you're just out there with raw emotion.

Now in the great artists of all, from literature to painting, you probably could see a very good balance among those three throughout their career: "Man … great, deep thoughts, fantastic technique, and what passion!" Now when you're learning and develop something, you're not going to have those three balanced. You gotta' accept it: "For now, my head is going to be stronger than my heart." You can't get uptight about it and feel guilty and say: "I'm becoming like a machine, there's no heart in here", or the opposite: "It's all feeling – I don't know what I'm doing." These strengths are good, too, for awhile.

You see, the path of the artist is to balance these three eternally and to work on that balance. If anyone ever balances all three at the same time all the time, they wouldn't be on the planet any more; they'd be in Nirvana. They would be out there in the ozone, because that means perfect balance between all the aspects of what life is really about. The ability to handle things in the mind, the ability to translate it to people through communication and the ability to be able to learn something technically and do it well – that's the challenge.

So I have no problem when I talk to a cat and say: "Look, this is where you are right now – go with it. Remember you have to come back over here though and you've got all your life I hope. This is a long road you're on. The art road is forever. It's not five years and then you get a degree – it's forever. I have to assume that you're going to understand the balance thing, that you're going to pay attention to this other stuff. I want you to put down this transcription, go out and live a little bit, travel a little bit, see the world – love gained and lost. I also want you to sit down and read. I want you to put in some hours and learn to play that instrument. This is what I expect from you and from myself. You will play that balancing game forever. That's what's coming out in your playing. So when you hear a player displaying one of those three things, you know that he's hitting that one hard right there. But it's balance that you're looking for ultimately."

Impressions

COLLINS: I'd like to just mention a couple of the artists you've played with and get kind of a spontaneous response ... Richie Beirach.
LIEBMAN: Richie's a true artist. He has pursued his own thing. It is very hard to come up with a style. This music is only 100 years old now but it has moved at the rate of 400 years of classical music in those hundred years. Nobody sounds like him. You hear two notes; you know it's Richie. And I would hope it's the same with me. Very few people care to do it; to go out on an artistic limb. Finding yourself is psychologically like going in front of gun-fire. You don't know if you're going to come out, you don't know what it's going to be worth – it's scary. This guy did it and we did it together, which is why we had a long and strong alliance. For that, he will always be one of the top in so far as gaining my respect.

The thing that made us a common alliance, a common heart, was we're both very dramatic. And of course the thing that we had to learn – I know I had to learn – was how to control that – how not to just lay it all out at the first moment. See, when I saw Coltrane, I mistook that for completely laying raw emotion out. It was my mistake. He was weeding it out slowly but it was incredibly intense. I learned from Miles how to parcel it out because he was the master, at least on the horn, of giving you a little bit at a time and making you come back for more. He would say, "You don't have to spell out the whole thing, bro'! Leave it to the rhythm section! You're goin' to that chord, but you don't have to – do you need to play the I chord?

Do you really need to play the turnaround?" That's how I'm translating it. He was saying that if you lean this way musically, implication and innuendo are enough. Let the others take it. You don't have to spell it all out. He'd have you on the edge of your seat. And that's where I am now, emotionally, when I play: I try to parcel it out, hold back. When I was younger it was all out on the floor – all out right away ... as fast as I could.

COLLINS: Another name: Elvin Jones.

LIEBMAN: Well, of course, from a musical standpoint, he is the drums. First of all, he was with Coltrane. So to play with him was like a dream come true; to play with that kind of feel behind you and understand that deep, deep time – I mean just incontestable swing, especially at certain tempos that no one else can play. So to play with him was a tremendous experience.

But even more important with him especially, even more than Miles, was Elvin as a person; what he brings to the music, to see that and be with him every night, and to know him: his commitment, his power, his sincerity, conviction and truthfulness when he would get on that bandstand. He would draw the audience in. I never saw anything like that! To play with a kind of guy like that, and then of course, compounding it by going on and playing with Miles immediately after Elvin was great. Miles' thing was: "Get on the bandstand, man; you better be ready, baby, because this is the most important thing you do in your life" – and anything could happen.

So, this combination of an amazing tower of strength – a pillar of incredible strength and reservoir of the ocean which was Elvin – and going to this mercurial, temperamental, "on top of the case" Miles, who quivered with electricity when he was on the bandstand...by the time I was done with those two over four years, I didn't even know until later how heavy it was. I was still in a cloud for a couple of years. It took me until the 1980's, really another five to ten years to really understand, to really absorb it. And now I can even talk about it, the lessons playing with those two guys. Those were the masters and to play with them on a steady basis meant that I was very fortunate to have that. I want to stress again – not because of the music so much – because that you'd learn anyway – but the people, the way they did it. To see their lives, then to be close to them – it's amazing – what an experience!

The IASJ

COLLINS: I do want to ask you about the *International Association of Schools of Jazz*.

LIEBMAN: You know, I travel so much in the year that I get to really know a lot of people all over the world. And it came to me how cats in France didn't know who cats in Germany were. Or Norway didn't know the musicians in Spain or the teaching that was going on.

Borders really separated the music. So I wrote to people over a three-year period starting around '86: "Are you interested in uniting?" I called a meeting in Germany and lo and behold, twenty people from fifteen countries came representing a dozen schools. We met for our fifth year at the New School last June (1994).

It's a small organization at this time. We have very little money. My goal is different from the International Association of Jazz Educators' (IAJE) – the most important thing for me about IASJ is cross-cultural communication. That's my little slogan: "cross-cultural communication." I want kids to get together and use the music to understand each other, period. I don't really care what they play. To tell the truth, these things are secondary. The main thing is that a kid from Denmark is with a kid from Israel, from Japan. And this is what happens at our meetings. On Monday we form groups from our 50-60 students. Some of them can't even speak a common language to some of their combo partners. By Friday they're playing an amazing concert. I mean this is real work. The teachers, who are also from everywhere, get them going and by Wednesday, I have the teachers leave the room. This is not a clinic; it's a workshop.

I'd say 300-400 kids from maybe 30-40 countries have passed through and have gotten the address of a person they can stay with in Berlin or wherever. They've gotten gigs. I think we're really helping form a network of young students. Of course, they move on; new students take their place. But the idea of this school thing is to get the kids to interact. That's the only thing that means something. So it's really an organization built on trying to personalize relationships using jazz as the vehicle – jazz is the means to the end. Jazz will live; there's enough good guys out there. I care that it can be used – it's the old statement for music – as a universal language. I mean, these people communicate. And then they start talking politics, maybe; and they start talking about their country; and maybe these guys will know each other. Who knows what this can really come to? It could be a lot more than playing *All Blues* together.

That was the impetus of it and now we're in the throes of a non-profit organization. It's a pain in the neck, but we've met in New York, Graz, Sienna, Dublin, and The Hague...Our sixth will be in Tel Aviv in early July. You get to the end of the week and you see these kids sittin' there palsy-walsy who couldn't even talk to each other in the beginning of the week. It feels pretty good.

COLLINS: I always think about the statement you had on the back of one of the *Quest* albums; you defined the quest of an artist in a couple of sentences. What do you think is the next step in your quest?
LIEBMAN: Well, I don't think in terms like that any more. When I was younger I thought very dramatic; you learn later that everyday is

The Future

what's most important – not this monumental Nirvana at the end. You realize you've done everything you wanted to do. So I realize that it's the everyday thing that's the most important. First of all the personal, the family, the kid...that's number one. Number two is your effect on people through your work. For us, it's through music; and in our case, it's very much through education. We are affecting young people. Forget that they love Coltrane – that's really not the point. We're talkin' 22 year-old kids from all over the world who are going to do something – and certainly not a lot of them are gonna be playing jazz in fifteen years. We're helping form people and that's a heavy responsibility. That's the teacher thing that there's no end to – you just do. We do that all day.

The artistic side of me is to just keep getting that soprano to feel like it's my arm. Wouldn't it be nice to have an instrument feel like a toothbrush or feel like it's your shirt. And to be so natural with your instrument that it's a complete translation of your feelings. This is a goal until the day you die. You just want to keep playing continually better and improve at translating your feelings to the people who are interested – not to everybody, or you have to dilute your message – through your medium (in our case it's jazz, and in my case right now the soprano saxophone). The number of listeners may be small. They will grow very slowly, but there will be enough that you'll feel good about.

But if you think that you want to talk to everybody at the same time, then don't go into a heavy art form because you're going to be disappointed. And that is I'm sorry to say, the sad state of jazz in a lot of ways now. It's inevitable: something is underground, it becomes over-ground; everybody knows about it and it loses its center. The music has become trivialized and subject to the whims of the mass media marketplace. Everybody sounds the same. Of course I'm generalizing, but something of quality doesn't have to be popular. Yet every once in a while you do see that one student, that one person who comes up to you – usually a grown man or woman – and looks at you straight in the eye and you know this one knows what's going on.

That's the one you look for; that's the one out of the hundred. The other ninety nine I just want to understand that this is a heavy thing and they should respect it. But that one, I expect him to go out and take care of business. They must do this because we need this positive influence in the world. Jazz is still a wonderful thing. So if you're heavy and you know how to do that, please try to do something good with it because this world needs it. It's bad out there.

COLLINS: On a personal note, I started as a player, as a lot of kids do. I got involved, went to the university, started to learn some things, went on with it – and all of a sudden, before I knew it I'm teaching.

I enjoy that and the reasons I pursue it are the reasons you talk about: you learn a lot about yourself, you learn about really what you're doing, how you can express that. Now I'm having a problem trying to balance my artistic pursuits with doing the teaching gig. I know with all the different things you do, you've got to experience that dilemma.

LIEBMAN: I do. I have a very busy life. Still, I answer every student's letter. You have to find a way to balance it because the teaching thing is as important as the artistic thing, but you can't do the teaching thing without the input from the artistic side because it doesn't feel right and then you're not validated, especially teaching a performing art. You have to be involved in the field I feel, to teach certain aspects of it – and to be excited about it. My artistic work is my inspiration for teaching. If you don't have that, then the kids know and then they don't get the real buzz. They can get the information from a book. They're supposed to get the buzz from you. That's what you really are doing as a teacher. You're turning a kid on.

Like Joe Allard; I didn't know what he was talking about until later. Coltrane – I didn't know until later. It made me realize more and more that what you're doing as a teacher is inspiring students. And unless you're turned on, they're not going to be turned on. So this is the dilemma of the teacher in the performing arts; how to keep the artistic input hot, keep the fire going so that you are burning with it and the kid gets it. Without that you're not going to be effective as a teacher. It's a real dilemma of balance.

3   The Artistic Triangle ("The 3H Club")

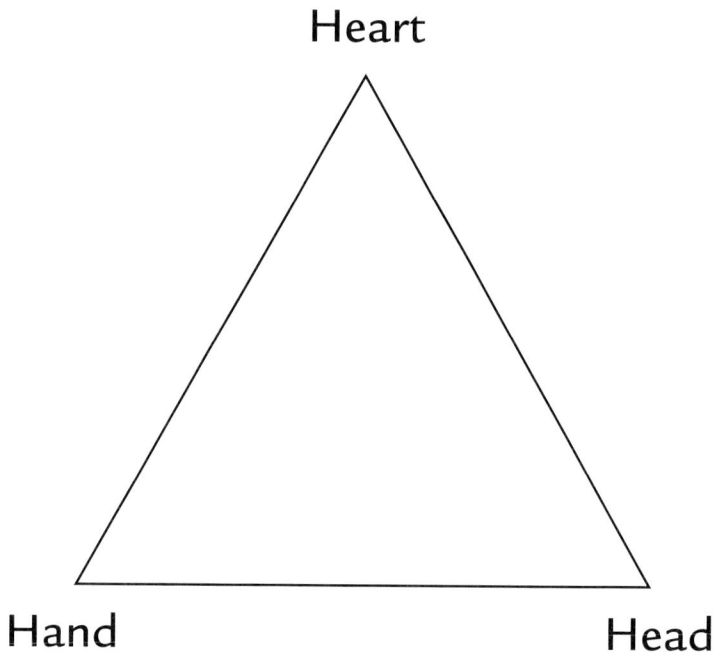

Heart
S o u l = E m o t i o n = A r t i s t :
emotional health; matters of the heart; sense of humanity; higher consciousness; passion; sprituality

Hand
B o d y = T e c h n i q u e = P e r f o r m e r :
physical health; mastering the craft; disciplined practice

Head
I n t e l l e c t = M i n d = T e a c h e r :
mental health; training the imagination; curiosity; morality; ethics; search for beauty and truth

My Ten All-Time Jazz Recordings

This is the "desert island" question often asked of musicians (or for that matter writers, playwrights, painters, poets and creative artists in general). That is what would be the indispensable recordings if you were only limited to ten? It does make you think about what makes an artistic statement lasting rather than transitory. For me, it means that when I hear something, one of the ways I judge it would be to ask whether I would still listen to it in say, ten years. I think that when one refers to a "classic" record, it means that the music transcends time and place. This is defnitely a worthwhile goal for an artistic vision.

As is often the case, one's major impressions are made early on during the first years of exposure to the particular art. For me, that was the middle 1960's and the chosen recordings are all from that period. It doesn't necessarily mean that nothing has impressed me since those formative years, but it does point out the importance of early reactions in forming a personal aesthetic. These are not in any particular order, but it is no secret that Coltrane was my major influence.

1. CRESCENT (JOHN COLTRANE): To pick one (or in this case two) recordings from someone as prolific as Coltrane or Miles Davis is extremely difficult. But this recording stands out because of the first two compositions called *Crescent* and *Wise One*. The first reason is that the time feel, which this unbelievable rhythm section attained here is the pinnacle of their particular brand of relaxed, laid back swing. And Coltrane's solos are a combination of modal and chord change ideas, completely varied in the shapes of their lines and rhythms. It sounds as if the solos were written out beforehand because of the unity of ideas and overall structure.

2. LIVE AT BIRDLAND (JOHN COLTRANE): The most exciting record of my choice, this was at the time of release (1963) a prime example of what it was like to see the group live. In fact, I often saw the quartet at Birdland in New York and this album is heavy with nostalgia for me. At one point when Trane is about to enter after McCoy Tyner's solo (on *The Promise*), Elvin Jones executes a roll with the bass drum and rest of the set which still brings goose bumps out. Also this recording features a heavy dose of soprano saxophone and was probably instrumental in inspiring me to concentrate on that horn years later.

3. SKETCHES OF SPAIN (MILES DAVIS): The combination of Miles' sound, lyricism and Gil Evans' arrangements results in probably my

all time favorite record in any genre. This is an example of music surpassing style, time and place. Like some of Bach and the late quartets of Beethoven, this music evokes such strong images that it is difficult to call it merely jazz. Also the ethnic overtone, here of Spain, was a harbinger of things to come in world music decades later.

4. FOUR AND MORE (MILES DAVIS): Again, a live recording which is incredibly exciting and at the same time, because of the ryhthm section (Williams, Carter, Hancock), groudbreaking in the musical sense. This record crackles with energy and enthusiasm with Miles riding the wave of his, at that time, new and young trio.

5. SPEAK NO EVIL (WAYNE SHORTER): This was one of a series of Shorter recordings on Blue Note in the mid 1960's when he was with Miles Davis. They are all full of some of the best crafted compositions in the history of jazz. This recording in particular strikes a group groove which is the pinnacle of great solos with swinging accompaniement. Along with Wayne, there is Hancock, Elvin Jones, Ron Carter and fluent, deep playing by Freddie Hubbard.

6. SUNDAY AT THE VILLAGE VANGUARD (BILL EVANS): From the early 1960's, this is the ultimate piano trio recording with the special magic that Bill, Scott LaFaro and Paul Motian achieved. This music is so personal that it makes me feel extremely sensitive when I hear it. Bill had it all for me – touch, lyricism, swing, harmonic depth and deep feeling. He influenced all intrumentalists.

7. A NIGHT AT THE VILLAGE VANGUARD (SONNY ROLLINS): My other major saxophone influence was this giant and along with Elvin Jones, this recording is Newk at the height of his be-bop playing. The technical aspect of his saxophone playing would make this a gem in itself, but also it swings incredibly hard.

8. KIND OF BLUE (MILES DAVIS): Much has been written about what is probably the most famous small group recording of modern jazz. The simplicity of the blues in contrast to the innovative modal approach demonstrated by this all star cast places this on most top ten lists.

9. THE REAL MCCOY (MCCOY TYNER): The modal side of McCoy (who also recorded some be-bop type albums under his leadership at this time) is heavily featured with great compositions and a stellar band of Elvin, Ron Carter and Joe Henderson. Again, wonderful modern small group playing which inspired so many musicians.

10. MAIDEN VOYAGE (HERBIE HANCOCK): One of the first well known examples of the use of suspended chords on the title tune, this was yet another great example of wonderful group playing and compositions.

There are some common threads throughout this list. First of all, four of my choices are live recordings. I think this is important because it highlights what jazz always represented to me which was the ideal of "The Solo". This means that symbolically the artist walks out on a tightrope with a safety net below (the other musicians) and proceeds to try and walk across, taking chances along the way and always experimenting with different approaches to the same desired goal. Also, besides the several choices each of Miles and Coltrane, almost all the other recordings feature the sidement from each of those respective bands during the early to middle 60's – Carter, Shorter, Williams, Hancock from Miles; McCoy and Elvin (on five of my choices) from Coltrane. It becomes rather obvious what bands I was listening to during this important stage of my development.

192　APPENDIX: MY TEN ALL-TIME JAZZ RECORDINGS

with McCoy Tyner in Paris, rehearsing for a concert, mid '80s (Private collection)

What Jazz Means To Me[1]

First of all, let me distinguish art from craft, not only in relation to jazz but all similar endeavors. Craft implies mastering technique to such a degree that the craftsman is competent enough to skillfully reproduce the general impression of the chosen art form. For a jazz musician, this simply means that one is trained enough to sound convincing using the rules and customs of the music. Art on the other hand goes beyond mere technique to portray the personal feeling of the artist towards whatever (s)he chooses. As Aristotle wrote: "The aim of art is to represent not the outward appearance of things, but their inward significance." A perennial challenge for all of the performing arts is the contradiction (or hopefully reconciliation) between entertainment and art. (In this sense, art also equals education.) If art instructs and ideally inspires, can it also entertain as it is asked to do? This in itself warrants a separate discussion.

Taking the above into consideration, much of what is called jazz does not qualify as art in my opinion. Therefore, "what means jazz to me" is extremely personal, for it is the manner through which I present my deepest feelings and thoughts to the world at large. After all, words, either verbally or written can be attributed to the speaker or writer's motives and on these grounds alone can be attacked as less than credible. But music, which literally goes into the air and is not tangible, is inherently devoid of human frailties, leaving it as a very personal message between artist and listener. Think about it – have you ever heard someone play resentful or selfish music, or even on the other hand, caring music? The fact that music is in the "ears of the beholder" (to borrow a cliché), opens it up to the heart and soul of the listener. If one speaks or writes, the message may indeed be loaded with subtle innuendo.

On a more abstract level and to clarify some of the above, a spontaneous, improvised art such as jazz purports to be, magnifies the moment. The art of improvising implies that the past or future are irrelevant. There is no time for value judgements or censoring when one is improvising. If only because of the amount of information which has to be filtered, the jazz artist must be in the now, present 100% or (s)he cannot accomplish the task at hand. (S)he would then have to rely on past habits or future projections, rather than immediate feeling. In fact, the constant struggle of the jazz player is just that; to stay in present time, psychologically and musically speaking. This allows the artist to interact both in relation to the vibrations felt from the immediate environment and audience, as well as the very real interaction hopefully taking place among all the musicians.

[1] published in: "Jazz And Dance", Djazzex Dance Company, Netherlands, 1995

From a totally different standpoint, jazz for me represents the ultimate synthesis of independence and dependence. Except for the occasional solo performance, the common small group format demonstrates participatory democracy at work. Though jazz challenges one's ability to express individuality, it also demands cooperation and teamwork for the greater musical good. There is a delicate balance called for between selflessness and ego, personified in trying to achieve a unified ensemble sound and equally, memorable individual solos. The social skills which are prerequisite for any interaction in everyday life are called upon in group playing, but using the language of music as the vehicle.

Jazz also requires fine tuning of the intellect as well as physical coordination on the highest level. The intellect has to have stored an incredible amount of technical, mathematical-like data in order to reproduce this information upon demand in the spontaneous jazz setting. Improvisation also demands immediate problem solving abilities in order to delineate the proper responses to both the musical challenges inherent in the music itself, as well as the necessary reactions in order to handle the consequences of group interaction. In common with some sports (especially basketball because of small team size), combining mind and body into a smooth flow is an eternal dilemma. Also, there is the matter of simultaneously expressing thought and feeling. In a musical gesture, how much is a mental cognition ("this is what is called for") versus raw feeling ("I can't explain what I played")?

Finally, the quest for an individual and recognizable sound or style which is one of the guiding parameters of playing jazz emphasizes an aspect I refer to as the "freedom thing". What an audience is really seeing/hearing is the ultimate expression of individual freedom. Especially in totalitarian societies, this rendering of man's need and legitimate right for self expression is potent and symbolic for all who hear the music. The "cry" in the sound of jazz cannot be denied by anyone who is the least bit sensitive.

Jazz means many other things besides that it is my major activity and vocation. I have learned more positive things in both the spiritual and mundane world directly from listening, experiencing and playing this music then would've been possible through all the religions and philosophies that are available. Added to this are the incredible personal relationships and deep human beings that I have encountered through this music. Without exaggeration, jazz has been the major force in forming me as a person.

Selected Quotations From:
Miles Davis and David Liebman – Jazz Connections: An Oral History[1]

- One of the things I learned from Miles was about leadership; how to lead a band, when and how to make decisions on the bandstand, how to work in the studio. In other words, how to organize the music. Miles could take a lead sheet or whatever and know when to play the melody, who should play what, who should double, when to leave things out, when to stop. Judgements concerning form were his greatest asset. Form means the whole thing from how to piece things together to when to go loud and soft. It's like a jigsaw puzzle and his ability to put that together was unmatched in music as far as I'm concerned.

- Miles did not doubt his instincts. If he felt you (or he) should play, you played then! It wasn't like there was ever a moment of indecision.

- He'd leave things in the middle of the air when he played. He rarely went to the end of the 32nd bar in a song form and resolved it to the top. He'd stop and go, maybe leave 4 bars out or 8. Then he'd come in on the 3rd bar of a phrase instead of the first bar. He had unusual starting and ending points, unusual places to begin or end a phrase. What I realized was that he was thinking about the rhythm section; that they need space to be inventive. If you leave space, they will fill it up. Then you have them to play off of. Miles was one of the greatest listener/players of all time. Of course, we all listen when we play, but his ability was beyond cliché. It seems his mind was constantly shifting between the rhythm section and himself. He had incredible perceptive abilities.

- Another thing about Miles was his ability to hear the bass. I'm not just talking about the rock period. His way of hearing from the bottom to the top was remarkable. I don't have that yet. Usually you hear the lines on top and the harmony because that's in the middle – the drums are obvious to everyone. His interaction with bass players was uncanny: Paul Chambers, Ron Carter, Dave Holland, even Michael Henderson, and of course Marcus Miller. He could play off of the bass line and use it as a reference. He would hear the bass and actually included it somehow in his lines.

1 Edward Mellen Press, 1996/97

- Miles was always the guy who could play the "wrongest" note and make it sound great. He could play a C# on a C chord, but the way he would intone it, bend it, place it, blow it, would make you say: "That doesn't sound wrong!!"

- One can listen to records forever, but until you stand next to another horn player and actually witness it from three feet away, you can't realize a lot of what I'm saying. What you see is this amazing ability to consistently mold a note, all the time it is ever-changing. An ability to do that means he's placing an importance on not so much what you play but how. This means where you place it in the rhythmic scheme, how you express it, when or when not to play it.

- He didn't seem to verbalize or didn't care to, but in truth, his style is very thoughtful, almost planned. His greatest genius was to continually change the environment around himself. The rhythm section changes, the sound of the instruments, the music; but he's still playing the blues, the same kind of lines. Like Duke, he looked beyond his own playing for how it all sounds. Look around you – look at your presentation – look at the arrangement. It's like being the director of a show or movie. He's doing everything at the same time.

- You want to cry almost, especially when you hear the ballads. The guy had a sound. He had a way of expressing beauty and poignancy that was so touching to whomever listened; this will above all remain as a beautiful, lyrical voice. There have been a few others: Stan Getz, Chet Baker, Bill Evans – but combined with this incredible perspective over several generations and the influence that the sidemen have had, the cumulative effect is staggering. When it boils down, it is the beauty above all that shines through and what makes people remember someone. He had that beauty.

Proposal To Form The International Association Of Schools Of Jazz (IASJ), 1987

My friends:

First of all, I bring you all greetings from Caris and myself, hoping that this note finds you and your associates in good health; and of course, best wishes for the holiday and New Year season.

As you are aware of, I have been teaching seminars and workshops worldwide for some years now. Most of you have seen me teach and/or perform, either alone or in conjunction with my closest associates. Because of my wide travels and experiences, I am in a very advantageous position to make some observations about jazz education.

It is becoming increasingly clear that jazz has finally attained the status of a bona fide art form with a well established legacy. Of course, there is still far to go in matters like funding and so on, but in general the situation has vastly improved over the past decade. Accompanying this positive development is the fact that there is a growing demand for education in the field. This is apparent from the proliferation of schools and associations all over the world featuring jazz education, as well as the large numbers of interested students. It is precisely because of this global growth that I feel it is time to form a network and put like-minded people in touch with each other.

Jazz has truly become universal. It has largely extended beyond its American roots to embrace all nationalities. More and more, the majority of students are from outside the U.S. To my mind, even the word "jazz" itself is an anachronism. This field could better be described as contemporary improvised music. With this description, there is the implication and the reality of a true fusion of all contemporary musical idioms. This means the mixtures of peoples and musical heritages from the world community. Cannot jazz include Spanish, Israeli, Danish, Japanese, etc. influences all together?

Of course the answer is obvious. The fact that groups regularly integrate music from all cultures and styles is taken for granted by contemporary improvising musicians. Notable examples include the group Oregon, the Spanish and Indian influenced music of John McLaughlin, and even in recent Miles Davis groups, there have been percussionists from Denmark and France. With the artists already mixing together, it follows that the educational philosophy offered to young students should be similar. I am proposing that a network be set up whereby we could institute a wide variety of programs attempting to achieve the goal of high level communication between various centers of jazz learning. By "we", I am referring to the private type of jazz schools (for at least the beginning). There are many possibilities and avenues of cooperation:

- An exchange program between schools including both students and faculty.
- A newsletter listing events and student/faculty achievements; also including articles and comments on various musical or other subjects.
- A yearly meeting/seminar at each of the participants schools; where eventually hundreds of students could be together.
- Multi-national big bands, small combos, sax ensembles, vocal ensembles, brass ensembles, etc., with the possibility of appearances at festivals, T.V., etc.

The possibilities are endless!!!

If such a program could really get going, governments, corporations, foundations and cultural societies would see a great opportunity to help us; the media would have something truly approaching brotherhood to focus upon; the musical interaction could result in widened work opportunities for all involved and most important, the art would be constantly rejuvenated and energized if only because of the participation of so many young people. Even curriculum and texts could be helpfully shared and improved upon. This could be a true United Nations of Contemporary Improvised Music. The underlying premise is that jazz, an already acknowledged universal music and language, serve as the context and rationale for the fostering of cross-cultural communication and inter-cultural creativity.

The classical musicians have been doing this sort of things for years. It is time that we begin to organize; small at first, slowly, but truly in a spirit of cooperation.

At this time I am interested in your reactions and comments. Please write to me at my home address indicated on the first page. If there is enough positive response, we can move on from there.

You all know me personally, some better than others. You are aware of my organizational and leadership powers if you have ever seen me teach. And hopefully, there is your recognition of my artistry. You can be sure that I wouldn't begin such a project without realizing its difficulty and potential. I have been looking for a way to spread the power of this music for some years. I hope you can help me realize this potential to really affect the world in a positive manner.

Sincerely yours,
David Liebman

Appendix: Proposal to Form the IASJ

Note: In 1989, the IASJ was formed and at present (1996) includes schools and individuals from 35 countries on every continent.

from the first meeting of the IASJ in Rottenburg, Germany, 1989 (© Hans Gruber)

8   The Return of the Tenor

The following lines and notes were written for a 1996 release "The Return of the Tenor – Standards" (Double Time – USA). They are a pretty clear description of my feelings about playing the tenor again.

The Tenor – The Return of the Tenor may sound like a sci-fi flick, but really it is nothing so dramatic. I could never give up the soprano, which after exclusively concentrating on for 15 years does at its best feel like an extension of my entire physical and mental being. But the tenor beckons for several reasons, both musical and personal. I am approaching 50 years old a few months from this writing and I'm marking off the occasion with some special projects: a new, updated *Self-Portrait of a Jazz Artist* (Advance Music) as well as a solo project which will serve as a follow-up to the *Loneliness of a Long Distance Runner*, recorded near my 40th year for CMP in 1985 (which is by the way one of my personal favorites). Coming to terms with the big horn has been looming in my head as a kind of mid-life challenge. After all, I began tenor at thirteen years old with my first teacher, Nat Shapiro, and went on to study with the legendary Joe Allard. Until 1980, it was one of the constants in my teenage and adult life as well as a vehicle of inspiration through Coltrane and Rollins which propelled me towards my life's work of playing and understanding jazz. It's time to "fess-up" which I will do as honestly as possible here.

One of the reasons I put the tenor down, besides wanting to see if concentrating on soprano would further me artistically, was because the style that I played in (referred to as post-Coltrane) was by the late 1970's becoming too common and clichéd for my taste. I figured that the next (one or two) generations of Trane-inspired tenorists would extend the language beyond what Steve Grossman and myself had done (especially when we recorded "Live at the Lighthouse" with Elvin Jones in 1972) and that would be that!! To my ears, by and large this has not happened, at least at a level prominent enough to have a major effect. Outside of some very individual tenorists who have constructed a unique approach, it is my feeling that with our culture's emphasis upon and rewarding of conformity rather than originality, much creative energy has been increasingly stifled in the past decade or so. What I mean is that I haven't heard much on the tenor in these 15 years that impresses me beyond great flash and technique.

The result of this feeling is that I am personally less self-conscious about my Coltrane roots and in fact am not deterred from facing this head on; something I was not mature enough to do when I was younger. Also, to manifest two different aspects of one's personality on each horn doesn't disturb me as it did when I wasn't really confident about who I was. I know myself better now and the confusion of identities I was experiencing playing tenor, soprano and flute is no longer a problem. I'm not worried about sounding like someone else as I feel that the point has been made on soprano.

I must admit that friends and associates who knew my tenor playing were very supportive and made me feel they missed my sound and approach. After all, where an instrument begins is in the sound. One can only do so much manipulation of technique and equipment before the inborn physical and mental attributes of an individual will assert themselves to form a personal sound. I don't know where my tone comes from, but I do know what other tones I like and dislike. Now when I hear my tenor, I realize that the sound is rather distinctive. Finally, after recently recording on the tenor in two, as of now unreleased free jazz settings (which incidentally takes me back to the 1960's scene where I began) and then doing this present set of standards in early 1996, I hear how differently I treat the two horns. I know for a fact that by being so close to Miles Davis' playing for a few years in the early 1970's, I consciously and unconsciously absorbed some definite trumpetisms on the soprano – in general, a way of finessing the music – playing over, around and under it. To be honest, pushing a lot of emotion through the soprano by and large is not very attractive aesthetically to my taste. I have been guilty of it, so I know!! In my better musical moments I have used the soprano as a kind of gliding voice, beguiling the rhythm section, cautiously "tiptoeing through the tulips" in a sense, but the tenor is different!!

It's a wild animal, a bucking bronco. With it, I tend to go more directly head to head inside the music. Maybe this translates musically to more chances taken, more densely packed lines, more roughness and use of overtone combinations in the sound, more vocalizations, freer and faster rhythmic groupings, a pronounced Rollins influence, etc. For sure, it feels like a major piece of machinery compared to the "fish" horn. The tenor is back in my arsenal for the time being.

9 Postscript

The act of improvisation is symbolic on several accounts. The quest for excellence and beauty while searching for the unknown is in itself an affirmation of the life force. This striving is a reflection of human existence in all its manifestations. The species is not satisfied with only sustenance and shelter.

Trying to hear, think and play that special musical sound in the heat of the improvisational process is what motivates this kind of artist to continue the search, just as all men strive towards higher goals. Feelings and intellect attempt to combine and balance each other.

Improvisation is also an affirmation of the need for the human spirit to express itself. Man's yearnings, his joy and suffering, all his feelings need to be expressed in some manner. This need cannot be suppressed for long by a totalitarian society of other persons, nor by natural forces, all of which at times conspire to thwart man's achievements. Communication of all of these feelings to others is one of the major functions of artistic creation.

Finally, the spontaneity involved in this art form underscores the act of being alive in the moment; to take advantage of every breath and opportunity to live for the now. Jazz improvisation in itself may or may not be relevant to our changing world, but the spirit realized in it touches all those who play or listen to it.

Books and Records

A Personal List

The following books and recordings have been among the most influential in my development.

Books

GOLDMAN, ALBERT, Ladies and Gentlemen, Lenny Bruce, Random House, New York.
VAN GOGH, VINCENT, Dear Theo: Autobiography of Vincent Van Gogh, edited by Irving Stone, Doubleday & Co., New York, 1969.
HODIER, ANDRÉ, Jazz, Its Evolution and Essence, Grove Press, New York, 1956.
BERNSTEIN, LEONARD, The Unanswered Question: Six Talks at Harvard, Harvard Univ. Press, Cambridge, Mass., 1976.
LENDAVI, ERNO, Bela Bartók, An Analysis of His Music, Kahn & Averill, London, 1971.
STRAVINSKY, IGOR, Igor Stravinsky, Poetics of Music, Harvard Univ. Press, Cambridge, Mass., 1982.
NKETIA, J.H. KWABENA, The Music of Africa, W.H. Norton & Co., New York, 1974.
HINDEMITH, PAUL, Elementary Training for Musicians, Schott Music Corp., New York, 1949.
KHAN, HAZRAT INAYAT, The Sufi Message of Hazrat Inayat Khan-Vol. II- The Mysticism of Sound, Camelot Press, London, 1963.
DIMONT, MAX I., Jews, God and History, Simon & Schuster, Inc., New York 1962.
THREE INITIATES, The Kybalion, Yoga Society, Chicago, Illinois, 1940.
SWAMI NIKLILANDA, The Gospel of Sri Ramakrishna, Ramakrishna Vivekananda Center, New York, 1969.
DEROPP, ROBERT S, Drugs and the Mind, GrovePress, New York, 1960.
VEBLEN, THORSTEIN, The Theory of the Leisure Class, Viking Press, New York, 1962.
FROMM, ERICH, The Art of Loving, Harper & Row, New York, 1956.
JUNG, CARL, Memories, Dreams and Reflections, Vintage Books Edition, 1965.
KRISHNAMURTI, J.- The First and Last Freedom, Quest Books, 1954.
NEVINS, ALLAN & HENRY STEELE COMMAGER, The Pocket History of the United States Pocket Library.
BEARD, CHARLES A., An Economic Interpretation of the Constitution of the United States, The MacMillan Co., New York, 1962.
CALDWELL, TAYLOR, Great Lion of God, Fawcett-Crest Books.
BOULEZ, PIERRE, On Music Today, Faber and Faber, London, 1978.
COKER, JERRY, Improvising Jazz, Prentice Hall, Englewood Cliffs, New Jersey.
– , Listening to Jazz, Prentice Hall, Englewood Cliffs, New Jersey, 1978.

Berlioz, Hector & Richard Strauss, Treatise on Instrumentation, Kalmus Piano Series, 1948.
Sessions, Roger, The Musical Experience of Composer, Performer and Listener, Princeton University Press, Princeton, New Jersey, 1974.
Copland, Aaron, Music and Imagination
Persichetti, Vincent, Twentieth Century Harmony, Norton & Co., New York-London, 1961.
Schoenberg, Arnold, Fundamentals of Musical Composition, Faber and Faber Ltd., London, 1967.
– , Structural Functions of Harmony, Norton & Co., New York, 1969.
Kochevitsky, George, The Art of Piano Playing, Summy-Birchard, Princeton, New Jersey, 1967.
Zukov, Gary, The Dancing Wu Lei Masters, Bantam Books, New York, 1980.
Neustadt & May, Thinking in Time, Free Press, New York, 1986.
Fuller, Buckminister, Critical Path, St. Martin's Press, New York, 1981.
Borges, Jorge Luis, Labyrinths, New Directions Publishing, New York, 1964.
Assorted poets, Japanese Haiku, Peter Pauper Press, Mt. Vernon, New York, 1964.
Hesse, Hermann, Siddhartha
– , Magister Ludi, Bantam Books, 1969.
Dostoyevsky, F., The Idiot, Penguin Classics, England, 1955.
Kazantzakis, Nikos, The Last Temptation of Christ, Simon & Schuster, New York, 1960
Michener, James, The Source, Random House, New York, 1964.
Wilson, Colin, The Mind Parasites
Grossman, Albert, Elvis, Avon Books, 1981.
Malcolm X, The Autobiography of Malcolm X, Grove Press, New York
Schoenberg, Harold, The Lives of the Great Composers, Mcdonald Futura Publ., England, 1980.
Clavell, James, Shogun
Shirer, William, The Rise and Fall of the Third Reich
Mailer, Norman, Of a Fire on the Moon, New American Library, New York, 1971.
– , Miami and the Siege of Chicago
Kafka, Franz, The Trial, Vintage Books, New York, 1969.
Anonymous, I Ching, translated Richard Wilhelm, Bollingen Series XIX, Princeton University Press, Princeton, New Jersey, 1984.
Gridley, Mark, Analysis of Jazz Styles, Prentice Hall, Inc., Englewood Cliffs, New Jersey, 1978
Schuller, Gunther, Early Jazz, Oxford University Press, Inc., New York, 1968
Anonymous, The Tibetan Book of the Dead
Gould, Glenn, The Glenn Gould Reader, Alfred A. Knopf, New York, 1984.
Schuller, Gunther, Musings, Oxford University Press, New York, Oxford, 1986.
Piston, Walter, Orchestration, Norton & Co., New York, 1955.

RIMSKY-KORSAKOV, NIKOLAI, Principles of Orchestration, Dover Publishing, 1964
COGAN AND ESCOT, Sonic Design, Prentice Hall, New Jersey, 1976
CHAMBERS, JACK, Milestones I and II, William Morrow, New York, 1985
UHLEHLA, LUDMILLA, Contemporary Harmony, Collier MacMillan, Ltd., London 1966, Advance Music, 1994
BROOK, PETER, The Shifting Point, Harper and Row, New York, 1987
GLEICK, JAMES, Chaos, Viking Press, New York, 1987
HAWKING, STEPHEN, A Brief History of Time, Bantam Books, New York, 1988
CAMPBELL, JOSEPH, The Power of Myth, Doubleday, New York 1988
– , Myths To Live By, Bantam Books, New York 1972
WHITFIELD, CHARLES L., The Child Within, Health Communications, Inc., Deerfield Beach, 1989

Records

COLTRANE, JOHN
　Live at Birdland, Crescent, Meditations, Ballads, A Love Supreme, Plays the Blues, Giant Steps, Coltrane, Impressions
DAVIS, MILES
　Sketches of Spain, Kind of Blue, Round Midnight, Miles Smiles, ESP, Four and More, My Funny Valentine, Live In Europe
EVANS, BILL
　The Village Vanguard Sessions, Live at Montreux Vol. I, Trio '64, Conversations with Myself
SHORTER, WAYNE
　Speak No Evil, Night Dreamer, Ju-Ju
HENDERSON, JOE
　Inner Urge
COREA, CHICK
　Now He Sings, Now He Sobs; The Brain
HANCOCK, HERBIE
　Maiden Voyage, Empyrean Isles
LITTLE, BOOKER
　Out Front
DOLPHY, ERIC
　Live at the Five Spot
KONITZ, LEE
　Motion
WILLIAMS, TONY
　Spring
MINGUS, CHARLES
　Let My Children Hear the Music, Black Saint and Sinner Lady
ROLLINS, SONNY
　A Night at the Village Vanguard, The Standard Sonny Rollins
HUBBARD, FREDDIE
　Body and Soul, Hub-tones

COLEMAN, ORNETTE
  New York is Now, Free Jazz
GETZ, STAN
  Focus, Sweet Rain
BLEY, PAUL
  Footloose
TYNER, MCCOY
  Tender Moments, Expansions, The Real McCoy
THE ISLEY BROTHERS
  The Heat is On
SLY AND THE FAMILY STONE
  Fresh
HENDRIX, JIMI
  Band of Gypsies
THE BEATLES
  Sg't. Pepper's, Magical Mystery Tour, Abbey Road, The White Album
THE CREAM
  Disraeli Gears, Wheels of Fire
BROWN, JAMES
  Live at the Apollo
WONDER, STEVIE
  Songs in the Key of Life, Innervisions, Music of the Mind
GAYE, MARVIN
  What's Going On
EARTH, WIND AND FIRE
  Spirit, All'n All, I Am
MITCHELL, JONI
  Ladies of the Canyon, Blue
TAYLOR, JAMES
  Sweet Baby James
CROSBY, STILLS AND NASH
  Crosby, Stills and Nash
REDDING, OTIS
  The Immortal Otis Redding
THE BAND
  Music From Big Pink
BARTÓK, BELA
  Six String Quartets (Budapest String Quartet)
IVES, CHARLES
  The Concord Sonata (John Kirkpatrick)
DEBUSSY, CLAUDE
  Preludes, Vol. 2 (Monique Haas)
STOCKHAUSEN, KARLHEINZ
  Gruppen for 3 Orchestras (Symphony Orchestra of Hamburg)

DEBUSSY AND RAVEL
    String Quartets (The Julliard Quartet)
STRAVINSKY, IGOR
    Symphony for Wind Instruments (Swiss Orchestra/Ansermet)
BEETHOVEN
    The Late Quartets (The Fine Arts Quartet)
BHAVALU
    South Indian Music; Impressions (Nonesuch Records)
SANTAMARIA, MONGO
    Yambu
THE ALI BROTHERS
    Indian vocal (Odeon Records)
GHOSH, PANALLAL
    Indian flute (Odeon Records)
KHAN, VILAYET
    Sitar (Odeon Records)
SHAKUHACHI MUSIC
    A Bell Ringing in the Empty Sky (Nonesuch Records)
SHANKAR, RAVI
    The Music of India (Angel Records)
DEPLAYA, MANITAS
    Flamenco Guitar (Connoisseur Society)

Discography

* designates recordings as leader
† designates recordings as co-leader

1967	Och Hans Vanner, Lars Werner, Love (Sweden)
1970	*Nightscapes, David Liebman/Carvel Six, CBS/Sony (Japan)
	Hino's Journey to Air, Terumasa Hino, Love TP (Japan)
	Brief Replies, Ten Wheel Drive, Polydor
	Peculiar Friends, Ten Wheel Drive, Polydor
	The Best of Ten Wheel Drive, Polydor
1971	My Goals Beyond, Mahavishnu John McLaughlin, Douglas
	Genesis, Elvin Jones, Blue Note
	Merry Go Round, Elvin Jones, Blue Note
1972	†Open Sky, Open Sky Trio
	Mr. Jones, Elvin Jones, Blue Note
	On the Corner, Miles Davis, Columbia
	Live at the Lighthouse, Elvin Jones, Blue Note (re-released 1990) Vols. 1+2, Blue Note
	Jazz Jamboree '72, Elvin Jones, Polskie Nagruna (Poland)
	From a Whisper to a Scream, Esther Phillips, Kudo
1973	Berlin '73, Miles Davis, Jazz Masters
	*First Visit, David Liebman, Phonogramm/Phillips (Japan), (also released in 1980 by West), 1992 Westwind
	People and Me, Abbey Lincoln, Inner City (Nippon Phonogram, Japan)
	*Lookout Farm, David Liebman, ECM/Polydor (Germany)
	†Spirit in the Sky, Open Sky Trio, P.M.
	En Concert, Miles Davis, Europe I (France)
	Miles and Beyond, Miles Davis, Lyfe
	Call It What It Is, Miles Davis, JMY
	Another Bitches Brew, Miles Davis, Jazz Door
	Black Satin, Miles Davis, Jazz Masters
	Palais des Sports, Miles Davis, Lyfe
1974	Dark Magus, Miles Davis, CBS/Sony (Japan)
	*Drum Ode, David Liebman, ECM/Polydor (Germany)
	Get Up With It, Miles Davis, Columbia
	Somesvilles, Fred Thompkins, Festival

Appendix: Discography

Ljubljana Jazz Festival '75, Na Koncertinom Podiju (various artists) Jugoton (Yugoslavia)	*1975*
Year of the Ear, Baird Hersey, Bent BRSI	
*Sweet Hands, David Liebman, A&M/Horizon	
Live From Onkel Po's Carnegie Hall, (various artists with Lookout Farm), Polydor (Europe)	
Father Time, Frank Tusa, Inner City (Enja-Germany)	
Passing Dreams, Badal Roy, Adamo	
Ashiribad, Badal Roy, Trio (Japan)	
†Forgotten Fantasies, David Liebman/Richard Beirach, A&M/Horizon	
Bittersuite In The Ozone, Bob Moses, Mozown	
From Russia With Jazz, Prince Igor Yahivelich, Different Drummer	
What'cha Gonna Do For Me, Steve Satten, Columbia	
*Light'n Up Please, David Liebman, A&M/Horizon	*1976*
Wishes / Kochi, Masabumi Kikuchi, East Wind (Japan), Inner City	
A Place Within, Link Chamberlain, Muse (*also released as: What's New, David Liebman, Jacobson Tobacco Road (Germany))	
Main Force, Elvin Jones, Vanguard	
*The Last Call, David Liebman, Ego (Germany)	
New Moon in Zytron, Jame Zytro, Pacific Arts	*1977*
Bishop's Bag, Bishop Norman Williams, Theresa	
*Pendulum, David Liebman, Artist's House	*1978*
†Omerta, David Liebman/Richard Beirach, Trio, Breaktime (Japan)	
Tiger in the Rain, Michael Franks, Warner Bros.	
Flaming Spirit, Ric Drexler, Claremont	
*The Opal Heart, David Liebman, Enja (Germany)	*1979*
Matsuri, Chin Suzuki, CBS/Sony (Japan)	
All in All, Masahiko Satoh, CBS/Sony (Japan)	
Faun, John McNeil, Steeplechase (Denmark)	
Secret Places, Nina Sheldon, Plug	
City Connection, Terumasa Hino, Flying Disc (Japan)	
Dancing on the Table, Niels Henning Ørsted Pedersen, Steeplechase (Denmark)	
*Doin' it Again, David Liebman, Timeless (Holland)	
"Mr. Foster", Al Foster, Nippon/Columbia (Japan)	
Who's Who, John Scofield, Arista Novus	
Family, Bob Moses, Sutra (also titled: Devotion, Soul Note, Italy)	
Wheels of Colored Light, Bob Moses, Open Mind (Germany)	
Home, Steve Swallow, ECM (Germany)	
*Dedications, David Liebman, CMP (Germany)	
*What It Is, David Liebman, CBS/Sony (Japan) Columbia (USA)	

1980   DAY DREAM, Terumasa Hino, Flying Disk (Japan)
        HEADS UP, Stone Alliance, PM Records
        *IF THEY ONLY KNEW, David Liebman, Timeless (Holland), MCA - Impulse (USA)
        SUSTO, Masabumi Kikuchi, Columbia (Japan)
        MINERVA'S OWL, T. Akase, Continental (Japan)
        MOUNTAINS, N. Ino, Nippon/Columbia (Japan)

1981   IMPRESSIONS OF CHARLES MINGUS, Teo Macero, Palo Alto
        CLEAN SWEEP, John McNeil, Steeplechase (Denmark)
        WINGS, Chin Suzuki, Trio (Japan)
        FUSION SUPER JAM, Aurex Jazz '81, EWJ 80210 (Japan)
        VISITING THIS PLANET, Tisziji Munoz, Anami Music
        *MEMORIES, DREAMS, REFLECTIONS, David Liebman, P.M. Records
        HEARING VOICES, Tisziji Munoz, Anami Music
        †QUEST, Liebman/Beirach Quartet, Trio, Breaktime (Japan), Palo Alto (USA)
        SO NO ONE ELSE CAN HEAR, Jimmy Cobb, CVR
        COUPE DE TÊTE, Kip Hanrahan, American Clave

1982   †EARTH JONES, Elvin Jones, Palo Alto
        MISTLETOE MUSIC, (various artists), Palo Alto
        *"LIEB" CLOSE-UP, David Liebman, CVR
        †SPIRIT RENEWED, David Liebman, Bob Moses, Eddie Gomez, Timeline Records
            (France 1991)

1983   SPIRITS OF HOPI, Jill McManus, Concord
        MARS, Steve Masakowski, Prescription Records
        THINGS WE DID LAST SUMMER, John McNeil, Steeplechase (Denmark)
        PICADILLY LILLY, University of Miami, Concert Jazz Band
        INTROSPECTION, Jukkis Votila, Finn Records, Polydor (Finland)
        VISIT WITH THE GREAT SPIRIT, Bob Moses, Gramavision

1984   *SWEET FURY, David Liebman, From Bebop to Now (Canada)
        THE SPELL, Klaus Ignatzek, Nabel (Germany)

1985   *PICTURE SHOW, David Liebman, PM Records
        TENDER MERCIES, Klaus Ignatzek, Nabel Records (Germany)
        †DOUBLE EDGE, David Liebman/Richard Beirach, Storyville (Denmark)
        †THE DUO LIVE, David Liebman/Richard Beirach, Advance Music (Germany)
        NEW HANDS, Lars Danielsson, Dragon (Sweden)
        †GUIDED DREAM, Tolvan Big Band with David Liebman, Dragon (Sweden)
        *THE LONELINESS OF A LONG DISTANCE RUNNER, David Liebman, (Germany)
        ACOUSTICAL SUSPENSION, Teo Macero, Teresa Gramophone Dr. Jazz FW

1986   THE STORY OF MOSES, Bob Moses, Gramavision
        †QUEST II, Liebman/Beirach Quartet, Storyville (Denmark)

APPENDIX: DISCOGRAPHY

INNER VOICES, Paolo Fresu, Splash (Italy)
INNER RHYTHM, Robert Jospe, Tundra

*HOMAGE TO JOHN COLTRANE, David Liebman, Owl/EMI Records (France), Blue Note (USA) 1987
†MIDPOINT, Quest, Storyville (Denmark)
*THE ENERGY OF THE CHANCE, David Liebman, Heads Up
†A TRIBUTE TO JOHN COLTRANE, David Liebman/Wayne Shorter, King-Paddle Wheel (Japan), Columbia Records (USA)
RAH, Billy Hart, Gramavision
ABRACADABRA, Jeff Palmer, Soul Note (Italy)
MEN'S LAND, Michel Portal, Label Bleu (France)

†NEW YORK NIGHTS, Quest, Pan (Japan) 1988
*TRIO & ONE, David Liebman, Owl/EMI (France)
†NATURAL SELECTION, Quest, Evidence
UNEXPECTED, Zaviot with David Liebman, Jazz Is (Israel)
A SIP OF YOUR LIPS, Ricardo Del Fra, Ida (France)
VOICE OF THE NIGHT, Ed Sarath, Timeline (France)
DAY AND NITE, McGill Jazz Ensemble with David Liebman, McGill (Canada)

*TRIO PLAYS COLE PORTER, Red Records (Italy) 1989
*TIMELINE, David Liebman, Owl/EMI (France)
VISIONS, Tom Harrell, Contemporary
†CHANT, David Liebman & Richard Beirach, CMP (Germany)
SAIL AWAY, Tom Harrell, Contemporary
SOMETHING ELSE, Jack Bruce, CMP (Germany)
†NINE AGAIN, David Liebman & Franco D'Andrea, Red Records (Italy)
*TOMORROW'S EXPECTATIONS, David Liebman & Caris Visentin with the Ronan Guilfoyle Trio, FMC (Ireland)
SCHOENBERG IMPROVISATIONS, Harry Pepl, Amadeo (Austria)
*THE BLESSING OF THE OLD, LONG SOUND, David Liebman, New Sound Planet (Italy)
THE HOUSE ON LEFFERTS BLVD., Yosi Levy, MCI (Israel)
HOMECOMING, Abbey Rader, Cadence

EXATON, Christian DeLezier, Exaton (France) 1990
MANU PEKAR AND GUESTS, Columbia (France)
*THE TREE, David Liebman, Soul Note (Italy)
*ONE OF A KIND, David Liebman, Line Records (Germany)
†OF ONE MIND, Quest, CMP (Germany)
†WEST SIDE STORY TODAY, David Liebman/Gil Goldstein, Owl/EMI (France)
PACIFIC RIM, Phillip Kahn, Borland International
PORTAL, GURTU, CINELU, LIEBMAN, LIVE IN LILLE, Sari Seeri (France)
BESTIAL CLUSTER, Mick Karn, CMP (Germany)

1991   *CLASSIC BALLADS, David Liebman, Candid (England)
        LOOKING FOR THE LIGHT, Phil Markowitz, CB Records
        *CLASSIQUE, David Liebman, Owl/EMI (France)
        POEM, Lars Daniellson, Dragon (Sweden)
        FRESH ENOUGH, Lars Daniellson, Bellaphon (Germany)
        BLUES FOR MCCOY, David Panichi, Spirit Song
        CONVERGENCE, Gunnar Mossblad, Mossblad Music
        SO IN LOVE, Craig Fraedrich, Positive Music
        ANADOLU, Aydin Esen, Columbia/CBS Sony
        THE MOMENT, Chin Suzuki, One Voice (Japan)
        SAILING STONE, Motohiko Hino, Fun House (Japan)
        LAST DAY IN MAY, Ed Sarath, Konnex (Germany)

1992   *SETTING THE STANDARD, David Liebman, Red Records (Italy)
        STRANGER IN BROOKLYN, Mike Zilber, Owl/EMI (France)
        *TURN IT AROUND, David Liebman, Owl/EMI (France)
        TURNADOT, Bob Belden, Blue Note (Japan)
        THE YIN AND THE YOUT, Paul Wertigo, Vera Bra (Germany)
        *JOY, David Liebman with the JMU Ensemble, Candid (England)
        SAX LEGENDS 1 AND 2, various artists, Paddle Wheel (Japan), Evidence
        LIFE'S A LESSON, Ben Sidran, Go Jazz (Japan)
        *THE SEASONS, David Liebman, Soul Note (Italy)

1993   *BESAME MUCHO, David Liebman, Red Records (Italy)
        KEY OF THE MOMENT, Peter Weniger, Mons (Germany)
        TALES FROM THE REEFS, Bocle Brothers, One (France)
        IT'S THERE, Motohiko Hino, Fun House (Japan)
        KING OEDIPUS, Peter Herbert, Milenium (Austria)
        TIME CHANGES, Jerry Hahn, Enja (Germany)
        RH FACTOR, Reuben Hoch, Bellaphon (Germany)
        THE GATECRASHER, Andreas Manndorf (Austria)
        KLANG DEBÜTS, MHS Big Band St.Gut (Austria)

1994   †FAR NORTH, Liebman, Daniellson, Christensen, Stenson, Curling Legs (Norway)
        *MILES AWAY, David Liebman, Owl/EMI (France), Blue Note (USA)
        PARTICULAR VERNACULAR, Bill Gerhardt Planet X (Holland)
        TRUE IMAGE, Jarmo Savolinen, Challenge Records (Netherlands)
        GULF, Intergalactic Ballet, TipToe (Germany)
        †FALLING STONES, David Liebman with Marc van Roon Trio, Mons (Germany)
        *SONGS FOR MY DAUGHTER, David Liebman, Soul Note (Italy)
        †GRAPHIC REALITY, David Liebman and Miku Narunsky, Owl/EMI (France)
        LATIN JAZZ DANCE, Afro Blue Band, Milestone
        ZYPHOID PROCESS, Scott Cutshall, CMP (Germany)
        FROM ME TO YOU, Ulf Radelius, DEP (Sweden)
        WHEN GRANNY SLEEPS, When Granny Sleeps, Storyville (Denmark)

ADVENTURES, Ken Sangster, Jazz Focus (Canada) 1995
MR. X, Mordy Ferber, Ozone
NEW YORK RENDEZVOUS, Didier Lockwood, JMS (France)
†IN THE SAME BREATH, David Liebman, Wolfgang Muthspiel, Mick Goodrick, CMP (Germany)
*VOYAGE, David Liebman, Evidence
PRAYER FOR MY FATHER, Valery Volkov, Sigma International
MISS YOU IN NEW YORK, TSquare, CBS/Sony (Japan)
ADVENTURE PUBLIQUE, Papaq (France)
IF I ONLY KNEW, Reuben Hoch, Bellaphon (Germany)
*MEDITATIONS SUITE, David Liebman, Arkadia Jazz

NEW YORK BREED, Conrad Herwig, Double Time 1996
*RETURN OF THE TENOR – STANDARDS, David Liebman, Double Time
THE ART OF THE TRIO, Daniel Humair, Label Bleu (France)
†WORLD VIEW, David Liebman, Jean Paul Celea, Wolfgang Reisinger, Label Bleu (France)
†LIVE IN NY, Liebman, Daniellson, Stenson, Christensen, Dragon (Sweden)
AND INTO THE LIGHT, Greg Waits,
DIS-TANZ, Michael Nicks, Transes Europeenes (France)
*NEW VISTA, David Liebman, Arkadia Jazz
AN ECHOED SMILE, Matt Balisteras, Palmetto
THE MUSIC OF ALEC WILDER, Vic Juris, Double Time
THOUGHT PROVOKING, Rick DellaRatta, Stella
†ANSWERED QUESTION, Liebman, Markowitz, Sunshine Digital (Japan)
HOMEPAGE, Uli Rennert (to be released)

Publications

Books
LOOKOUT FARM – IMPROVISATION FOR SMALL JAZZ GROUPS, Almo Publications, 1976
CHROMATIC/NON DIATONIC SCALES, Jamey Aebersold, 1988
SELF PORTRAIT OF A JAZZ ARTIST, Advance Music, 1988/1996 (French, 1997)
DEVELOPING A PERSONAL SAXOPHONE SOUND, Dorn Publications, 1989/1994 (German 1993, Japanese, 1994)
A CHROMATIC APPROACH TO JAZZ HARMONY AND MELODY, Advance Music, 1991 (French, 1993)
SAX LESSONS WITH THE GREATS, DCI, 1994
GUIDE TO THE ROAD, Jamey Aebersold, 1994
THE ART OF RECORDING, Jamey Aebersold, 1995
EXPRESSIVE TECHNIQUES, Dorn Publications, 1995
MILES DAVIS AND DAVID LIEBMAN – JAZZ ENCOUNTERS, Edward Mellen Press, 1996

Videos
THE COMPLETE GUIDE TO SAXOPHONE SOUND PRODUCTION, Caris Music Services, 1989
THE IMPROVISER'S GUIDE TO TRANSCRIPTION, Caris Music Services, 1991
THE DAVE LIEBMAN GROUP LIVE IN ISRAEL, View Video, 1997

Published Music
EIGHT JAZZ ORIGINALS OF THE '70S (Vol. 19 of Play-along Series), Jamey Aebersold, 1979
THE WORLD'S GREATEST FAKE BOOK, Sher Music, 1983
30 COMPOSITIONS, Advance Music, 1984
A MOODY TIME for saxophone quartet, Advance Music, 1985
THE GREY CONVOY for saxophone quartet, Advance Music, 1985
QUEST: STANDARDS AND ORIGINALS, Advance Music, 1988
THE NEW REAL BOOK VOL 2, Sher Music, 1988
THE LONELINESS OF A LONG DISTANCE RUNNER for saxophone quartet, Caris Music Services, 1994
ATONEMENT for string quartet and solo instrument, Advance Music, 1994
REMEMBRANCE for woodwind quartet and solo instrument, Advance Music, 1994
RELENTLESS for woodwind quartet and soloist, Advance Music, 1994
THE NEW REAL BOOK VOL 3, Sher Music, 1995
ODE FOR LEO for cello and soloist, Advance Music, 1997

Transcriptions
THE DUO LIVE, Advance Music, 1986
TRANSCRIBED SOLOS FOR PLAY-ALONG SERIES VOL. 26, Jamey Aebersold, 1990
TRANSCRIBED SOLOS FOR PLAY-ALONG SERIES VOL. 19, Jamey Aebersold, 1991
IMPROVISATIONS OF DAVID LIEBMAN 1979-1995, Editions Henry Lemoine, 1995

Periodicals

San Francisco Bay Guardian, 1971
Musician Magazine, 1978-80
Jazz Life, Japan, 1978-82
International Musician and Recording World, 1982-84
Coda Magazine, 1985-86
International Association of Jazz Educators, 1984 (ongoing)
Saxophone Journal, 1988 (ongoing)
Jazz Changes, 1994 (ongoing)
Oggi, Italy, 1995 (ongoing)

Play-Alongs

Vol. 19 Play-Along, Aebersold Publication, 1979
Vol. 26 Scale Syllabus, Aebersold Publication, 1982
The Jazz Workshop Series (Advance Music):
The Jazz Workshop Series – The Blues, Advance Music, 1988
The Jazz Workshop Series – Modal Jazz, Advance Music, 1988
The Jazz Workshop Series – Classics and Originals, Advance Music, 1988
The Jazz Workshop Series – Jazz Drumming (Billy Hart), Advance Music, 1988
Contemporary Idioms, Dorn Publications, 1995

with wife Caris at IAJE Convention, Atlanta, USA, 1995 (© Jamey Aebersold)